The Grief Collective:

Stories of Life, Loss & Learning to Heal

About the Author

Dr Marianne Trent is a Clinical Psychologist in The NHS & in Private Practice. She specialises in Trauma, Grief, Anxiety & Depression. She lost her own Father in 2017 and during his ill-health formed 'The Dead Dad Club.' The Club comprised a group of friends and colleagues who understood grief and who allowed her to process her complex feelings, usually via messages on Messenger and WhatsApp at strange times of the day and night. 'The Dead Dad Club' was such an invaluable source of support to her that she wanted to recreate the same for people who were not fortunate enough to know lots of amazingly empathic people in real life. The Grief Collective is exactly that – an opportunity for readers to learn about grief and be supported with it by the experts – the people who have endured it.

This is Marianne's first book although she also appears in Amy Brown's book 'Let's Talk About The First Year of Parenting'.

Marianne is a regular blogger, writing about mental health related topics and concepts. She has been interviewed live on the BBC News and written for The Guardian, Platinum Magazine and Grazia Daily.

Website: www.goodthinkingpsychology.co.uk
Instagram: @GoodThinkingPsychological
Facebook: Good Thinking Psychological Services
Facebook: The Grief Collective Book
YouTube: Good Thinking Psychological Services
LinkedIn: Marianne Trent

About the Author

The Grief Collective: Stories of Life, Loss and Learning to Heal.

First published in the UK by KDP, 2020.

Copyright © Dr Marianne Trent 2020.

All rights reserved.

ISBN: 9798690947736

Also available as an e-book.

The right of Dr Marianne Trent to be identified as the author of this work has been asserted by her in accordance with the copyright design and patents act 1988. Marianne has asserted that individual case study contributors will maintain the copyright for their own unique stories.

This book is sold subject to the condition that it shall not, by way of trade and otherwise, be lent, relent, resold, hired out or otherwise circulated without the publisher's prior consent in any form, binding or cover other than that in which it is published and without a similar condition being imposed on the subsequent purchaser.

Edited, Indexed and Proof-read by Dr Marianne Trent

Cover Photograph: Damien Trent
Cover Design: Damien Trent
Author Photograph: Damien Trent
Photographs on page 327 by Paul LeBlique, Rob Marsh & Marianne Trent
Photograph on page 328 by Unsplash

Where to get support: A Quick Guide

Bereavement:

Cruse Bereavement - 0800 808 1677

Winston's Wish - 08088 020 021 (For Bereaved Children

The Good Grief Trust
www.thegoodgrieftrust.org

Grief Encounter (supporting bereaved kids)
www.griefencounter.org.uk

Losing a Child

The Lullaby Trust – bereavement support after the loss of a baby or child

SANDS stillbirth and neonatal death charity

Oscars Wish –
www.oscarswishfoundation.co.uk

Child Bereavement UK

Mental Health

Samaritans - 116 123

Shout TEXT helpline - 85258

Mind - 0300 123 3393

RETHINK - 0300 5000 927

SANEline - 0300 304 7000

Respect – Men's Advice Line - 0808 801 0327

Campaign Against Living Miserably (CALM) (for men) - 0800 58 58 58

Papyrus HOPELINEUK, for under 35's feeling suicidal or anyone concerned about someone like this - 0800 068 4141

The Mix (Under 25s) – 0800 808 4994

Where to get support: A Quick Guide

Abuse & Violence

National Domestic Abuse Helpline - 0808 2000 247

National Centre for Domestic Violence - 0207 186 8270

Action on Elder Abuse - 0808 808 8141

Victim Support - 0808 168 9111

Children & Young People

Childline - 0800 1111

NSPCC - 0808 800 5000

The Mix (under 25s) 0808 808 4994

YoungMinds - 0808 802 5544

For a summary of ideas discussed as useful within this book please see the Helpful Resources and Ideas section on pages 322 & 323.

Contents

About the Author 2
Where to get support: A Quick Guide 4
Contents 6
The Grief Collective: Stories of Life, Loss & Learning to Heal .. 10
About This Book 11
Why write this book? 15
Where did the idea for grief stories come from? 16
A Note on 2020 17
About the Cover Image 18
Anonymity 19
What to Do Now You're 'In the Club?' 19
The Stories 21
Holly's Story 22
Shades of Grief: 28
Personal Reflections by Iris M 28
Rachel's Story 36
Elishia's Story 42
Kate's Story 47
   Kate: An Adult Perspective 50
Kerri's Story 54
Dave's Story: 59
Grief and The Order of Things 59
Natalie's Story 68
Tracy's Story: 72
A Story of Hope & Healing 72

Contents

Sarah's Story 78

Hannah's Story 81

Sue's Story 84

Kim's Story 87

Katie's Grief 91

John's Story 97

Mel's Story 100

Chelsea's Story 103

Katie & Sam's Story 108

Marianne's Story: 111

The Man who inspired the Collective 111

Liz's Story: 129

A reply to Marianne 129

Joanna's Story 132

Mia's Story 137

Losing Mum: 143

Jane's Story 143

Jody's Story 146

Amber's Story 152

Lindsay's Story 160

Claire's Story 165

Vicky's Story: 168

Bonfire Night 168

Marina's Story 173

Joanne's Story 177

Rebecca's Story 187

Kara's story: 190

My Darling Angel Baby Jessica Lou 190

7

Contents

- Samantha's Story 204
- Yvonne's Story 213
- Eleri's Story 215
- Diána's Story of Losing her Strong Pillar 218
- Laura's Story 224
- Mariella's Story 225
- Lockdown; 227
- Nikki's Story 239
- Katie's Story 244
- Fran's Story 250
- Sonia's story 254
- of Grief and Loss 254
- Lucy's Story 258
- Surina's Story: 263
- I'd like to get off this rollercoaster please (p.s. strokes suck) 263
- Vanessa's Story 270
- Hold my Hand in Death: 273
- Her Name Was Leah 276
- Lynsey's Story: 289
- Grateful for the time we had, with nothing left unsaid 289
- Alice's Story: 292
- Guilt – A Stronger Emotion than Love 292
- Hena's Story 300
- Maxine's Story 302
- Bernice's Story: 308
- Grief to Anger to Love 308
- Yasmin's Story: 312
- When a Child 'Dies' 312

Contents

An email to the Contributors 317

.... 317

Reflections on Writing 318

Emotional, Practical & Mental Health Support for Contributors
.... 321

Helpful Resources and Ideas: 322

Acknowledgements 324

Compassionate Flow 1 327

Compassionate Flow 2 328

Index 329

The Grief Collective:
Stories of Life, Loss & Learning to Heal

Written, edited & compiled by
Dr Marianne Trent,
with case studies generously
contributed by people who have
experienced grief in their lives.

About This Book

In August 2020, Tim, a fellow Psychologist posted in one of my favourite Facebook groups to ask if anyone fancied taking part in a book writing challenge. More specifically, 'Does anyone fancy writing and publishing an entire book in a month?' Now, for anyone who knows me, you'll know that I love a challenge, and for a number of reasons this was one I just couldn't resist!

I've known my dear friend Kara, who'll you'll read about later, since 2007. It's fair to say that these days our lives are pretty different to the seemingly carefree and hedonistic lives we were leading when we met as Assistant Psychologists at St Andrew's Healthcare. Back then, in between the dancing and the curry clubs and the superb psychology work, we would use work emails to discuss the intricacies of our lives. Even then, she would say to me: 'Marianne, you have to write a book one day!' Whilst this wasn't the first time I had thought about writing, I loved knowing that I'd always got this little cheerleader in my corner who supported my creativity and spurred it on. Every now and then she would say: "When are you writing that book?!" It was in fact her who alerted me to the book writing challenge and as soon she'd tagged me I knew that I was jumping aboard! With hindsight, maybe all those years ago she knew she wouldn't be able to resist a book writing challenge herself one day too and knew that my love of words and grammar would come in handy for my proof reading of her own beautiful book!

I knew immediately which book it was I would 'write' in a month. This very book you hold in your hands was an idea I'd had soon after my dad died. Initially, I wanted to call it 'The Dead Dad Club'. I know the title is potentially quite shocking, but there is a reason. When my dad was palliatively ill and in the time after he passed, I used to speak to a number of people about how I was feeling. I affectionately called these people my

'Dead Dad Club!' It felt like a club because I tended to get much better containment and support and discussion from these people who were already 'in the club' and understood grief. However, I knew that the book would hopefully go on to feature a wide variety of different loss stories from parents, children, siblings, colleagues, friends, even much-loved pets. I knew it was never going to be a book 'just' about 'Dead Dads,' although of course there are a fair sprinkling of those within these pages too. In terms of Acceptance and Commitment Therapy (often known as ACT), it can be useful to be frank about topics because there's less ambiguity and less room to hide. Loss doesn't get any easier by packaging it in fancy words. However, I know that we're all at a different stage on our 'grief club' journeys and some prefer 'passed' to died.' A friend and contributor, Kara actually, although I promise I do speak to other people too! Anyway, she suggested she wouldn't want to read a book called 'The Dead Dad Club' because her Dad is alive and well and she wouldn't want to tempt fate. I can appreciate that. A fellow story writer said that if they were struggling with the loss of a Mum they would never think to pick up a book called 'The Dead Dad Club!' Another excellent point! Another contributor also said that whilst she was okay with it and appreciated its frankness, that it might potentially upset other loved ones who were now having to fathom a way through their lives without their much loved people who are depicted within these very pages. So it was that: 'The Grief Collective: Stories of life, Loss and Learning to Heal', was born. It does what it says on the tin. It still suggests the 'club' element but also encompasses different types of grief; not all of the grief you read about within these pages will feature death.

Whilst my ideas for the book were already formed, it is only this challenge which gave me the impetus to actually 'put pen to paper.' Well, that bit about a pen is of course a creative lie – the whole thing has been edited, written and collated on my laptop. My handwriting is dreadful and if I'd had to personally scribe it with my trusty ballpoint I'd have needed about 3 years even just to decode what I'd said on the first page let alone get it published in a month! An assistant psychologist friend once proudly presented me with a handwriting pen. I was excited for a moment, but nope, it didn't help! I'm thankful for computers which make book creation and calls to action a much simpler process.

So it was, that in September 2020 I started asking for grief case studies on my Good Thinking Psychological Services social media channels. I created a 'grief brief' which explained the project and gave details about what I was hoping might be achieved with the book. However, the description was deliberately non-specific. The emphasis was very much on how important it was to hear each individual's own unique experience of grief. When someone expressed an interest in contributing to the project, I sent them 'the grief brief' and asked them to put something together if they would like to. The only caveat being that it had to be ready before the end of the month!

The case studies, or 'stories' as they're referred to in this book, started to come in. When I began to read them I was so humbled and honoured that people had put them together because I asked them to and that they were so willing to share them with me, to share them with you! It's honestly one of my greatest privileges in life so far. I also think that it demonstrates my point that once you're in 'the club' that you just know how to talk to others about grief and that it's in fact okay to talk about and important that we do. I began to get even more excited about what a potentially useful resource for people on their own unique grief journeys.

Each story is wonderful and they're all their own. I edited them and changed some of the order and the flow and tidied up the odd typo here or there and asked for clarification in some areas. But I hope you will find that you can hear each person's individual voice and writing style. By the way, for anyone who doesn't know, the word 'cwtch' is Welsh for cuddle or hug! You would have heard Bristolian in one story but I'm sorry to say that I did change all of the 'cant' to 'can't' in that story so now it may just be me who reads that particular one in Bristolian! With that in mind, some of the stories I can read in the accents of those people who have written them because I know them personally. Others, I don't know at all and yet all of these people have been so kind and generous in sharing their stories with us. See what other voices and accents you can 'hear' too!

The stories vary in length and style. I purposefully haven't grouped them in terms of loss or length. I think there is so much to learn and to gain by reading about another's life without necessarily knowing in advance which 'genre' it falls into. That said, if you did want to read about particular types of losses then there's an index at the back of this book which will give you a helping hand on which page to start.

Why write this book?

I'm a Clinical Psychologist and I often work with grief. Loud and clear, time and time again I get the message from my clients that people don't want to talk to them about grief. People can't handle it and want to gloss over it and cheer them up. This isn't how being a human works. We're mammals and as such we live in groups and form connections with one another. Our complicated human brains mean that we are going to have a variety of difficult and painful emotional experiences. We can't exist by ignoring these and glossing over them. I experienced this first-hand after the passing of my Dad. People could see I looked awful. People could see I was tearful; but they didn't want to ask; they didn't want to 'rock the boat' if it was still *just about* afloat! If you're still in the depths of grief and are struggling to imagine a way forward without your loved one then I hope that you will find this book useful.

Where did the idea for grief stories come from?

In my work and personal life I love a story. I love knowing about people and how their lives have been. It helps me think about people for work and in my personal life to have a rich tapestry of human examples to draw upon. I really love the work of Irvin Yalom who writes case studies about his therapeutic work with patients. I also seem to recall from my training days there is also a book by Patrick Casement which does the same using clinical examples. Growing up, when I was in sixth form, I also read a book called 'Women on Top' which was case studies written by women about their sexual fantasies. It was such an interesting style of book and my decision to write this book about grief and bereavement has been inspired by this style of writing. The explanation you just read was taken directly from my 'grief brief' to contributors. As such, you'll notice that Dave mentions this in his story which made me smile and I hope it does you too!

A Note on 2020

The beauty of books is that they can live on indefinitely. Therefore, I can't know what year it is you'll be reading this in. I'd like to briefly mention that 2020 has been a challenging year for, well, pretty much the whole world really. 2020 is the year when COVID-19 became a worldwide concern. It also brought with it a higher than normal death rate and impacted on people being able to spend time with their loved ones whether they were healthy or unwell. The day I wrote this page was 29/9/2020, it was the day that the BBC reported that that it has now been estimated that 1 million people worldwide have died as a result of COVID-19. It's hard to comprehend the amount heartbreak and suffering this will have involved.

COVID-19 and it's far reaching implications are depicted and discussed within a couple of the stories within this book. However, you'll notice that many of the story contributors experienced the grief they've written about many years ago. Sometimes it can take a while for the dust to settle on grief and bereavement in order to talk about it. Therefore, it might be that the calls to action requesting grief case stories just came too early for people affected by the pandemic. Therefore, given that at the time I write this, we are still in the midst of this global event, there aren't loads of COVID-19 references. I hope that if you've been affected by grief through the pandemic, either as a loss to your own health, occupation or the loss of a loved one that you find this book to be a great support in navigating your grief journey nonetheless.

About the Cover Image

On the 26/9/2020 I woke up bright and early to work on this book. One of my jobs that day was to do some editing and to figure out how to a) design a cover and b) what to feature on it. I posted as much on my Good Thinking Psychological Services Facebook Page along with a photo of a box of Aquabeads my son had dropped all over the table. People quickly started to comment: That's it! That's your cover, that's totally what grief is like! And so, with a little photo re-shoot the cover was born. I hope you like it.

Anonymity

Some contributors have asked for their names to be changed and / or those of their loved ones. This has been done. However, to further protect identities, I've not told you which are real names and which are not. I've also referred to everyone by their first name only.

What to Do Now You're 'In the Club?'

Who doesn't love being in a club right? One of my earliest memories of being in one was when I was at primary school. I'd stolen my Mum's self-adhesive Kay's catalogue stamps and taken them into school with me to use at the top of the membership forms for whatever club it was we were forming that day! I hope that you'll find being part of our grief collective helpful. To me, membership of the DDC meant messages; lots of messages passed between me and my friend / colleague / confidant. Messages usually sent via messenger or WhatsApp, sometimes via text. Is it just me who seems to have a particular method for contacting certain people? Some friends are WhatsApp, some messenger – others like to have actual phone calls! Anyway, as you'll know, life doesn't always move in a linear fashion and actually some of the members of the DDC only experienced their loss after my dad had died. When my Dad passed it's likely that these people perhaps wouldn't have known what to say or wouldn't have wanted to 'rock the boat'. They weren't part of the original club, however, as a founding member of the DDC, when they experienced their loss then 'rock the boat' I did and have continued to do! I'd sooner someone say 'thanks for checking in, but I'm actually good today,' than them feel isolated with no support. Once you've read this book I'd like to invite you to create your own grief community and help indoctrinate people into 'the collective' and let them know that it's always okay to talk to YOU and that you'll always have time, always be able to handle their emotions, their fears and indeed their tears. On days where you're not feeling strong enough to support others then I hope that you are well supported too.

I'd love to know what you think to this book and whether it's been as useful as I hoped it would be when I first dreamed it up! I can only hope that it will be anywhere near as useful as my own, original 'DDC' was to me. If there's enough interest then maybe one day we will have the Grief Collective 2, although I can't imagine I'll want to write it in a month next time! Many of the original members of the DDC have kindly shared their stories with us within this book and so you are now all honorary members of the DDC too; welcome to the club! The club which no one actually wants to join! Whilst I can't promise you a toaster, or a kettle like I may have falsely promised my primary school friends with their stamps, I can promise you warmth, acceptance and validation within these pages.

Speaking of pages, we've set up a Facebook page for this book too. If you'd like to join us it's The Grief Collective Book, see you there!

The Stories

1
Holly's Story

It is twenty years since I 'lost' my Mum. All these years later I find myself working as a clinical psychologist in specialist palliative care. You'd think I'd have steered clear of this area as it was all so painful and intense. But, if anything, death is our connecting, universal, human experience. It is unquestionably profound. In Buddhism there is a phrase along the lines of: 'it is only at the moment that we understand the certainty of our own death that we truly begin to live. Perhaps the ability to hold our own personal fragility close is what gives life greater meaning? I certainly see the emotional impact of the work on myself and my colleagues, but I also see the vicarious resilience. When I've asked what motivates staff to do this work, I've heard the expression 'them today, us tomorrow,' I never lose sight of that. Keeping this in mind is levelling. It keeps things real and gives perspective to the day to day. It's deeply compassionate and really very beautiful.

What's interesting though is that I'm frequently mindful of the language used in relation to grief, death and dying in my work. It's striking to me that I often avoid using the word 'lost' (after all, our loved ones aren't 'lost'; we know exactly where they are) yet it's the first word that came as I began to write this. Because really and truly; my Mum is lost to me. And I was lost without her. I didn't know my way. She was my navigational point. I am still lost at times. One of the things said frequently in palliative care is that there's 'one chance to get it right'. And whilst there were a lot of things that weren't right about my own Mum's death, the thing that stands out (the humdinger of the whole experience for me) was the nurse who sang to her as she died. That is something unforgettable.

Holly's Story

I had taken some convincing to go home to shower after days of sitting next to my Mum's bed, helping with self-care, massaging her feet, singing to her. I didn't want to leave. But the nurse assured me that she would sing to my Mum in my absence (Mum always sang to us when we were ill, anxious, upset. I can still hear her beautiful, deep, rhythmic voice in my mind). It seemed the most natural thing in the world to sit and sing (and for the record; I am no singer.) But it brought a certain energy to the room. It was comforting. This small act of deep compassion by a nurse (who for the record also couldn't sing) is something that I will never forget and will always be grateful for. And how do I know she didn't just tell me that she sang to my Mum? Because the first thing she said when I returned was "she didn't like the Beatles did she? So I switched to Elvis and she settled again." I cannot tell you how many times the memory of this has given me comfort.

My Mum died of a subarachnoid haemorrhage. She was doing some Christmas food shopping for a friend. She hadn't felt well but the person that she was (evacuated in the war as a child and so part of that unstoppable generation of 'get on with it'), meant that she wouldn't let a grim headache, of 2 days duration, stop her from helping out a friend. I thought about that for a very, very long time. The fact that she sat in the middle of the shopping centre, clutching her friend's shopping, bleeding from the brain, totally alone. Our brains are brilliant at torturing us like this. I had intrusive images and auditory intrusions of the ambulance siren that took her to hospital for the longest time. For a good six month hearing a siren would make my stomach turn. And of course, these were completely fictitious; I had generated them to build the story and connect with what that life shattering moment had been like for her. This precious, gentle woman, who meant the world to me, was now facing the end of her life. She collapsed two days before Christmas and died on New Year's Eve. The last words she said to me as we sat listening to the chimes of Christmas day on the radio from the nurse's station, were "Is it Christmas? Oh, Merry Christmas darling". She slipped into a coma a few hours later and never regained consciousness. There was nothing remotely merry about that Christmas.

I tell myself how blessed I was to have had those last words. To have had moments when she was first in hospital when we could talk and I could tell her how much I loved her. She retold my sister and I stories from her childhood. In the past we'd have rolled our eyes and said "yes, you've told us this story before!" But knowing those moments would never happen again made every fibre of my being come into sharp focus. I remembered her telling me that she had a horrible moment after her own Mum died when she couldn't visualise her hands. She went hunting through boxes of photographs to try to bring back the memory of them. I remembered this and spent so much time looking at my Mum and her hands, committing them to memory. I needn't have bothered. I have her hands. My sister has her hands. I look down at my hands and I see that she is part of me.

I spend a lot of time in my job talking about death and dying and am often struck by how many families just don't talk about it. It's taboo. It's 'dark.'. It's 'depressing'. But that wasn't the way things were in our family. My Dad died when I was two-years-old. My Mum talked of him often and in doing so kept him 'alive' for me; I had a Dad, he loved me dearly, but he wasn't able to be there. This is 'continuing bonds' in action. So, we spoke about his death, my grandparent's death and at times about the future and my Mum's death. She was a very spiritual person and when her brother died (at 33 years old; the same age as my Dad and Grandad strangely) she told us that she "felt him there, giving me comfort". So the joke would start about "well don't think about coming back and giving me comfort!" We would laugh and I remember saying "you can come and give me comfort in a dream. But not in real life." That was our deal. And for about 6 months after my Mum died, I had the same dream over and over and over. It was me sitting with my head on her knee, sobbing, telling her I couldn't cope without her, telling her I missed her. She would stroke my hair, tell me it would be OK and I would wake up (usually in tears) but feeling close to her. The dream was in some ways such a perfectly ordinary interaction. But the ordinariness of it made it all the more real. Then one night I had the dream, but the conversation was different. She said to me "I can't keep coming to you like this anymore. I have to go away now. But you don't need me. You can do this on your own." I protested, but she assured me it would be OK. I have never dreamt that dream again since. I find it quite mind-blowing to think either we have an absolute innate ability to access that bond and receive comfort when we need it; or, there is an alternate dimension out there that we know nothing about that perhaps I need to keep an open mind to! Either way, my mind (or my Mum) called it right. It was at that time that things began to feel more bearable. And in some ways there was a changing from the pain and distress to a desire for things to be more meaningful and different in some way.

I tormented myself about the fact that I turned down an invitation to see my Mum just a few days before she collapsed because I had a pile of Christmas presents to wrap and no other time to do it. How pathetic does that sound now? I say to people that I work with all the time; we make so many decisions every day with the information we have to hand. I didn't know my Mum was about to die. I didn't know she was unwell. So in my head I can tell myself I made a choice with the frivolity of assuming I would see her over Christmas and we would be spending time together then. But that thought process doesn't cut it when it comes to the knot in the pit of your stomach and the self-loathing that you picked a pile of rubbish presents over precious time. Again, our brains are masters at making us feel bad. I was working full time, studying a few evenings a week, scuba diving twice a week, trying to get to the gym; I had friends and a fiancé that I also wanted to spend time with. I felt I had no time (or I thought at the time that I had no time. Truth is we can always make time). Of course, hindsight is a beautiful science. Had I known, I would have spent every moment with her. But I didn't know. We never know. That is something that I absolutely take away and remind myself of regularly. I have never since cancelled a person over a task. It's a simple life rule and it helps me. This is the best advice I can offer to people in this situation; we can't undo things, we don't have a time machine. All we can do is to choose to view things differently and choose to commit to a different path in the future. If not, those layers of guilt can be corrosive.

The first Christmas after Mum died, I found the thought of presents so distasteful that they sickened me. I talked about it with my sister who, luckily, was on the same page. We agreed on a book with meaning (a 'chicken soup for the soul' kind of book; or for me, the veggie version.) Instead of gifts, we would ask what people wanted in the way of a 'doing' task or activity (this was my sister's idea). So I could offer to wash her windows or help out with some decorating (or go with her to 'Go Ape' which was what she actually requested). As the years have gone on, the joy of Christmas has returned. I've since had a child of my own (which incidentally, no one tells you how painful that experience is without your Mum). It brings back all those loss feelings quite acutely for a time. Who is there to remind you how heavy you were when you were born? The story of your weaning? Crawling? Sleeping? These are all aspects of your life story that have new meaning as you face those things with your own child. I felt simultaneously closer to her and yet further away than ever. Becoming a parent gave me more understanding of her. It was painful.

I think if I had a pound for the times people say that being around children really helps, I'd be a very wealthy person. It's probably why our caveman ancestors lived in kin groups with the whole generation. Being around young people and their joy and enthusiasm is very healing. So despite the newfound pain of missed connections with my Mum, I had the joy of new life and seeing the world through the eyes of this new little person.

Holly's Story

Another important part of keeping the bond alive, for me anyway, is the whole 'what would Mum say?' thing. It's the metaphorical t-shirt that we wear and this is powerful for me. I know Mum loved Christmas and got so excited about it. So the traditions that were meaningful to her (drinking a sherry whilst making the family Christmas cake) become the traditions I carry forward; along with the story. So every year as I do this I talk about 'Nanny Fox' and we get out the sherry glass and have a toast. We smile, we laugh, we remember.

Loss is brutal. It's a sucker punch to the gut. It gets easier, but it doesn't go away. And sometimes new life experiences make the loss reappear in full glory (the night before my wedding was another corker; a deep wave of sadness hit and I lay crying cuddled up to my wonderful bridesmaid.) But, what does change is the fact that we can carry it much more lightly when we remember, when we smile, when we take parts of that special person forward. I'd like to send a huge, huge hug (from the written word if that's even such a thing) for all of you going through this experience right now. It will get a lighter load to carry. I can promise you that. But whilst it's heavy; share it. Because we in the club understand.

2

Shades of Grief:

Personal Reflections by Iris M

Over the past six years, grief has visited me in various different guises: first, the sudden death of my adored dog after he was hit by a car; next, the unexpected and tragic death of my brother-in-law, due to medical negligence. This was followed by the successive deaths of my beloved Grandparents, the cornerstones of my childhood, and most recently, the death of a family friend, aged only 17, by suicide.

Over these past few years, I have really come to understand, in an almost visceral way, how death is so intimately bound to life. It is the other side of the coin, it's part of the deal, it's in the small print. Before that day, six years ago, when my husband walked through the front door with no dog and bloodshot eyes after taking our terrier out for his usual evening walk, I'd had the luxury of never really having to consider it. But eventually, death is something that will touch us all. Sometimes we will be on the periphery of it, at other times we will be at the very heart of it. Sometimes it will come so close that we can feel it bristle the hairs on our arms, then gratefully, pass us by.

This is an everyday account of grief. I am not a writer, but I am a human being who has suffered loss and I believe there is value in sharing the everyday stories of grief, in revealing its various shades. Generally speaking, we are not very adept as a society, or perhaps even as a species, at having these conversations. So when I was offered the chance to share my own experiences, I decided to accept the challenge as a small gesture to whoever should read it. I invite you to share in my experiences and hope that, in some small way, it may help you to make sense of, or become more acquainted with, your own. As grief is an inevitable part of living and loving, it is a universal human experience. And if there were ever a time to pull together as human beings, to connect, to support, to share, it is in the depths of grief.

Grief has made the world around me look and feel different. At times, it has felt as though I were in a black and white film, seeing only variations of grey around me. I have felt slowed; as if the weight of loss was pulling me down like quicksand. Grief has cracked me wide open and left all my vulnerabilities exposed, I have felt as though I am unravelling, struggling to find solid ground to stand on.

There was a significant period when I was afraid to be alone with my thoughts. I filled every quiet moment with podcasts and audiobooks. I am passionate about music, but there were times when grief made me too anxious to listen to music of any kind. I was fearful that it might provoke some emotion I couldn't bear. I struggled with watching films and television programmes for the same reason; I felt too fragile, too brittle. I couldn't tolerate the emotional turbulence.

For a long time, grief robbed me of the ability to fall asleep effortlessly. I would lie awake, my mind churning and fearful, listening to the church bells near my house chiming each hour away. I would often wake in the middle of the night too. In the early hours of the morning, when the world is at its most lifeless and lonely, grief always felt at its most overwhelming and terrifying. I was filled with a vague, yet pervasive, sense of dread.

My grief has been messy, ugly and unbecoming. In the depths of grieving, I was often preoccupied, there was a dark shadow looming over me, I smiled with a little less enthusiasm, I zoned out when being spoken to, I was snappy or behaved like a slightly prickly teenager. At times I may have appeared cruelly apathetic, radiating all the charm of a scrap of sandpaper.

In conversation, it often took me much longer to formulate my thoughts and when I finally did, I would lose them again in an instant. My grief has made me feel like a computer with a large program running continuously in the background, slowing down all my other functions. It is constantly there, whirring away, quietly draining my energy. I am always processing, updating my system with this new information that I have to assimilate.

There are times when I have longed to have some outward marker of my grief. A little sign that says: 'I am not quite me, be gentle'. At these times, I have thought about the old tradition of mourning clothes and how they alerted those around the bereaved person to their loss. In Victorian times, it was the convention for widows to wear full mourning clothes for 2 years. The colour of the cloth chosen for the clothes lightened as mourning went on, moving from black to grey, violet, mauve and finally, white. Perhaps a part of me envies the protection given to the Victorian widows; the unspoken understanding conveyed by their clothing. I wonder whether, in modern times, we have lost something of the respect for the process of mourning and the time and work it entails. In our instant society, where we seek to fix things with the click of a button, do we really allow the time and space we require to grieve? Where does grief fit in to our often over-scheduled lives?

Whilst dealing with my most recent losses, I have been a mother to three children under the age of six. Subsequently, I have learnt that the work of grieving when you have small children to look after, presents a particular challenge. Attempting to contain someone else's feelings when you feel completely overwhelmed by your own, is a daunting task. As is feigning delight in a painstakingly constructed Duplo tower, when you feel as though your insides have just been scooped out. For me, this situation was at its most testing when my beloved Grandmother died just three months before my third child was born. It's very hard for the tide of grief to flow naturally in this situation and, to a certain extent, I found myself needing to detach entirely from my feelings of grief when I was looking after my new-born baby and two other young children. I just couldn't find a space for it amidst the relentless daily chaos of family life.

What I discovered though, is that the work of grief cannot be side-stepped effectively for very long. It caught up with me and demanded to be seen to. It started to show up in unrecognisable ways. Grief does not always look the way we expect it to. My levels of general anxiety increased; a phobia I had long had under control began to mushroom; I was sleepless and carried painful tension in my neck and shoulders.

There came a time when I was forced to make space. I had not been truly myself for so long, that I had almost stopped noticing the difference. I had become acclimatised to feeling utterly flat. In blocking out my feelings of grief, I had inadvertently blocked out all other feelings too. I couldn't remember the last time I had been subsumed by joy. This realisation only dawned on me when I went to see a psychotherapist. At this point I didn't even think I was going because I needed to talk about my losses. I couldn't make out the shape of my discontent; I just had a growing feeling of unease, a sense that I could be better, something was amiss.

It is fascinating to me that it took a conversation with someone else to shine a light on my grief. I had detached myself so adeptly from it, that it had become completely unrecognisable to me. I needed someone to gently turn my head back towards it. I found I was greatly soothed by the experience of having my grief seen, recognised and acknowledged by another. And there was something unexpectedly powerful about the fact that this person was someone I had never met before. I also found that talking to a therapist freed me from having to worry about looking after her feelings, something I would tend to do when talking with friends. Sometimes I tried too hard to neatly package my grief when presenting it to others, to make it more palatable somehow. With my therapist, I could more easily offer it up raw and unedited.

After a couple of sessions of therapy, I knew that I had to actively encourage and welcome the feelings I had been pushing down my priorities list. I had to make a special effort to create space for them and this meant, at times, deliberately *provoking* them. Sometimes I used music to do this; listening to the bleakest songs I could bear, helped me to connect to those dormant painful feelings. At other times, I looked at photos or watched videos of the person I was grieving for. Another thing that worked well for me, as someone who has always found writing very therapeutic, was to write to the person I had lost. Somehow this made it easier for me to access my thoughts and feelings; my pen always seemed to know what I needed to say. And in some strange way, writing a letter felt like making contact with the ones who were gone.

There are many different things I could cite as being helpful to me on my various paths of grief, with each thing assuming more or less importance at different points along the way. Finding a physical release was a huge help. I started running to literally work the uncomfortable feelings out of my body. I took up yoga which helped me to feel grounded and more connected to myself. Yoga gently fed my body and soul in a way that I could never have anticipated, and still don't fully understand.

I worked hard to carve out space for myself amidst the relentless march of the daily routines. Making space often meant snatching opportunities to go out for a walk and just allow my brain to whir; to find somewhere to sit, with a beautiful view and just watch; to go for a drive and turn the radio off. I said 'no' to things and cancelled unnecessary plans, all in a bid to make more room to feel and to be. Allowing myself to 'just be' was the state I had been running from when I filled every waking hour with audiobooks and podcasts, too afraid to meet with my thoughts. But I have learnt that sometimes the work of grief needs space, and silence.

I avoided spending too much time with people I didn't feel I could be genuine with. Having to act a particular way, or put on a jovial mask when you feel echoingly empty inside, quickly becomes exhausting. Since seeking authenticity in my interactions was so important to me, I tried hard to surround myself with the people who 'got it'. This involved seeking out the people in my life who asked 'how are you?' and really wanted to hear the answer.

I found huge comfort in spending time in nature and taking pleasure in the small things. The unchanging rhythm and flow of the natural world offered me solace, through reminding me that we are a part of something much greater than ourselves.

Ultimately, I found things that helped to make the pain a little more bearable and did more of them. I learnt that there is no timescale for grief and sometimes, I have needed to remind myself that I don't lose the right to grieve after a certain period. Grief will take as long as it takes and in some ways, I would suggest that is never really 'done', it just morphs and takes on a different form over time.

In moving forwards, I have found rituals to be helpful, but as with many aspects of grief, this is an extremely personal choice. I have chosen to celebrate the birthdays of my loved ones but prefer to pass over the anniversaries of their deaths. I take great pleasure in enjoying the things my loved ones would have – listening to the music they loved, doing the things they enjoyed. Through these acts I find my ways of honouring them.

I have also chosen to have a lot of photographs of my loved ones around the house. I want to see them every day, I want to smile at them and sometimes, I even want to talk to them.

I also take great comfort from paying attention to all the little ways my loved ones are still with me; noting language or turns of phrase I have inherited from them, traits we may have shared. When someone dies, they leave so many small gifts behind them, just waiting to be noticed.

Death is the very thing which gives life meaning. Within loss there are valuable opportunities to learn and grow. When my brother-in-law died suddenly, leaving my sister-in-law and her four young children, I watched the life of a family ripped apart in a day. And so I have watched, over the course of the last five years, a family slowly, very slowly, come back together again. They have reformed, found a new rhythm. As the years have passed, the tougher days have become fewer and fewer. The human heart has an incredible power to heal; it has been humbling to see my sister-in-law, someone who was so utterly shattered by loss, find the courage to love again, wholeheartedly.

Having met death so frequently over the past six years, I have a profound sense of the fragility of life. As a consequence, I have resolved to be more generous with my expressions of love and care; to be more open-hearted. Along with this, I try never to wait, to show anyone what they mean to me.

As I write this, I am in the midst of grieving for a young family friend who took her own life. I have just discovered that the heartbreak caused by the loss of a young person, is a very particular shade of black. It is an awful disruption to the natural way of things. What's more, suicide is like acid poured on the wounds of grief.

I go out for an evening with friends, I chat, I laugh, I enjoy my food. Then just after the dessert is served, I am lost to thoughts of her. My friends are talking but I am not really listening, I have departed for a while. I return to my place in the flow of things and manage to reconnect. But in the car on the way home from the pub, I feel the heaviness, a sickness rising up my throat. She is still gone, nothing has changed. I can go out, I can chat and laugh with my friends, but she cannot. The permanency of death winds me. It will always be this way; for as long as I am here, she will not be. A heavy sigh leaves me. There is no reprieve from this fact. Like grasping a handful of nettles, my work now is to boldly hold this truth, clench it and feel it sting, over and over, until it no longer hurts me so much. The only way to go through the pain, is to truly *feel* it.

> Gratefully, my previous experiences of loss allow me to hold on to some hope. Like the mourning clothes of the Victorian widows, I

know that shades of colour will gradually return to my life. Along with the black days, there will also be grey, violet, mauve and white. As time passes, more possibilities will slowly unfold before me, even those I never thought would be possible. And once again, I will be a witness to the humbling capacity of the human heart, to heal.

3
Rachel's Story

Thursday 19th July 2018, the date my life changed forever, forever etched in my memory, a single point in time that turned my life upside down. It was around 4.30pm, my 4-year-old daughter was finishing her dance class while my two-year-old son played with his cars in the waiting area. I got a call from an unknown number so I ignored it, it rang again so I answered it; a voice I didn't recognise saying 'your husband has collapsed, the paramedics are working on him and they want to speak to you.' What happened over the next few hours was a bit surreal. I think my body was in shock and I just concentrated on getting someone to watch the kids, asking my parents to drive 3 hours to have them overnight and getting his family together to drive the two hours to the hospital. There were phone calls from the air ambulance doctor which gave me hope, at that point I didn't really contemplate that he wouldn't survive.

Early that morning he was getting ready to go away overnight for a work outing. He had lost his wedding ring about 6 months earlier and it dropped out of his drawer whilst he was packing, he was so excited to have it on again. Fast forward to around 1am on Saturday 20th July and I am holding his hand in the hospital, staring at that ring, having to say goodbye, I didn't want to let go of his hand. In hindsight, I feel this was fate knowing that his time was going to be up that day and foreseeing me holding that hand.

The hardest thing I have ever had to do is to tell my children that morning that Daddy wasn't coming home. My daughter wondered why her grandparents were there and I had to explain that Daddy's heart had stopped beating and we wouldn't be able to see him again. It wasn't until later that night that emotion started to hit her and I'm not sure I will ever feel pain like that again. The next few weeks were a blur of talking to the coroner, arranging the funeral and starting to go through all of the other formalities. In a way it gave me something practical to focus on. The feeling of loss in the pit of my stomach didn't leave me and looking back, I'm not sure how I managed it all. The choices for the funeral, especially what music to play (music was his main passion and I didn't want to let him down by choosing the wrong song). We had never discussed our plans for such occasions; we didn't contemplate that it would happen in this way.

I tried to read a lot about grief in the first few months, trying to make sense of everything. I struggled to find reading material which were aimed at young widows and which talked about the practical steps of grief. I had so many questions swirling around in my head. What should I be feeling? What would be coming next? When could I expect this intense pain to start to dissipate? I now think that this is because, similarly to parenthood, there is no one right way to do this. Each journey is individual and each circumstance surrounding the passing of a loved one is different. There isn't a right way or a wrong way of processing your grief, just whatever helps you to do it in as healthy way as possible. There was a good book called 'Always and Forever' which a friend bought for my children. My daughter really enjoyed reading this and would ask to read it every night. We would often cry together reading it and when the time was right for her, she stopped asking for it every night. She will still ask for it now and again, but we can now read it without the rawness of emotion we once had. I also found a good online blog which talked a lot about moving forward which helped and I joined a national young widows charity where there was lots of posts that made me realise I wasn't alone in how I was feeling.

It was through this charity that I met someone who has become a very good friend who lost her husband around the same time as me and who has a son the same age as my daughter. Having someone who understands exactly how I feel is invaluable. We tell each other things that we wouldn't tell those close to us and we just get it. Our kids have also got an incredible bond and the fact that they don't feel different from each other means they don't feel alone in their circumstances. It's funny how life brings you together with certain people and I know that we would have been friends if we had met under other circumstances as we get on so well, I'm lucky to have her in my life.

I was lucky enough to be offered a set of grief counselling sessions through a local hospice. These were invaluable for helping me to process a lot of things. I replayed what happened that night over and over in my head (I still do this sometimes). We addressed the guilt of whether there was something I could have done, the anger of what happened and a lot of personal reassurance. It still stays with me that 'if you do not look after yourself you will not be able to look after others'. I have had to tell myself this a number of times when trying to take on too much and make sure I give myself room to breathe. Everyone kept telling me I was strong but I didn't feel strong. I felt like I was just about surviving and that's in essence what I was doing. I made lots of decisions on my own which was tough, I was used to sharing all of those things.

I started to write a journal every day to put down all of my thoughts. I made a list in it of all the things that I missed about him and whilst I was writing this piece on grief I picked up that journal and read this list to reflect on it. It made me smile as there were some things that he did that I hadn't thought about for a long time and it's good to capture all of the little memories you have of someone. I made photobooks for the kids of all the photos of them and Daddy and the things we had all done together. It was incredibly hard to put together at the time, looking at his face staring at me from the computer screen but we often now spend time looking through these books and I will tell the kids stories of the places we visited and the things we did. Sadly, my son was too young to remember his Daddy properly, so this is one way he can feel connected to him. I also had memory bears made from some of his clothes for the kids and when they were delivered it was strange but it felt so powerful to hold something in 3 dimensional form that was a part of him. When the lady who made them said she had enough material to make another one I had to have one made for myself so I can hold it now and feel there is something there of him.

I made the decision, a few months after he passed away, to move to be closer to my family. It was hard, emotionally and physically doing it all on my own when my grief was still raw but I'm glad I did it and I didn't once question my decision. It was a fresh start for us and made such a difference to have my family on the doorstep. The hard thing about moving to a new area is having to explain our situation to all the new people we meet and who don't know our history. I have come to terms with the fact that this is just part of our story now but it doesn't make it any easier trying to get it into conversation or having to deal with the awkwardness of people not knowing what to say when you tell them. I find I can talk quite openly about death and about what happened as I have lived with it for a while but people who haven't, tend to close up and divert away from asking too many questions. People naturally find death a difficult subject and they don't want to say the wrong thing or upset you, I'm sure I was like that before I had to deal with a close loss. If people were more open to the normality of it, society would be able to support each other better. I like to talk about my husband, what he was like, the things he liked doing and funny stories about him. I will often talk to the kids about how daddy used to say this or do that and how much like him they are. It keeps the memory of him alive and I wish there wasn't so much fear around talking about grief.

People talk a lot about the waves of grief, how they come and go. I find this to be very true as time passes. The emotion comes less often but when it hits it can be like a tidal wave, knocking you off your feet and taking your breath away.

Sometimes it is obvious milestones or anniversaries where you can almost see something coming but other times it can be totally out of the blue and just hit you when you aren't ready. You learn to let it out and let it pass. Sometimes it passes quickly, other times it takes longer, there are no rule books for our feelings. I often find myself thinking 'I can't remember what it was like to not have this grief always there, in the background waiting to strike.' I am not sure it will ever go away; you just get used to having to process it. My heart still feels badly bruised and I'm not sure it will ever completely heal. I also get intense pangs of jealousy when I see other families together and know that we will never have that ideal scenario. We would often say how much we had achieved in our lives and we did that together. It's not the same facing the future without the other half of yourself.

I find myself worrying a lot more now about certain things and it's hard not having that other person, your support network, to talk to about it. I constantly worry about what if something would happen to me. How would the kids be able to deal with that? I worry about how we will continue to be financially secure, how I can balance work, looking after the house and the ever-growing list of extracurricular activities? However, one thing I have learnt is that you don't know what the future holds and you can't spend all your time worrying about it. Sometimes you have to enjoy the present, but that doesn't stop the worries lingering there.

I think the worst thing as I look to keep moving forward is knowing what my children are going to miss out on. You spend all your time trying to give them everything you can and I will never be able to give my children the one thing they really want or need. I do my best to make up for it as much as I can but there will always be a big hole left in our lives. I do, however, believe that we can be happy and we are on a regular basis. We talk a lot about Daddy being in our hearts and I truly believe we carry him everywhere we go. I have two amazing children who bring me so much joy and have already achieved so much in their little lives. In some respects, we have maybe even become closer because of our grief and the emotions that we have embraced together.

Life will never be as full as it was and there will always be a hole, something missing from all we do but we continue to keep moving forward and I know that I am blessed to still be here to enjoy every day.

4
Elishia's Story

I struggle to comprehend the process of grief. It has been one whole year since my dad passed away/died - it feels like a lifetime ago and at the same time, I can recall it like it was yesterday when we had to say goodbye.

Dad's illness came as a shock. No symptoms until it was too late. Diagnosed in January 2019, palliative care in February, and died in September. He'd just turned 54. I had just turned 28.

I took it for granted that my parents would be around forever. I envisioned they would see me graduate with my doctorate, my dad would walk me down the aisle on my wedding day, they would retire by the sea and have their grandchildren stay over at weekends and during the holidays. I feel angry and cheated that this vision has been cruelly taken away from me. Now, I have to imagine a new future without my dad physically here...and that hurts!

My dad; a fun-loving, carefree and funny man. He was forever cracking jokes, using humour and an absolute wind-up merchant. Besides that, he was caring, generous and so hardworking- a perfectionist in many ways! I take comfort that I have adopted many of his traits, even if the perfectionist trait is frustrating at times.

So, when my dad became ill, it was heart wrenching to watch. The symptoms were horrific. I felt helpless. We couldn't fix this for him no matter how hard we tried, and then the horrible guilt trap consumed me. I felt guilty all of the time. Survivor's guilt perhaps, guilt for being happy, for being sad, no matter what I did or how I felt, I felt guilty all of the time. Thankfully, the guilt has eased in time, and I can now appreciate that I did my best to care for my dad and did everything I possibly could.

Dad's care and treatment at the beginning of his diagnosis was unfortunately poor. The prognosis was not shared very sensitively, and he ended up in hospital a few days later. He had given up. He had been told he had 2-4 months to live. With my threat and drive systems activated, I requested a second opinion and his care was taken over by another care provider. His prognosis was still the same, treatment still relatively the same but there was something different that this provider had...hope! I strongly believe that it was this that helped dad to fight and outlive his prognosis for a further few months. Even when everything felt bleak, hope gave us the resilience to get back up and the motivation to carry on and fight.

The week of my dad's passing and the arrangements for the funeral are still a blur for me. Mum and I were running on adrenaline to get us through the days. A year later, I am unable to remember much about the funeral other than it was a beautiful service.

After the weekend of the funeral, I started the biggest journey of my career to date- the Doctorate in Clinical Psychology. I had worked so hard to get to this point, and now it felt tainted. Adjusting to two big transitions was really hard. It felt bittersweet. I was happy I had the opportunity to tell my dad I had secured a place on clinical training; but now I was starting this journey without him. I wouldn't be able to tell him about the course, my placements, the topics I had learned. I noticed I felt really angry, really sad, and every little thing felt like a trigger. Life just carried on as normal for everyone else (or so it appeared), and I just wanted to shout, "I have just lost my dad" and cry. I didn't want to put on a brave face and smile behind gritted teeth. I was exhausted from putting on an act, pretending

I was okay. Behind closed doors, I noticed I would be hard on myself for not keeping it together, questioned my sense of coping and compared myself to others who were also grieving convinced they were coping better than I was. On reflection, I did not give myself the kindness or credit I deserved. I had just lost my dad and yet here I was still carrying on. This for me has been a very valuable learning point. I now own my grief, and I am not ashamed to grieve.

I get really annoyed when people say to me "it will get easier." I find it insulting to the people we have lost. Instead, I remind myself the pain of losing someone we love <u>**NEVER**</u> gets easier; our life just seems to grow around the pain, so we have some better and some not so good days...and that's okay. For me, this is much more comforting. A kinder way to notice my pain. The pain button analogy is also another helpful way to acknowledge my grief. I don't necessarily believe that the ball of grief gets smaller; but I have noticed that over time the ball does not hit my pain button as frequently as it did during the early stages of my grief. Don't get me wrong there are still those days or triggers when my grief ball is bouncing frantically like a ping pong ball on my pain button, but I allow my pain to be there, make room for it knowing that it will eventually pass.

I also remind myself that there is no estimated time of arrival or end point to our grief. We grieve for as long as we need or want to without the pressure of others or society telling us different!

People shy away from grief, avoid asking how we are, avoid talking about our loved one out of fear they will offend us or trigger a shower of tears. This frustrates me too. Talking about my dad is deeply helpful on so many levels. I remember and reminisce the good times, yes it makes me sad, but it also makes me happy, and I feel grateful that people want to remember him with me. This for me is comforting and meaningful.

There are lots of little things that help me in times of need:

- Symbolic representations e.g. seeing robins and butterflies with a strong sense and belief that my dad is still around me.
- A cancer awareness badge on my lanyard at work which I hold close to me if something has triggered my pain button, and I patiently wait for the storm to pass.
- I talk to my dad, I wish him goodnight, I kiss his photo, and therapeutically arrange flowers at his grave symbolising I am still caring for him...so many little things that help me.

A year on and life feels a little brighter than it first did. I have good days and I still have bad days too. Indeed, the good days are much more frequent now, but I accept and allow my bad days to be there, knowing that my anger, sadness and hurt will pass.

I owe so much to my dad; I wouldn't be where I am today if it wasn't for his guidance, teaching and direction. Further, this unfortunate life experience has helped me grow and develop both personally and professionally.

I would like to end my story by sharing the final paragraph of my eulogy to my dad:

"And finally, here's my thank you to you Dad for all that you have been and for all that you are. You might not be here physically with us anymore, but we will forever carry you in our hearts. You will live on through us and we will continue to make you proud. Until we meet again Dad to do it all over again. We love you."

There are a few other useful bits and pieces you might find helpful:

- The fried egg analogy. I think it is based on Dr Tonkin's model of growing around grief. Imagine a fried egg... Our grief is represented by the yolk and the white bit surrounding the yolk represents our life. Society thinks the yolk part of the egg decreases in time; but actually, it's the white bit surrounding the yolk that changes. During our early stages of grief, the white bit is small so we can only see our grief (yolk). But as our life expands/grows/develops, we start to see more white surrounding the yolk. The yolk is still the same size, our grief has not decreased, our life has just grown around it.
- Podcasts on grief- Psychologists off the clock e.g. bearing unbearable loss.
- The quote: Grief is the price we pay for taking the risk to love (Owen, 2019).
- Also "in our pain we find our values, and in our values, we find our pain."

5

Kate's Story

5a – A Belfast Child

As a child of "The Troubles" grief was everywhere. The distraught faces of people on the telly who had lost loved ones in such a senseless way; the lady down the street who had lost a cousin or an uncle etc. Put simply, all around an awful lot of anguish and far too much loss. But mostly it was removed, detached & belonged to someone else. For that we were thankful.

When I was about age eight, Joan, a little girl I would sometimes play with was shot & two days later she died in hospital. She was out playing in the street with her friend & they were both caught in the crossfire when a paramilitary group opened fire against the police. I'd never lost anyone I knew before & although I really didn't know Joan all that well as she lived in Liverpool but was back in Belfast staying with her grandmother, she was the first person I had met who had died. A couple of days after she passed, an older friend of mine & one my mother thought should "know better" said, "Shall we go & see Joan"? So at age 8 with a 10 year old friend, we knocked on the door of her Grannie's home & announced – "We have come to see Joan". People in Ireland were and generally still are, brought home to rest for a few days before the funeral. Laid out in their coffin for family, friends & neighbours to come & pay their respects. I don't know if I felt grief about Joan that day because I was just so scared. But I experienced something traumatising in the tormented faces & anguished cries of Joan's parents & grandparents. Her grandmother was brushing her hair which really freaked me out. The curtains were closed & in the small dark room even her little coffin seemed huge. People were kissing her. I think I just pretended. I couldn't quite make my lips make contact with her pale cold face. By the time I walked the 10 minutes home I was hysterical & had wet myself. My mum was furious at my ten-year-old friend for taking me & I think she was also a bit cross with me for doing something so 'silly!' I cried that day until I fell asleep at bedtime. After this, I bed wet fairly regularly, I was afraid of the dark & wouldn't settle to sleep unless someone stayed with me – this carried on until I was about 11 years of age. As such a young child it was less of a sense of loss / grief for me & more the realisation of what death really was & what it looked like. Death was dark & people squealed loudly & the house smelled strange & everyone said things like "they would never be the same again". I was scared rigid about death & dying then & for many years that followed, well into my adulthood & I'll admit even now it's something I can fixate upon especially when someone I care about is unwell. "My name is Kate & I catastrophize everything". I hardly remember the times I played with Joan, or how she sounded or what she wore because I was so young & it was so long ago. But the image of her in her coffin is as clear now as it was 48 years ago.

Fast forward to 1975....my big brother Paul & his best friend Alan were inseparable. Alan hung out in our manic, overcrowded little terrace house & he was so "cool." He & Paul played guitar & mesmerised me with their coolness. They also went fishing once a week. One week Paul couldn't go. I can't remember exactly why, but sense Dad wouldn't let him go as a punishment for some misdemeanour or other. The next day there was a knock on the door from Alan's Aunt. He was dead. He had gone fishing with another lad & on the way home they had both been shot in a paramilitary "tit for tat" killing. I knew Alan far better than I knew little Joan & his death was so much closer & more tangible. My brother was broken, I didn't know what to say and as distraught as my mother was, mostly she was

Kate's Story

just "glad" it wasn't Paul that bled out in A & E. A phrase I recall with such clarity is – "thank God it wasn't our Paul". Paul was broken, he cried all the time – my cool big brother bent double in grief. It scared me – really scared me. Every year, for more than 20 years, Paul put a memorial in the Belfast Telegraph on the anniversary of his best mate's death until Alans mother asked him to stop as it was just so upsetting for her. It's true to say in the years that followed until Paul's death in 2006, he spoke about & carried on grieving for his friend.

My experience of grief as a child is very different to my adult experience. Although I vividly recall images in pictures, like still photos in an old movie - snapshots of chaos & pain, mostly I connect with how it felt. It was something beyond my comprehension & control.

Helplessness - wanting everything to be "normal" again & desperation when my childlike efforts to kiss it all away made little or no difference.

As some small act of remembrance about once a year I scroll through the names of all those who lost their lives in the conflict & pause a moment when I see their names.

(Joan Scott – died 30th May 1972 – aged 12)

(Alan Raymond – died – 22nd June 1975 – aged 23)

5b
Kate: An Adult Perspective

As a small child & until close to when I started high school, I said my prayers every night. I'm not all that sure why I did this as it wasn't something we were told to do. But I think it made me feel safe in unsafe times. My prayers were always said in a certain order. I started with a general "thank you for today" with perhaps a bit of a moan about the bits that didn't go so well, then a kind of "wish list" to God for the next day. Followed by the Lord's Prayer & finally but most importantly, my "God Bless" list. It went like this - "God bless Daddy, Mummy, Terry, Alan, Paul, Anne, Norman & God Bless me". Always in order of oldest to youngest. I recall feeling a bit worried because one day I would be the only one left because of course people died in order of age & so as the youngest I'd be alone one day with no close family. Of course, as I matured I kind of knew this wasn't the case but that's how I saw it back then.

You can imagine even as an adult how, all bent out of shape I was when death came to my family in the wrong order. My brother Paul hadn't been well likely for some time but he lived alone, was somewhat estranged from my dad & being the kind soul he was, wouldn't have wanted any of us to worry. In early 2006, we found out Paul had been diagnosed with end stage Hepatitis C. I could write for hours about all that happened. but fast forward to late October, Paul was in hospital & fighting for his life. It's all a bit of a blur, although I recall one instance when he was literally drowning with aspiration pneumonia, I'd not left his side for over 24 hours, it was the middle of the night, he was blue & he needed to be ventilated, but there were no intensive care beds to be had. Such was the depth of his distress & mine, I actually begged the doctors to just fill him up with morphine to ease his pain; I just wanted them to let him go. Of course, they couldn't do that & eventually he was ventilated. Within a few weeks & various attempts to get him off the ventilator, Paul died in hospital. I had to come back to England, where I live for a couple of days to organise childcare, unpaid leave & to work a couple of days. I got the call to say Paul had died when at the home of a family I was working with; I buckled to my knees & screamed. That wonderful woman put her arms around me & held me close while I sobbed. Sometimes even now if I see her in town, she gives me a hug. I'll be eternally grateful to her for her kindness & understanding at a moment when I felt I just couldn't breathe.

Even though I knew Paul was going to die, the sense of loss was unbearable & coupled with the fact I wasn't there when he passed, I felt I'd let him down & I'd never forgive myself. The birthday card I left for him went unopened. The rawness of my loss was intensified by the despair of my mother, sister & brothers, but especially my mother. As a family, we all pulled together. I visited him twice a day at the funeral home & sat talking to him sometimes for an hour or more. Indeed, there was almost always someone with him those couple of days. And as well as tears there was a lot of laughter in that room. Being able to do that really helped me accept that he wasn't here anymore & allowed me to say things I'd perhaps not been able to say. In Ireland, funerals are only 2-3 days after the death so there was a lot to do & arrange. All the planning helped me & we all made sure his send-off was fitting for him. I went shopping the day after he died to buy him a crisp white new grandad shirt to be buried in, (he'd have hated a collar & tie). Going into so many shops bursting into tears & telling the story of needing an extra small grandad shirt for Paul. In the end I could only get a large so had to trust the undertaker to make sure it looked the part - it did. His biker friends did a guard of honour of his coffin whilst it was carried down the road. We played Pink Floyd "Wish you were here" as he was carried in & Lynard Skynard "Freebird" at volume, as he was carried out from the funeral home. Paul died a long & horrible death - had an abysmal few months of ill health before he passed. I hated that then & still do. All we could do was our best for him & I think we did that. I just can't imagine suffering that way & Paul did it with strength & humility. Only once since he died, have I seen Paul in a dream back when I was in South Africa in 2008. It was a comforting dream & I woke crying as I didn't want the dream to end. I hope I see him in my dreams again one day.

Less than a year after Paul, my dad died. Strangely I was in the air on my way back from an event in Portugal with Paul's fiends when dad died. Some may say he had a "millionaire's death". He was close to 90, passed in his sleep & in his own bed. Our relationship had at times been tricky & shamefully I used to think I'd not feel anything when he died. But of course I did. I went straight to the undertakers from the airport & spent a while talking to him & fixing his hair. There lay an old man who did the best he could for his family & so I was able to say goodbye & shed a tear.

Both Paul & dads passing were expected.

On New Year's Day 2017 my eldest brother Terry was found dead on his dining room floor. No warning, no illness – no time to even contemplate what was going to happen. He was there – then he was dead. My mother had called me the previous evening worried as she was unable to get hold of him on the phone. I dismissed her concerns & said he was probably out. When he was found, his dinner was still in the hot oven, the table was laid & his little dog was lying beside him. I could hardly comprehend it. He had spent a day or two with me a few weeks before & I'll be forever grateful we had that time together. Even though it was more than 10 years since Paul & Dad had died, it felt unreal. Unlike Paul, Terry had grown-up children who pulled together, arranged the repatriation flight from Manchester to Belfast & paid amazing tributes to him. My poor mother was & remains broken, stuck in grief. I find it really hard to speak to her about Terry or Paul as she cries every day & I can't help her. Changing the subject when she wants to talk about them is cowardly, but I just can't say anything to make her feel better & not being able to do anything makes me feel impotent.

More recently my beautiful dog died. She died in my arms whilst my other dog lay on the floor beside her and a vet she knew did her the ultimate kindness. And believe it or not, losing her opened up the flood gates & I cried for her, for Paul, Terry for Dad & for everything else sad in the world. There was no funeral to arrange to distract me. And something about the innocence & vulnerability of family pet really made my heart so sore.

When someone you never imagined being permanently separated from dies, it leaves such a painful void. You feel hollow & lost. Not yourself anymore. Like the mask of "devil may care" has slipped so far you could use it as a bib. Being naturally a bit cheeky & brash, I just didn't know how to be vulnerable or how to grieve properly, if there even is such a thing. I kept busy, filled my day with "stuff" & avoided talking too much about it.

I often didn't know if I wanted people to speak to me about my loss or just pretend it hadn't happened. I was so afraid I'd cry at work which I inevitably did. With hindsight rather than being asked how I was, I would have liked to be asked "Tell me about Paul / Terry / your dad, your dog – what were they like?"

Death / dying snaps at your heels like a yappy terrier. It may not draw blood today or tomorrow, but sure as eggs are eggs, it will.

6
Kerri's Story

> "Hi Marianne,
>
> Nice to hear from you and your awesome book venture. Well done you. Sounds like a great project. Hope you're doing well?
>
> Strange that you emailed when you did. I had just spent the night with a friend talking at length about how I'd managed to navigate Dad passing away. He commented that I'd been very strong and controlled and wondered how I'd done it. My thoughts on this are pretty clear, as per below. By the way, I am not remotely creative or a good writer! so apologies in advance! Feel free to chop up/ edit if it doesn't work or let me know if it isn't what you want. No obligation to do anything with it either, obviously. This is just a stream of my thoughts. Good luck with it all, K xx"

There are a few things that have helped me to cope with losing Dad - who was by the way, my favourite human on the planet. He passed away with very little notice and had been fit and healthy, so it was unexpected. But I also live on the other side of the world, away from my family, so bad news from home and the inevitable 24-hour flight that would follow, was always something I dreaded and hoped would never happen. This particular phone call was one I never wanted to receive.

It's now September 2020 and somehow, I've managed to navigate the 15 months since losing Dad with strength and poise. I often reflect on how I've managed to come through the heartbreak I always feared, relatively unscathed. The thought of losing my hero and my biggest supporter, was unthinkable to me growing up, but it happened last year and I have coped. I believe there are a number of things that have helped me and given me strength:

- Love. My relationship with Dad was so loving, positive and close, and the bond I had with him was something I always did (and always will) cherish. I think my adoration of him, the fact that the relationship was uncomplicated, and the fact that we communicated well, ensured there was nothing left unsaid. There was no conflict and our connection was strong. I think this really helped in my processing of losing him. He knew how I felt about him and I knew how he felt about me, and that was hugely comforting. I am very aware that I was extremely lucky to have had this luxury and I know that not everybody is as fortunate. I imagine that losing a loved one with whom you shared a difficult relationship would present more painful challenges.

- Gratitude. I always felt incredibly grateful to have had Dad in my life. He was such a special man, I would have been grateful just to have met him, but to have been raised by him was the hugest blessing. Such was the honour of being his daughter that my overriding feeling throughout the early stages of grief was one of gratitude. I do believe gratitude continues to help get me through difficult times, but it was ever-present during the first few months of this new chapter. I felt a warmth and a strength as a result of focusing on the positives of my situation. I felt lucky to have had him for 38 years of my life, and grateful that I didn't lose him at a younger age. I felt grateful that he had lived to see milestones in my life. I felt grateful that he didn't suffer. I felt grateful he had been a happy man and had lived a long and fulfilling life. I felt grateful that I got to spend his final days with him. I felt grateful for sharing the experience with my brother who was incredible throughout. I felt grateful for the amazing support I received from friends and family. I felt grateful for the person Dad had made me and for the strength I was finding to cope.

- I was pragmatic about losing him. It was something I knew I had no control over and somehow I found a way to accept it and not fight it. You have no choice. As I took the 24-hour flight to his hospital bed, I felt calm. I quietly prepared for and expected the worst, and thanks to the sensitivity and love of my brother during that difficult phone call, I knew what I was flying into. The inevitability of losing him, like we all have to, is something I accepted. I knew this pain was going to come one day. I knew I couldn't change it, cancel it, reverse it, hide from it. I had to approach it head on and the only way out of it was through it. The fact that we are all going to have to experience loss in our lives, the fact that it's unavoidable, and that there will never be a good time to lose a loved one, enabled me to be calm and accepting of the process.

- Another thing I believe that helped in processing the pain is that Dad prepared us well for his eventual passing. He talked about death in a non-fearing way. He didn't avoid it as a conversation topic and he made sure we knew he wasn't scared of dying. It would get mentioned gently from time to time and his philosophy around dying gave us strength after he had gone.

- Pride. In the days after Dad's death I remember dreading his funeral, but my experience of the day was uplifting and positive. I felt exceptionally proud of the man we were celebrating. I was proud of his life and his legacy and I was proud to be representing him. I sat tall, I listened to tributes about him and I shared memories of him with loved ones. I couldn't have imagined it would be like that but rather than focus on pain, I felt consumed by pride.

- Self-Compassion: In the weeks and months after Dad's death, I took time and space to care for myself. I put myself first. I was calm and quiet and showed myself kindness. I would take morning walks along the beach and became aware of a constant gentle breeze at my back moving me forward. I assumed this was Dad.

Don't get me wrong, I am so sad he is not here and I miss him terribly. I think about him always and wish I could talk to him about the news and sport and politics. I imagine how he'd respond to world events and wonder what his opinion would be on decisions I need to make. I wear his aftershave, I hold a blanket we were given from his final days, I read old text messages, listen to his music and watch old videos to hear his lovely voice. I find old birthday cards he wrote me. I see his photo on my phone every day. I contemplate getting a tattoo. I laugh at jokes he would tell, phrases he would recite and conversations we had 100 times. But I live my life.

I live my life like I always did, full of joy and adventure, because my life didn't stop when Dad died. It got sadder and emptier, but it didn't stop. I keep moving forward. I move forward with gratitude. And I feel his love every single day.

7

Dave's Story:

Grief and The Order of Things

I'm seventy-six years of age, so have met grief several times. Not that it affected me to a huge degree – death and its associated grief was expected in almost every case – but it has always been an intimately personal thing. Something I found hard to share or explain.

My earliest memory of death was my grandfather when I was about seven. He had collapsed and died in our street whilst returning home and was laid-out in the dining room of my grandparent's house, next door to and adjoining my parent's house. I had access to both houses, either through the front door that always had a key in it, or through a gate in the fence that separated our gardens. To me it was all one and I had every right to be wherever I wanted. I went and found Granddad and had a chat with him. It seemed natural and it didn't occur to me that I was unlikely to ever see him again. I was shoved off to a friend's house on the day of the funeral and the next I knew there were a lot of people back at my Gran's. It still didn't register though, not until a framed photograph was hung on the lounge wall, next to the fireplace where he usually sat. It showed a large pile of earth covered in flowers. The flowers were wreathes, and it was explained to me that that was Granddad's grave. I had difficulty with that – it didn't look like the piece of ground under a Horse chestnut tree that he and I had visited some time previously. And why was earth piled-up so much? Was he in that mound? He told me I could visit him there (in due course, once he'd died) and collect the conkers.

His passing didn't trouble me as such. He wasn't around but his 'stuff' was – his watercolour pictures still hung throughout my Gran's house, and all the paraphernalia an old man acquires still lay pretty much untouched. I was given some bits of it. Pens and pencils that he drew with, and a well-used Windsor and Newton watercolours tin box. I wish I had those now, but they disappeared at some time. So, grief was easy at that young age, and so it should be.

Later family deaths all occurred pretty much to order – Gran died when I was about fifteen. She had taken to her bed two or three years earlier. I remember it well as there was just her and myself at home. She told me she needed to get into bed - which by now was in the TV room, converted from the dining room when the new-fangled contraption arrived in time for the Coronation in '53. I had to assist in the removal of her Spirella corset! Not the best of tasks for a young lad but I survived - and so did she for quite some time. I know it was a Spirella job because she was the local Spirella lady, spending her days making the things to measure - until she retired of course. My first girlfriend, being a bit plump, was kitted out with a Spirella in next to no time. What affect it had on that fourteen-year-old God only knows! Anyway, Gran passed away shortly after being transferred to a local care home when her family could no longer cope. Grove Road Hospital – the name seemed to put the fear of Christ into any elderly Richmond resident! It was just a few paces from the cemetery. Anyway, her passing was routine to my teenage mind. I'd felt a loss when my dad woke me one morning with the news that she had died overnight. He said she was very old and it was to be expected. I accepted that and simply missed her occasionally. Gran was buried in the same plot as Granddad (now that, Marianne, really is 'Girls On Top!'). My uncle, still single, had lived with his parents all his life and continued to live in the house, so nothing changed in that regard.

Grief and The Order of Things

My Dad was the next to go and his passing was the first to register strongly with me. I was by now married with two young children. We had been to Richmond to see my parents. Dad had been suffering from 'flu. Mum was physically OK, but had suffered several minor strokes over recent years, affecting her speech and her brain, and putting quite a strain on Dad. He had been in bed all day whilst we were there and was obviously feeling very tired. Came the time to leave and he insisted in sorting out some change for the children. I told him to leave it until next time, but he wouldn't. Eventually he sorted it and we drove back to Maidenhead in the early evening. The phone rang shortly after we got in. It was my brother to say he'd had a call from a neighbour and it seemed Dad was in a bad way - it probably wouldn't be good news by the time we'd meet back at Richmond. I drove back and, sure enough, he had died, aged seventy-five.

The neighbour had persuaded the ambulance guys to take him to hospital as our mum was not up to dealing with anything. In fact, she had not been told Dad had died, but she knew and told us when we went to talk with her. I still miss him and wish he'd told me more of his life in India. His parents had met there and would never return to England. Dad had come 'home' in 1934 to see England for the first time - and met our mother, who later went off to India to marry him. They came back to England when she couldn't settle to the way of life 'out East'. All of this, I'd love to be able to talk to him about, but it didn't strike me to ask when he was here. He'd given up a very different life and had to start a new life here, in England, in a depression. I admire him for that and his gentle ways, I just wish we'd been closer somehow.

Uncle Bill, otherwise known as 'Ellis', who lived next door to my mum had never had a very good relationship with my dad but I have to say, he certainly came up to the mark once Dad had died, and looked after Mum to the very best of his abilities. He only bore the strain for about a year though, when he unexpectedly collapsed and crashed into the china cabinet! We had been quite close when I was a child, although his hot temper had embarrassed me on more than one occasion. As I reached my teens we grew apart. He didn't like motorbikes or my girlfriends (although he had enough of his own). I cannot say I missed him, he was simply too difficult a person to miss! I'm glad I knew him though, and we popped him away on top of Granddad and Grandma! Two years ago Lin, my wife, and I collected conkers for the first time at that plot that Granddad had shown me all those years ago. I'm sure the three of them would have smiled.

My mum lasted another couple of years before succumbing to another stroke. We had reached a point where we knew she could no longer be left alone in the home that she refused to leave. Frequent calls from good neighbours had told us she had been wandering in the street or hoovering the house at unlikely hours in the night. She was not in a state to be concerned by the fact it was Grove Road Hospital that she was taken to. Her passing was a relief for her and, without doubt, for us as well. I don't feel bad about that, there can come a time when life is not rewarding in any way. When that is reached, its time to go. I do miss her, but it doesn't hurt.

Then came a shock. I was in my office working on some project to improve the Company's lot when my secretary came in and said she had my brother on the 'phone – but she didn't think it sounded like Herb. She put him through and he told me he had just lost Eileen, his wife. She was 52. I couldn't comprehend what he was telling me. It just wouldn't sink in. His friend Jim came on and explained they were at London Airport, en route to Lanzarote, and had just boarded the terminal bus when Eileen simply died. There was no point in me going to the airport as Jim and his wife would bring Herb home straightaway.

Grief and The Order of Things

I couldn't think how I could bring myself to tell my wife, Lin. After a while I decided to go home and tell her. She was in the garden. I brought her into the house and told her Eileen had died. She didn't get it - why had I come home to tell her a person she hardly knew had died? No, 'our' Eileen had died. The news gradually sank in despite the natural disbelief and we sat together, stunned.

I was about thirteen when Herb and Eileen first started dating. She became like a sister to me even before they married - and when that happened three years later, I was Best Man. They lived with us in the family home, having most of the upper floor of the house. Herb and I worked together so I saw them both every day. We holidayed with them, went out and about with them, and we were pretty much inseparable until they started their family and took a flat in nearby Whitton. Still, we visited several times a week. Then they bought their first house and we gradually saw a little less of them. Nevertheless, we often went out together and holidayed together. When I met the young girl that would become my wife, Eileen accepted her without question, and she was the first person I told when we decided to marry. She said she knew we would.

Bringing up families meant we saw rather less of Herb and Eileen, but that didn't mean we drifted apart, far from it. We regularly visited each other and still shared holidays. So, Eileen's death was the first loss that I didn't really understand. I stood outside their house on the day of the funeral looking at the flowers that friends had sent - and the enormity of Herb's loss suddenly hit me, like a ton of bricks. I burst into tears and couldn't stop crying. Eventually the hearse arrived and we joined Herb in the first car. Bang, another ton of bricks! This shouldn't be happening. Herb should not be going through this. The coffin was too close. In our faces. I needed space. It was only a few minutes drive to the church but one that seemed to last forever. I couldn't wait to get out of the car. The service went by with me in a daze and Herb coping far better than me.

I felt guilty about that. Lin supported me superbly, as she always has, but it was a nightmare.

Back at Herb's house there were friends to meet. Another mountain to climb. And still Herb coped so well. After everyone had gone he told me he didn't know how he was going to cope. They had run their business together from the day it started, so on top of losing his wife he'd lost his business partner. I was going off to Singapore on business the next day. What awful timing, but I couldn't cancel, too many arrangements had been made. I phoned him at strange Singapore times of night to see how he was doing. And I kept waking up in tears. They were for him though, not Eileen, which perplexed me. I got back and he collected me from the airport. He was coping remarkably well in company but struggling like hell on his own. He got through it all though, and we did too. When Herb found Maria we welcomed her into our lives. She would never replace Eileen for us or Herb, but she is her own person and became part of our family. I am convinced she saved my brother from a very dark place.

I continue, after nearly thirty years, to miss my late sister-in-law. She was more a sister, the 'in-law' bit is irrelevant. Lin and I often talk of her and she is not forgotten. I know that the grief I felt when she died was for both Herb and Eileen. It was the most difficult time I'd experienced when losing family.

And then the latest death to contend with, my brother Herb, aged eighty-four. He died in May and its now September 2020, so not so long ago, but he had had a 'dress rehearsal' and that, in a way has helped the grief of losing him. Four years back and he was kick-starting his Velocette – no mean task at eighty. Fortunately, his friend Graham was with him and offered to have a go, but Herb was one of those determined people that didn't like to give in, even if to his own detriment. Finally, he got off the bike and staggered a little. Graham asked if he was OK? Herb replied: 'not really' and collapsed to the ground. There was no sign of life, but Graham started pumping away on his chest. Maria, Herb's wife, was inside their workshop and hearing the kerfuffle came to assist and 'phoned for an ambulance. She relayed instructions from the emergency services to Graham and Russ, her son, who between them kept up the CPR until the ambulance arrived. I got a call from Maria to tell me what had happened and Lin and I dashed off to St, Peter's Hospital, Chertsey. There, everyone was waiting for news from the intensive care unit. Eventually a doctor explained that everything possible was being done to keep Herb alive, but things did not look good – he had suffered a major heart attack and could not breath without assistance. What damage may have occurred to his brain was unknown and for the time being his body temperature had been reduced and he was in an induced coma. We could visit him but be prepared to see lots of tubes and wires. I went in with Maria and was completely shocked, despite the warnings. He looked dead and felt cold. A large tube disappeared into his mouth. I thought we had lost him, without any doubt, I was certain he would not recover, he was dead. Seven days later when I visited him, he was sitting up in bed and chatting to us as if nothing much had happened! He remembered nothing of the incident but otherwise was as lucid as ever, nothing lost.

On my first visit, at the time of crisis, I came away with an enormous feeling of loss – not simply of my brother but with every tie to my childhood and teenage years. I had never before experienced such a feeling, as if half my life's memories had been taken away. No more connection to my family, or Richmond, or Old Deer Park Gardens (our family home), or my learning years in the toolroom in Twickenham where we both worked, or those teenage years of motorbikes and so much more. It all was now pointless. I couldn't explain that to anyone, even Lin, the one person who I feel may have understood. It didn't last long, thankfully, as Herb's recovery was as unexpected as his supposed demise. Now he was getting about again, albeit with far less energy than before, but he was here and could be visited and could visit. Things were back to near normality – so much so that before too long we were having to nag him not to attempt to start any of his motorbikes. He got round that by buying an electric start lightweight, and managed occasional runs out to Bagshot Chippy on a Wednesday, one of his favourite meetups.

But the inevitable toll had been wreaked upon his old heart and lungs and when he went for his last check-up with his specialist the news was not good. 'I'll make another appointment for you in six months, but I don't expect to see you', and so it was. To say the least, it was unfortunate that this would come about in the middle of the most serious pandemic any of us are, hopefully, ever likely to see. When his heart and lungs deteriorated to such a state that every breath was a huge effort, he simply had to accept there was no alternative to hospital. But Covid-19 meant isolation. The hospital staff were certain he must have the virus despite two negative test results. A cruel way to go when your mind is as good as ever. He knew he had not got or had the virus, but nobody could visit in these hard times, whether or not he had it. He died of another major heart attack, alone in the hospital toilet. I'd spoken with him the previous day, when he told me he couldn't carry on much longer, it was just too difficult. I understood and told him so.

I shall be forever grateful to Graham, Russ and Maria for their efforts in keeping Herb going for that extra four years. It gave both he and I time to come to terms with the inevitable. And whilst I still feel that I've lost all those connections to my early life, I can now concentrate upon my feelings for my brother and I do accept he'd had a good life and a long run. I'll always miss him, I know that, but his death is, in the order of things, something I now accept. But I miss him.

All-in-all, I've managed the grief of life and death quite well I think. I've been lucky in that there has been little that one can describe as trauma, its mostly been natural and 'in the order of things'.

> I miss the people I knew and loved and sometimes feel quite sentimental, but that's something that's natural with age I believe.
> I'm sorry I can't speak with them but I know it won't bother me once I'm gone. That's life. I do not believe in anything after.

8
Natalie's Story

Grief. It's such a slippery concept. Just when I think I have a grip on it, it shifts. It's not tangible, linear, or time-bound. It manifests itself in different ways for all of us. Although we might share similar emotions and coping / non-coping strategies (which helps us realise that we're not alone), our individual life stories are inextricably linked to the way in which we think, feel and act around grief; our resilience to it. And so there's a loneliness to grief, other than the obvious missing the loved one who has died. And this is where talking about our experiences and sharing them can really help. We all need to feel heard.

My father died suddenly, 7 years ago from a heart attack. He was 65 years old and had just received his first pension payment. That always seemed very cruel. He was a wonderful father/friend/confidant and we were very close. Particularly, after the birth of my son, whom he adored. The shock of his death carried me through the first few weeks and it wasn't until after his funeral, when the phone stopped ringing and when there was nothing more to organise, that I felt the excruciating pain; the realisation that I would never see him again. This is when the crying started. I cried constantly. At home, on the bus to work, in the bathroom at work, all the time. I didn't care that it was sometimes in public. I couldn't have stopped even if I did. It wasn't a quiet, polite kind of crying either. It was full-on snotty nosed, red-faced, uncontrollable sobbing, which I decided quite quickly, had to stop. I focussed my attention on my family for the 2 years following that and tried to be there for their grief. I couldn't bear to deal with my own. What I hadn't anticipated was the havoc that our different experiences of grief would have on our family unit. I'd imagined my dad's death would bring us closer together and it didn't. It was an incredibly hurtful and confusing time and I felt I was losing my identity and my control in addition to my father. Loss upon loss upon loss. As if I had any control over anything anyway. That's when I began to press the self-destruct button. Not openly and obviously at first. I still considered myself to be highly functioning at work. But I withdrew from family and friends, started eating and drinking more than was healthy and gave way too much time and credence to my negative inner voice. After 2 years of increasingly destructive behaviour, I had a breakdown and that is when I sought help. 5 years after my father's death, I was ready to open up to a counsellor and this was the kindest and most important thing that I could do for myself. I was able to talk through the acute sadness and feelings of loss and abandonment that I was experiencing; the shame and guilt I felt about my own self destructive behaviours and my role as a parent; the isolation from my family and the anger I felt about that; and the absolutely paralysing fear I felt about moving on and what that meant. All these messy, knotty, complex feelings that needed unpicking. It was from this place that I could explore my grief, my vulnerabilities and start to rebuild what felt broken.

What helped?
-Talking to a person-centred counsellor. It took me a long time to feel ready to seek help, but when I did, boy was it worthwhile. To be given unconditional positive regard despite all the ugly emotions and broken-down bits about me, felt incredible. I finally started recognising what I needed and I gave myself permission to feel and be vulnerable and ultimately, to start healing.

-Reading. About the stages of grief; about loss. It can feel quite traumatic when you're in the absolute depths of despair, but when I felt I couldn't reach out to anyone else, I could always reach for a book. Understanding my grief and developing self-awareness was key for me. Finding Meaning: the sixth stage of grief by David Kessler, is an incredible book.

-Time to myself with myself. Before my breakdown, I didn't prioritise this and I'm not sure I'd have coped well with some time alone anyway. I had such a need to fill the void. When I started counselling however, not giving myself that time to grieve, started to become a bit of a theme in my story and so I recognised that I needed to make a change. The change was small but by carving out a little time each day just for me became important. It felt selfish at times, uncomfortable even. But really, it was an act of kindness that gave me the opportunity to tune in to my thoughts and feelings for a short while, accept them and move on.

What didn't help?
-Eating and drinking to excess. Sounds obvious really. It only fed the shame and sadness I felt, not my soul.

-Putting other's grief before my own. I'm a natural helper and always want to make sure that the people I care about are OK; that their needs are met; that I'm there for them. The trouble with that is, I forgot to look after myself and give time and space to my own grieving as a result. The irony is of course, that you can't help others if you don't help yourself. There's a reason that in an emergency on board a plane, you're asked to put on your own mask before you help others.

-'Shoulds' and 'Coulds'. When I think about my relationship with my dad, the breakdown of my family, my self-destruct period and the lack of emotional availability I had for my son during that time, it's easy to start should-ing and could-ing all over myself. To beat myself up for how I should have behaved and to think about what I could have done differently. I'm all about reflection but what can I do now about what happened in the past? How does that help me to move forward? It wasn't pretty, but I coped with things the best I could, with the resources I had at the time. Might I deal with inevitable grief differently in future? I do hope so, but now I'm trying to remain in the present and am stopping with the self-flagellation.

7 years down the line and my grief hasn't gone away. It never will. I miss my dad all the time. It's palpable. I still sob every now and again and sometimes unexpected moments arise where feelings are so raw and overwhelming that I'm knocked sideways. I can only say that I'm getting better at coping with my grief and that I'm at the point now, where I remember the love more than I feel the pain.

My love for him will never be done.
It's unfinished and I'm sometimes not sure what to do with that, but I think he'd probably say:

> *"Use it to love yourself Natalie and those around you."*

9

Tracy's Story:

A Story of Hope & Healing

At 9.15pm on February 10th 2019, I made a call to 999, this would be the first call of many I would make that night to say that my younger brother had ended his own life.

Let's rewind 20 minutes from that time when I was oblivious to the emotional rollercoaster that was coming and you would have found me stood in Kev's kitchen joking with his friend about how he was probably in a pub somewhere getting drunk and he'd rock up at closing time with a shrug of the shoulders dismissing why we were worrying about him. If only, this had been the case!

Kev was (after 19 months it still feels surreal saying 'was') Kev! I have never met anyone like him and never will, although his youngest son may give him a run for his money. Kev hated to be called by his full name, he would actively ignore you if you tried to call him Kevin. He was either referred to as Kev or Gerbs, I used both. 'Gerbs? Why that name?' Is often asked. Well for those of you old enough to remember the 80's you may recall a show called Roland the Rat, in the show there was a gerbil called Kevin. As kids do, we then started calling Kev gerbil and eventually it got shortened to Gerbs which stuck.

Kev was 36 years old when he ended his life, he was a Daddy to 2 gorgeous young boys (aged 4 and 5 at the time). He was an amazing Dad and loved his boys with all his being. How could he leave them? I still think about that question, and now I understand suicide a little more I know that his decision to end his life does not makes his love for children questionable, it was all about his mental health.

I have relived and dissected the weeks leading up to Kev's death a million times. The 'what ifs' were crippling. What if I'd asked this question? What if he'd said how he was feeling? What if I'd called him that morning? What if? What if.......?

Due to circumstances we spent a lot of time together in the 2 months prior to his death. We had trips to the cinema, days out in the park (my daughter who is now 7 still talks about how uncle Kev shut her and the boys in the boot of his car as they were sat in it changing out of their wellies – they found it hilariously funny!), nights drinking and the most fabulous day out at the zoo. I sometimes wonder whether he mentioned anything about how he was feeling when 2 weeks before he passed, we were extremely drunk together, maybe I just don't remember? I know that's a possibility as people tend to open up a bit more when drunk, but I have to come to realise that I can't punish myself for something that may or may not have happened.

Let's now get back to the evening of the 10th February 2019 and the days, weeks and months that followed – this is where it all gets a bit harder to write/look back on. There are several things that I can recall from that evening; 1) the physical pain in my heart - it actually felt like my heart was breaking into little pieces, 2) the desire to run away! One of my biggest regrets is leaving Kev's friends to deal with everything that night, I just couldn't function. In the same breath, I am so thankful to them both for shielding me and protecting me from that particular nightmare, 3) the nausea I felt and 4) the need to have my mum with me.

There are certain parts of that night that would result me in reaching out 6 months later for help.

The days that followed were a blur, I took on the role of contacting the coroner etc. My mum has thanked me quite a few times for taking on the responsibility of sorting out the more formal side of things. I was very open that it was for very selfish reasons that I took on this role – I wanted to keep myself busy and distract myself from the fact that Kev was gone, simple as that. Kev and I had several arguments over the years about how I would try to 'mother' him, so it was probably the most natural thing that I would slip straight into it. However, no matter how much I tried to distract myself, that pain in my heart would not go. I tried explaining to people how it physically hurt, but I'm not sure anyone understands unless they have actually experienced it too. That first week I lived off coffee, the thought of food made me so nauseous – I couldn't understand how anyone could eat. I enjoy eating, I suppose as I was so consumed by grief, I couldn't face doing something I enjoyed.

I went back to work after one week, again looking back this was a way for me to distract myself from dealing with my feelings. I also became a very angry person, angry at almost everyone and everything. Strangely, my anger was never directed at Kev although you could argue it was his fault I was feeling the way I was. The only emotion I had towards Kev was that of extreme sadness. I was so sad that someone could feel that ending their own life was the best option. After 19 months I still get the pain in my heart when I try to imagine how he must have been feeling that day.

Over the next 6 months, we had the funeral and the inquest to get through. I read a poem at the funeral, I remember sitting down after I finished and while a piece of music was playing I was shaking so much I didn't know how to stop it. The inquest was extremely tough. For some members of the family it was the first time they had heard the details in full. It was like being part of a horror movie where you know the outcome before everyone else.

2 months after Kev passed my sister and I went to the tattoo shop together and had a tattoo of Kev's fingerprint tattooed onto our arms in the shape of his heart. Next to it I also had a tattoo of some forget me not flowers (sky blue was Kev's favourite colour). In May 2019, I attempted an ultra-challenge, 106km walk and I ran a half marathon. I raised a fantastic amount of money for charity which would go towards funding telephone lines where people could call for help.

Fast forward to September 2019 and although I had been going to a monthly suicide bereavement group I did the bravest thing I could do and the one thing I wish more people would do, that was to ask for professional help. By this time, I was having flashbacks, not being able to sleep, was very emotional, constantly in a state of fear that someone else close to me would end their life and avoiding certain situations.

In February 2020 I was diagnosed as suffering from PTSD and I started a course of intensive CBT therapy. I had no idea what to expect of the sessions and I also didn't know whether they would work, but I owed it to Kev's memory and my family to give it my best shot. Also, how could I share posts promoting people to ask for help or try to get family members to ask for help if I wasn't prepared to do the same.

The CBT sessions were emotionally exhausting, in one session I spent the entire two and a half hours crying (proper ugly crying!). At the start of the session my therapist, who I must say was amazing and I owe a lot to, fully explained the purposes of reliving the entire night and saying out loud which parts were causing me the most distress. Out of respect for Kev I won't go into details of that night. In following sessions, we concentrated on the parts of the night that I was having flashbacks to, my therapist used an approach referred to as 'the laundry cupboard.' It involves taking out all of the memories from the night and filing them back into the brain. I have not explained it enough to do it justice so recommend you research it further. What I will say is, it worked for me.

My sessions were still taking place as the country went into COVID-19 lockdown, I chose to continue doing them over the phone. I had another 6 or so sessions over the phone, each of them getting easier. By the end of sessions I was sleeping better, the flashbacks had stopped (I still find myself thinking of that night but it's now when I choose to, not when my brain decides it wants to torment me with it). I had also started to do some of things I was avoiding. The worrying for other people had also reduced, it still remains, and I don't think it will ever fully disappear. I would never in a million years have thought Kev would end his own life, so if he can then anybody can, and nobody is safe – that thought scares me a lot.

Kev was very passionate about his local football team, so this year we have had his ashes placed in the memorial garden at the football ground, it has bought a lot of comfort knowing his resting place is at a place he loved – ironically the football ground was built on the site we used to play on as kids and therefore, holds lots of memories for us all.

19 months on and I have way more better days than bad days, I think about Kev a lot and always will but I know that while we all continue to talk about him and remember him (even the annoying traits) then he will live forever and never be forgotten. Maybe reading this and knowing there is light at the end of the tunnel will help people reach out or even realise that how they are feeling when bereaved by suicide is 'normal'.

A Story of Hope & Healing

If you have been bereaved by suicide, my advice for you is – look after yourself, if you are finding things hard then focus on getting through the next minute, the next hour, the next day and most of all never feel guilty for laughing or smiling or living. Your friend, husband, brother, sister, mother, father, son, daughter, brother in law or sister in law would not want you to be miserable. They ended their life to stop the pain for them, not to create pain for you. Keep their memory alive by doing things they would have encouraged you to do had they still been alive. And, most importantly ask for help in the same way you wish your loved one had.

Email from: Dr Marianne Trent
To: Tracy

Dear Tracy,

It's utterly beautiful. Thank you so much for taking the time to write it and for trusting me with yours and Kev's story. It's so powerful to read and my heart goes out to you. Loss is complicated and messy – loss by suicide brings along a whole host of extra hugely complicated feelings and experiences too. I'm so pleased you were able to access the right treatment for you at the right time and that it has helped you to process your experiences and to begin to heal.

Thank you once again and I'm so sorry for the loss of Kev.
Marianne

10
Sarah's Story

In my experience, people almost always apologise if they cry when discussing their grief. There seems to be a cultural belief in the U.K. that it is embarrassing to be seen crying or a fear that it may embarrass the other person. It does seem to be true that many people try to avoid the topic of grief after a brief offer of condolences, as they may not want to further upset the bereaved. Also, many people simply do not know what to say or how to cope with the subjects of loss and death.

I have not had much personal experience of grief, apart from losing my grandparents and I believe your loss can be affected by many factors, for example, your age, closeness to the person, other events occurring in your life at the time. When my Nan (who I loved very much) died, I had returned from working abroad in time to see her and say my goodbyes, something I felt very grateful for. I was able to be present at the end and I remember it being peaceful and felt reassured by it. In contrast, when I said goodbye to my husband's mother on her deathbed, it felt frightening watching her struggle for breath, as if she was clinging on, not ready to go.

With my Nan, I had lots going on in my life at the time, it felt like I didn't have time to dwell too much on the loss but I remember feeling sorry for my Mum and not really knowing what to say to her and not wanting to see her cry and feel bad. I think my faith also helped, picturing my Nan safe in Heaven and reunited with my Grandad.

Despite my own faith in the afterlife, as I get older, I do feel fearful of death and also have a fear of losing those close to me. I try not to think about it in any detail because I know the grief will be intense and painful. If I imagine losing a parent, child or my spouse, I cannot picture how I will recover from it.

A friend of mine lost her mother and was able to read the eulogy at the funeral, something I think I would be entirely incapable of doing. It seems we are often expected to be 'brave' and accepting of death, but I imagine myself being unable to contain my grief, unable to stop crying or to get through the day. I picture people from other cultures, wailing and ululating and feel that is surely a more natural response than the British 'stiff upper lip'. I remember a boy in my class at school died from a heart defect he was born with at the age of nine. I went to his funeral. It was overwhelmingly sad to see his mother's grief, how she had to be held up and supported. I cry at the idea of losing my children...but I also fear dying young myself and leaving them motherless and unprotected.

I agree with the idea that grief is like a club...one that I am not yet a member of and one that I am in no hurry to join. As a therapist myself, I think there is a massive need for professional support...a safe space to grieve, to scream and rant and open up on feelings of guilt, relief, anger...whatever the bereaved is feeling, a chance to express themselves without fear of being a burden to others or affecting other people with their own sadness.

Perhaps for people not yet in 'the club', it can be hard to completely understand or empathise with people dealing with grief. I think there is an idea about 'getting on with it'. "They wouldn't want to see you feeling like this." This may be true, but might not be particularly helpful. Everyone has their own way of dealing with loss. A friend of mine recently lost her mother but said it was almost a relief as she was in her nineties and had very poor quality of life. She was surprised at her sister's more emotional reaction, thinking that her death was only to be expected, but her sister was grief-stricken at the hole left in her life.

One of my therapy clients spoke about facing their own mortality as they reached the age that their mother had passed away. They had lost both parents and a brother and their other brother was seriously ill, so they felt themselves taking a step closer to death...the next one in line. They spoke of their intense grief and difficulty in coping with day to day life after caring for ill parents in the last stages of their lives, left bereft. The tidying away of precious, treasured possessions seemed cruel, a whole house of sentimental value to deal with. Practicalities to face on top of emotional distress. I cannot imagine having to pick through a lifetime of memories, deciding what to keep and what to get rid of.

Another client was distraught after the loss of a beloved pet and spoke to me about it because they felt 'silly' telling people they knew how upset they were about this loss. It can be easy to dismiss these feelings, writing it off as 'only a pet' but pets can be a valued family member, providing comfort, companionship and a sense of acceptance. For some people, their pet helps combat loneliness, isolation and perhaps helps with social contact so a loss can be devastating.

Death is a massive, scary issue, that we tend to avoid discussing but I think there is discomfort on both sides, with the bereaved not wanting to 'keep going on about it', as one client put it and the listener perhaps unsure what to say or how to help. The words 'time is a great healer' are a cliché but for many, the only option is to keep putting one foot in front of the other, until they have taken enough steps through grief to gain a tiny distance from it. Special events and anniversaries will bring up difficulties but many people will find ways of coping and moving on and talking about it must surely help to eventually get to a place where happy memories can be shared and the deceased remembered with joy.

11

Hannah's Story

It was Friday 31st March 2006; I was just 16 at the time and sat in a lesson at school using the computers. My dad had flown to Bahrain a few weeks earlier; he was a painter and decorator and was managing a project at the World Trade Centre there. He was due to have a meal on a boat the night before to celebrate finishing the project. He called me earlier on that day (he used to call me daily just to check in) and I remember him calling me his 'Princess' and his 'Baby Mole' - I'll never know where that one came from! I remember talking to him like normal, probably wanting to hang up the phone so I could get back online to talk to my friends, but I always made sure I said 'love you' before hanging up.

At around 11am, just before lunch time at school, my mum called my phone and I remember answering in lesson. She told me she was coming to collect me. She swiftly arrived at school and told me that we were going to my dad's parents' house. Earlier that day my Nan had a phone call to tell her something had happened the night before; the boat my dad boarded had capsized. 58 Brits had died.

I remember seeing a glimpse of the news and all I saw were body bags being dragged out of the water. My heart dropped and I was anxiously praying and hoping one wasn't my dad. We sat waiting for another phone call to tell us if Dad was one of the ones who had sadly died, and an hour or so later my Nan's house phone rang... my dad was dead.

My dad was one of the 58 British people who didn't make it. I remember my Nan throwing the phone across the floor, crying her eyes out. She was heartbroken and utterly distraught, so was I. I had so many thoughts running through my head; it didn't feel real, but that was the day my life changed forever.

I can't remember much from the following days - it's kind of blurry, like I've blocked it out. I was 16, months away from sitting my GCSE's and my world had just shattered. It didn't feel real at first, and even 15 years on sometimes it feels like he's just gone away and hasn't come back. Maybe because he died abroad and I didn't see it happen, and he wasn't poorly, I couldn't prepare myself for his death in any way. I actually have recurring dreams where he's not dead and has just gone away, which is comforting in ways as at least I still get to see him in my dreams.

During the weeks/months after his death I suffered terribly with panic attacks. I used to wake up during the night feeling like somebody was strangling me and I couldn't breathe. My heart used to pound out of my chest, my hands felt sweaty and my chest felt so tight; I literally felt like I was dying. Along with my panic attacks I had anxiety. Anxiety is like this constant bubble following you around, a constant burden that weighs you down, you can feel its presence hovering over you like a cloud. I struggled to cope so I reached out to a counselling helpline. They offered me CBT (Cognitive Behavioural Therapy). I didn't have to wait long for my first appointment, only a few weeks. At my first appointment I remember filling in questionnaires about how I was feeling, scaling my thoughts and feelings from 1-10. The sessions helped me because it was easier to talk to someone who knew nothing about me. I felt able to let everything out and not have anybody judge me as such. I did around 12 weeks of therapy, one session each week and I remember feeling a weight lift from my shoulders, learning how to cope, learning how to breathe when I felt anxious, learning about triggers and how to help my emotions.

In the years since my dad died, I've started my own family. I met my partner just over 1 year after my dad passed. I would have loved them to meet, just like I wish my dad could meet our four beautiful children. He would have been the best Grandad ever and I know my children would have loved him just as much as I did.

I also think back to 2018 when just weeks after giving birth to my fourth child my health deteriorated dramatically as I was diagnosed with a brain tumour. I had a tumour back in 1993, aged 3 and my dad was always very over-protective of me. This time my dad was not physically there to protect me, to be by my side or to just help look after the children but I do believe he was watching over me, making sure I got better again.

My dad was only 42 when he passed away, still so young, still so many years ahead of him to make memories, still so many laughs to be had and hugs to be given. Grief is a strange thing; the reality is you will grieve forever. You will not just 'get over' the loss of a loved one, but you will learn to live without them. You will learn how to deal with emotions, and you will heal in time. I still have my good and bad days, but I look back now and try to remember the happy times we shared, the time we had together... those 16 years I get to cherish forever. If I have learnt anything from my experiences it's that life really is short, don't take it for granted, because it could change within the blink of an eye.

12

Sue's Story

My father died suddenly just a few days before Christmas on the day of his brother's funeral. He had abandoned plans to attend because of snowfall overnight. It was after clearing the path he felt unwell and after saying: "Oh dear" he died of a heart attack. He was 61.

I was in my early thirties, with two children - one at school, one still at home. The vicar in my father's parish rang my husband who came home from work to tell me. At the time I thought that unnecessarily dramatic. A phone call from the vicar would have been quite sufficient. Dad was a very matter of fact person; he called a spade a spade and if someone had died, we said they had died; there was no passing-away in our house. So I asked myself how dad would have behaved; it seemed a good guide.

I'd been told that when my grandmother died at my parent's house my father had said to my brother: "Have you ever seen a dead body? Because if not, you'd better go and take a look at Granny before they take her away." So when I arrived at my parent's house, it seemed a good idea for me to take a look at Dad. He looked very peaceful and unmistakably dead – something I could detect without ever having seen a dead body before. I found that very reassuring and I would recommend anyone who has been bereaved to do the same thing.

Things were much simpler then when a death occurred. It was the eighties and before Dr Shipman's practices had been exposed. I've since been through the process upon the death of my mother and it's a great deal more complicated now.

With my brother and my mum, we sat down to discuss the details of the funerals and when the undertaker arrived mum announced that had our father been with us, he would have poured a glass of sherry for everyone. So that's what we did. I don't recall my mother crying; in fact I don't recall her grieving much at all ever. If she did, it wasn't on show. I didn't cry at the time and not much afterwards. At the time we were more concerned with whether the funeral would take place before Christmas and car insurance; if would be legal for her to drive the next day as the policy was in my father's name. Mum and I, being busy souls, agreed to get on with our pre-Christmas events, some of which were charitable in nature. Again, reference to what Father would have wanted was most useful.

And so it was that life went on. I had another baby and the children grew up left home and start having their own children. Then one day my persistent winter cough drove me to the GP. He sent me immediately for an X-ray and before I had much time to worry, I'd been diagnosed with lung cancer with an 8% chance of recovery. I did everything I could to heal myself; cutting out any food that could be construed as harmful, adding any that could be beneficial, taking supplements and subjecting myself to chemotherapy while employing Reiki and Journey Therapy in between treatments. And that's when Dad arose again.

Journey Therapy is based on neurolinguistic programming, re-programming though processes. Very soon into the session, where I'd chosen my father to be my imaginary accomplice on my journey, the therapist said I needed a new friend with me. I have no idea what it was that she detected in my responses; but she'd spotted something to do with my father that needed exploring further.

And so it was, about three and a half hours later, with the

contents of a full box of wet tissues in my lap, I opened my eyes - both literally and metaphorically speaking – to the truth that I had not grieved for the loss of my father. I bawled my eyes out during that session and expressed the real and raw grief that I'd clung onto for thirty years. I let it all out in what seemed at the time endless sobs.

The after-effects of the session were very interesting as my mind went on processing everything for quite a few weeks afterwards, that's how Journey Therapy works. Somehow, it removed any negativity; that's the only way I can explain what I felt and feel. To a great extent, nine years and a second session later, I can still say I'm still changed by what I experienced in grieving that day for my father.

Later, when telling this story to someone else, they said: grief goes to the lungs. Checking it out I see that Chinese medicine makes that association. How much my diet and supplements helped in my recovery, how much the chemo, how my therapy assisted, I do not know. but at the time of writing, following surgery to remove a couple of my lung lobes, I am official cured of the lung cancer.

I still miss my dad, and I still sometimes have a tear in my eye. Sometimes I cry because he's not here any more. I'm nine years older now than he was when he died. There was so much more I would like to tell him, so much more I would like to have shared with him and those feelings don't change.

Since his death I have had more experiences concerning death and this time I haven't buried my feelings but let them out. When the tears come I welcome them and embrace the sad feelings of loss.

I've learned that I must not bottle up grief, it's a very bad idea.

13
Kim's Story

Within the last 5 years, I have experienced two significant bereavements. Although neither were my 'immediate' family, they were my family none the less and they both affected me deeply. I feel selfish even saying that, as I consider that I was on the periphery of the loss, in that they affected others much more strongly than me. At the age of 27 my (now) fiancé lost his father to a heart attack. A complete shock, early hours of the morning where his mother attempted CPR and by the time we arrived, he had gone. As life changing as this was for the family for several reasons, the grief process felt relative to the loss and we have survived it.

Two years later I experienced another loss, which I am going to talk about here. Two days before going on a short holiday, I received a text message from my best friend saying she and her husband were now home from the hospital and along the lines of: *'we're going to enjoy some family time at home'*. To provide some context, her husband (also one of our best friends) had a lifelong condition and spent his life having bouts of hospital admissions which became normal to most around him. Three days later, whilst starting our second day away. I received 'the' phone call. I just knew. We communicated all the time, but as with many people today it was always via text. Rarely, if ever by phone really. I could not believe it, I wanted to scream, but I felt numb. It is fair to say, that we considered life may have been limited for him, in that he may only reach 40 or 50 years old. But by no means did we think this soon. Not at 27. Although he had several periods of hospital admissions, generally he was 'well'.

After nearly 30 years of friendship I thought I knew her well. And although we do know each other very well, to this day the regret I have for not going straight to visit as I received that message, to be with her and make sense of what she was trying to tactfully tell me, will probably take a very long time if ever, to go away. Although I do not hold any guilt per se, as when it came to his health, they were a private couple so I didn't wish to pry too much, but I just wish I could have been there for her during those final 48 hours. At the time I told myself that if *'things were that bad'* she would surely just come out and say it. Yet the kind being she is, she didn't want to worry me and only hoped I would read between the lines. But I didn't. On reflection, I accept that this was because of denial. We have of course spoken about this and I think denial also ran true for her. And saying the words would have just been too painful.

What affected me more about losing not only a close friend, was I guess losing someone my age, lifelong condition or not. And he was my best friend's husband. Triple whammy. I also had the strangest feeling of being able to imagine what it might have felt like for her. It is a level of empathy I have never experienced before. I genuinely felt the significance of her pain and felt that I also held her loss in some way, in addition to my own. Maybe seeing my mother-in-law lose the love of her life had scared me into worrying about the fact that couples lose their partners every day, and one day I may experience exactly that. As absurd and as unhelpful as this sounds, I ruminated about losing my partner just so I could tell her *'I know how you feel'*. Even when I imagined how it felt for her, I knew that my loss was just not the same as the pain intensity that she was going through. Hers was another level to mine and to most, just incomprehensible. I am unsure how, but I think I did somehow comprehend it. Even though I have thankfully not experienced it.

When I lost my father-in-law, those two weeks in between death and the funeral were a confusing, heart-breaking, busy blur, often with lots of visitors. But after the funeral, it almost felt like people forgot and as they continued with their lives, the support that was around at the time, seemed to quickly dissipate. This time around, I was not going to be a person who 'forgot'.

I found the loss of my friend incredibly painful, but what did not help was how I saw our friendship group carry on with life so blatantly. I understand that although it seems like it won't, life does go on and we do move forward with our grief. But I was lucky, I had my partner at home to comfort me and I was very aware of this. However, I observed friends to be so incredibly unaware of comments, conversations, and actions whilst in the company of a newly bereft widow. Our single friends would so candidly talk about dating, our married friends talked about sex and some would express that as she was lucky(!) that she was still young and that she had plenty of time to meet someone else. Shocking I know. But she did not want to meet anyone else, she wanted her husband. So why would people say that? Is that supposed to make her feel better? On several occasions my pain for her was so strong that my blood would boil at the insensitivity of others around her and the lack of comfort from some people. We now, on reflection (as we have talked it over, during many nights of tears and laughter) just believe that they either could not understand, were unable to show that they cared, or thought that by 'being normal' would help in some way. I cannot speak for everyone, but I would say, maybe don't try to be normal, don't try to ignore the elephant in the room. If you want to be helpful, sit with that discomfort or at least ask them if they want to talk about it. As your discomfort for not knowing what to say does not even come close to what they are going through.

However, a caveat to that is of course that we are all different, so maybe address it directly to know what works best for that person. But for me, just do not ignore it because you are unsure of what to say. Just say something.

As time has passed, the pain does become more manageable and for me, the pain genuinely eased tenfold, when I started to see her coming out of the woods. I have felt guilt with this feeling also, as if in some way she is responsible for making me feel better. I know that is not the case and it just means that by seeing that her life is a little easier and happier, makes my grief a little easier too. I could go on for pages about the scenarios, feelings, hurt and confusion that has gone along with my grief. However, it has taught me the importance of just being human and being compassionate. Being there for her, on reflection has no doubt helped with my grief but more importantly hopefully helped with hers, even just a little. We talk so openly about it all and how it affected her and me and everyone else around us, that I think we made some sense of it together. And when I am feeling a sense of sadness, I remind myself how proud I am (and how he would be) of her for finding the strength and resilience to be able to smile and laugh, even on the tough days whilst learning how to find happiness again. For her to get up every day and be the best mummy to their miracle twin boys, is the pure ray of sunshine that constantly reminds us, that Nick, you will never be forgotten.

14
Katie's Grief

My dad and I didn't always get along. During my childhood and early teens, our relationship was rocky at best. We fought almost constantly, with every evening marred by another shouting match. I often felt like he purposely distanced himself from me by trying to drive a wedge between us.

By the time I was 16, I had an after-school job, a busy social life and more independence. While still keeping me at a distance, my dad now regularly caught me in conversation when I came into the kitchen for a glass of water or a snack. He seemed interested in what I was learning in school, interested in what personal philosophies I was starting to develop and interested in what music I was listening to (which was always followed by a conversation about what I *should* be listening to). Over time, these five-minute conversations stretched into ten-minute conversations, then twenty. Eventually my dad and I could be heard in the kitchen for hours, debating life's big questions or discussing a book we had both just read. It started to be a nightly ritual that replaced our fighting.

After a while, it came time for me to start planning to go to university. As an 'army brat', my dad had grown up in American army bases all over Europe. The stories he used to tell of his adventures in Rome (like that time he got a job selling popcorn, but brought his own bags so he could make a profit selling extra popcorn on the sly) and Spain (like that time he got mugged and had to sleep in a field) made me feel like there was a lot I was missing out on having never left the United States. I applied to the University of Nottingham in England and after a few months of waiting for exam results, I was accepted. From that point on it was a whirlwind – busy packing, busy saying goodbye to my friends and busy doing all of the administration that comes along with moving to another country. When it came to sorting out my immigration documents, I had to make an unexpected trip to New York. My dad decided he would drive me there and back.

On the way back from New York, cruising down I-95 South, my dad lowered the volume on the radio. Without looking at me, he said, 'I know I was really distant when you were growing up. I just want you to know that it wasn't because of you. I didn't want you to turn out like me, so I stayed away.' His voice broke, which threw me because I'd only seen my dad cry once before, when his father died, but he continued, 'You've grown up now and I'm so proud of who you are. I'm your biggest fan. I love you, but it's going to kill me when you go to England. You have to go, but I'm going to miss you.' Without waiting for any kind of response, he turned the radio back up and started to sing along with John Denver. I turned to look out the window and wiped the tears off my face. We never talked about that moment again.

We adjusted quickly when I began university. The time difference worked well for us and we would speak every night on Skype at 10pm (my time, 5pm his time). We did this for two years and then one night he signed on and I could tell something wasn't right. He started talking and words started swimming in front of my eyes. Cancer... Lung cancer... Chemo... Radiation... I was in shock. My dad had smoked like a chimney since his early teens, but he'd always seemed like some sort of impenetrable fortress to me. We hung up after talking for a few minutes. One of our shortest conversations. He didn't want me to come home, I needed to finish out my degree. So, I stayed.

That summer, after I graduated, I went home to the States to apply for another visa and to spend some time with my family. My dad had been through chemo and radiation which had shrunk the tumours and his prognosis was (unexpectedly) good but had left him gaunt and weak. I spent the summer reading and talking with him, running errands and watching horrible made-for-tv movies, which we laughed at until we cried. From time to time he'd start a conversation with 'When I die...', which I would roll my eyes at and wave off, telling him not to be dramatic. 'Yes, yes Dad, I know. No bagpipes.' My visa eventually got approved and I got ready to come back to England. My dad asked if I would stay for Thanksgiving, which was then only a few weeks away, but I said needed to get back to England to get settled in before work started and take care of a few things. I promised I would come back as soon as I could and that I would definitely be back for Thanksgiving next year. I didn't know that it was going to be his last Thanksgiving.

It was May bank holiday. I looked down at my phone after having been sat at the computer working for a few hours and saw that I had three missed calls from my mom and a message asking me to call her back. Instantly, my mind started racing – dad had been doing well recently and had even started respiratory rehabilitation. He'd seemed really well when I'd spoken to him just the night before, so what could have happened between now and then? I called my mom back. She answered and I asked what was going on. The only thing I remember was 'Katie... dad died.'

I don't think I even said anything in response – I think I just hung up the phone. I remember sinking to the floor in my apartment, sliding against the wall. It felt like my ribs had split in half and that my heart was trying to sink as low as possible, pulled by gravity, but still locked in the confines of my chest. I sat there like that, sobbing, then just staring for what must have been a few hours. Sometimes it feels like I'm still there.

I called my mom back and we talked. I found out that my dad had killed himself with a gun no one knew he had. No note. No clear event or factor anyone could point to that had pushed him over the edge.

The next few months went in fast forward. I flew home. I helped my mom go through my dad's belongings. I helped pack up my childhood home and found my mom a new place to live. I flew back to England. I had a week off of work where I just stared at the wall. And then I pushed it all down again, painted a cheerful face on and 'got on with it'.

This was an effective tactic for a few years. I didn't talk about my dad unless prompted and even then, I wouldn't go into detail. I didn't talk about my feelings. I didn't need therapy. I didn't need to talk. I didn't want to talk. That was it. I felt like this was effective, but obviously, in reality, it wasn't. I was hurt and angry. Not at my dad, but at the world for being so unfair to him. After he died, a lot of my relatives reached out, trying to be helpful by saying things like 'that's awful what he did to you and your mom, how cowardly.' This made me angrier. Couldn't they see how much courage that had taken him? He struggled with his demons for so long without talking to anyone, fighting these epic battles in his mind - alone. I shifted the blame to myself. I was closest to him at the time. Surely, I should have known he was going through all this. I should have said something. I should have done something. I started to spiral. Friends noticed, but I shrugged them off, which strained my friendships and relationships. Even my mom, who I've been extremely close to my whole life and who had been my teammate through all of this process so far, suffered the consequences of this new low that I was feeling. I got to a point where I thought about killing myself too, though thankfully never seriously enough to manifest into action. It all culminated in a tearful afternoon sat outside a restaurant, sobbing into the arms of my boyfriend, saying that I wanted to die and that it was all my fault. My boyfriend, recognising this as something much more serious than a girl who had just had one prosecco too many at brunch, talked to me and made me realise that it was time to get some professional help.

I had let the idea that my dad's suicide was my fault fester in my mind for years. The first time I admitted that to a therapist, I cried for 10 minutes. That doesn't sound like a long time, but it is when you're crying in front of a stranger – trust me. But that day marked the first day of pulling myself up and getting back on some sort of healthier track. The therapist talked to me and showed me how my dad's suicide could never be my fault. She showed me ways I could properly grieve which I hadn't allowed myself to do before. She pointed me towards resources provided by the charity Survivors of Bereavement by Suicide, which described everything I had been feeling for years and helped me feel validated. I started to feel myself again. I began to enjoy talking about my dad again, telling stories of his misadventures and mischief.

As anyone who has ever been to therapy knows, it's not a quick fix. Sometimes I'm afraid that I'm always going to be a bit angry and bitter, but I think that's just a part of grief. It's catching yourself mid-laugh and feeling guilty because they would have found that funny too if they had been here to see it – but they're not. It's the pang I feel when I can hear my dad's laugh in my own. It's the sadness I feel when I think about the fact that my dad will never meet my children. It's grieving not only for what was, but also what remains and what you never had.

When I was helping my mom go through my dad's belongings after he died, I came across one of his old denim jackets. Inside one of the pockets was a barrette from when I was a little girl. I remember finding that and simultaneously smiling and crying. I think grief is a bit like that. You go forward through life and from time to time you find a little piece of that person in somewhere unexpected and it's painful and wonderful all at once. Just like how I still cry every time I hear 'My Girl' by The Temptations on the radio.

> I love that there are still snippets of my dad that I come across even after all these years. As much as it hurts to have lost him, I'm so lucky to have had someone it hurts this much to miss.

15

John's Story

When I was around six, I would have this recurring dream. In the dream I saw an image of my parents, on their wedding day. My mum in a white gown freckled with flowers, my dad with his auburn hair, parted to one side. As quickly as it had appeared, the image would suddenly stretch and tear and burst into flames, and I would wake, frightened by what I had seen.

When I was eight, they both died. My dad in the January of 2000, in a car accident. Two months later, my mum followed when the breast cancer she had beaten only two years before, had returned.

The experiences were different in that one was expected and one was not. There had been nothing to anticipate when my dad died; it just simply happened one Friday evening, when he didn't come home. Whereas when my mum was dying, it felt as though everyone walked around our home as if the floor were covered in eggshells. Whispered conversations in hallways, a nurse leaving as I arrived home from school. Despite this, I don't think I understood that she would die. I don't think I believed that she could die. I sat with her on the evening before she did, in the wooden rocking chair that swayed by her bed, staring at my mum for what would be the last time.

There are certain memories that come to mind when I think of them. The way they left dregs of red wine in their glasses on a Friday evening. My mum's infectious laugh, almost witch like. Sitting on the back of my dad's motorbike, as we drove through the woods. Despite these memories, whenever my parents come to mind, I inevitably come back to their deaths and how robbed I feel by it.

When I was younger, I would imagine that they had not died. That in fact, they had gone into hiding, and lived in a cottage on a small hill, hidden by trees. My mum made marmalade there, as my dad worked on the garden fence. The reality of death does not hit you as a child. The permanence of death does not register with a child.

I am fortunate that I have an older sister, and naturally we faced this loss together. We have managed (somehow) to remain best friends throughout the years. These days, when I find time to see her, we inevitably find ourselves drinking white wine, reminiscing about our childhood, and listening to my mum's favourite songs. This will usually involve singing our hearts out to Shania Twain, to the annoyance of the neighbours. Ultimately, she is the only person who can know the gravity of this loss. She told me once how she lay with my mum as she died. How she fell asleep next to her, and how when she woke, the bed was empty and all that remained was the scent of talc.

Grief has seemingly affected us both in different ways. In the years following, my sister turned to alcohol, to drugs and to men who treated her badly to manage her anger and loss. Comparatively, I remained constant, if not something of a wallflower. Yet, as the years went on, I felt as though I was holding myself together with elastic bands, as if I were constantly running, dodging bullets. I knew that my grief would not leave me unscathed forever, and when I turned twenty-one, I welcomed anorexia home, like a crow who had pecked at my window for a decade. What followed were painful years of weighing cereal, shivering in the summer, and crying over bowls of soup. Eventually, I was able to recover, to move forward on a path which was not defined by where I had been and what I had lost, but where I chose to go next.

John's Story

I lived with my grandparents after my parents had died and I am certain that they did not expect to inherit an eight-year-old boy as they neared sixty. It would be unfair to say anything other than my life with them has been good and that I have been loved. However, as I have grown older, I have felt the lack of my parents' presence more and more. I think of how my mum would have loved a gay son. How my dad, with his love of motors, would have loved buying me my first car. How I would have cried on my mum's shoulder when I broke up with my first boyfriend. How they both would have sat in the audience, proudly, as I graduated. But instead of what might have been, I cling to the very few memories that I do have.

A fortnight before her death, my mum took me to have my ear pierced. The stud they tried to place in my tiny ear wouldn't fit, so she took her own diamond earring out and placed it in my ear instead. I wore this to school the next day.

Now, when I tell people that I grew up with my grandparents, something almost rehearsed spills out of my mouth – I'll say how 'fine' it had been and how I've been given everything that I could possibly need. People often accept this and probe no further. But on a rare occasion, I will confide in a friend, usually over wine, who will ask about my parents. I will tell them what I remember, which ultimately comes back to the details of their deaths. The knock on the door as policemen delivered news of a collision. The smell of talc in my mum's room. The curdled milkshake she had left on the bedside table. By the end of shedding my history, I am usually in tears. In that moment, I think that perhaps I can let go of the weight that has lived in my chest for twenty years and that I have carried since I was a child.

And in that moment, I think I will be ok.

16

Mel's Story

My Dad, George, was the kindest soul I have ever known. Quietly confident, unassuming and generous to a fault. As a young child I always feared the loss of him. He smoked Benson and Hedges. It seemed like everyone smoked back then. My Dad was handsome, immaculately dressed, smelt wonderful and always saw the good in people, even if they did not deserve it. My parents divorced when I was five years old so Dad's place was a little oasis of calm I would retreat to, drink coffee, have a cigarette and put the world to rights. No matter when we visited, he greeted us all with a big bear hug as if he hadn't seen us for years. He was just different and incredibly special.

When he was diagnosed with Cancer aged just 60, we felt our world implode. Every ounce of my being wanted to protect this kind, gentle man. What was this beast that would ravage his body and take him away from this life and those who adored him? How could someone so pure of heart be treated this way? I remember lifting him up his hospital bed after his first operation. It was like lifting a small rag doll. He rallied and moved back to his home, never once complaining.

We heard the cancer had returned and that he had just a few months left to live on the morning of my 28th birthday. That was 17 years ago and remembering those words still burns. We kept it quiet from Dad that he would not win this fight. We faced a massive wall of discontent from the medical teams who seemed to believe he would be better off knowing his fate. We disagreed.

As his family, we felt his body was already broken, so why break his heart?

Dad went into the Hospice on Christmas Eve, which felt especially cruel as families everywhere were preparing for a time of togetherness, whilst we were preparing to say our last goodbyes. Dad hung on until December 30th and passed away in our arms, after all of us reminded him that he was an amazing Father, we were so thankful he was *our* Dad and we would always love him. The first person I called was my best friend Kate. She picked up the phone and simply asked, 'Has he gone?'. Kate got it. I called my friend John; he knew how this felt. He was in 'The Club' a few years before me. We could sit in a comfortable silence together, both familiar with 'The Dad Grief'.

About 3 days after he died, I had one of those 'special dreams'. The ones where it feels totally real; he was there, normal, healthy and so close to me. I woke up feeling at peace and although incredibly raw, felt safe in the knowledge that he was no longer suffering and felt he would never leave my side. Every little thing I encountered was a sign; a white feather, a visiting robin, every song on the radio felt like Dad was still with us.

The next few weeks were a blur. Although we had time to prepare it didn't make losing him any easier. Dad had 6 children, all strong characters and having them around was a massive help. I didn't cry at the funeral. That was private. After the funeral I was relieved for the distraction of work. I sometimes worked a 12-hour paramedic shift, got home and changed and worked in a nightclub until 2 or 3am. I craved anything to avoid having time alone and sit and feel that loss. I heard the phrase 'bereavement burnout'. A person wanting to be so busy that there was no time to stop and think.
That first year was the hardest. The immense anger I could feel about people who still got to live; murderers, thieves, people who did bad shit. What kind of God could do this? How was

this fair? The ache of a heavy heart was the first thing I felt when I woke and the last thing I felt at night. Months passed and I would realise I had not thought about him for a whole hour, then 2 hours and then something would happen make to make you belly laugh. Then came the guilt. My beautiful Dad is dead. How *dare* I feel happy?

Some days I would be fine and then out of the blue, the grief would hit me like a tidal wave which left me clambering to the safety of the shore, desperate for breath.

I feel my Dad sent my husband to me. He sent someone to make me smile again and have fun. My Husband gets quiet and treads carefully around the special dates; Dad's birthday, the day he passed. I know why. He does not want to upset me. But the opposite is true. I want to talk about him. It keeps him with us. We were the lucky ones. Not everyone gets an amazing, inspiring Dad.

The things I know about grief. You don't miss them any less, but you learn to live with it. Cliché, I know, but very true. My friend Kate nailed it when she said this of grief: 'There is no way to avoid it. We can try and hide from it, or go round it, but sometimes we just have to accept it, and drive straight through the middle of it'. Drive straight through the heart of it, like it does ours. We do come out the other side. From a personal perspective, I feel as long as we still talk about them and remember them, these beautiful souls are never far away. For anyone going through this. It does get easier. I Promise.

Love you Dad. xx

17
Chelsea's Story

Losing my dad after his short battle with cancer was so difficult. At only 60 years old, he was far too young and had so much life left in him to give. That's what hurts the most. My dad was my biggest supporter, my best friend, my biggest critic and my hero all in one. He would never judge and always be there with a listening ear, he had the driest sense of humour and we always bounced off each other when telling stories. When he was diagnosed with cancer it came as a shock and took me by surprise. Initially, when I was told it was mouth cancer I wasn't that scared. I did a lot of research on the Internet and hoped that some minor surgery would help remove the tumour. How I was wrong. The surgery was much bigger than anticipated with the doctor informing us that due to my dad's reoccurring blood clots, he only had a 30% chance of surviving the operation. That's when I started grieving.

After seeing my dad off into surgery at 7am, I didn't know whether that was the last time I was going to see him. I recall being sat in the car thinking that was it for us, I was in shock and I really had no idea what was to come. However, Dad was hopeful; he always had a positive mental attitude, which he had drilled into me and with that I had a glimpse of hope that he was going to get through this and out the other side. After what felt like forever, I received a call from the hospital that he had come out of surgery and that he was recovering well. The anxiety that I had been carrying around all day had suddenly vanished; I knew my dad was strong enough to get through it. He wasn't ready to leave just yet.

The next few weeks were so hard trying to keep it together, ensuring dad was ok at hospital and that he was being looked after, and performing sufficiently at my new work role in a busy psychiatric hospital. Dad loved hearing about my work stories, and despite him not being able to verbally communicate with me because of the surgery, he held my hand and smiled. I knew he was thankful to have me by his side. At this point I was exhausted, both mentally and physically. Dad was in hospital over Christmas, so that's where I spent it; that didn't bother me, as I knew deep down this may be his last. However, with commuting for my new job, travelling back and forth to the city hospital each evening and the constant worry about Dad in the back of my mind, it was starting to wear me thin.

At this point, the anticipatory grief had begun. As strong as I knew my dad was, the cancer had spread so quickly and there was only so much the doctors could do for him. I kept my hopes up and my fingers crossed that deep down he had the strength to get through this. I knew I had to keep a smile on my face for him, to be the strength that he needed. My friends were checking in on me asking how I was and how my dad was getting on. I really appreciated this, but it's difficult for anyone to really understand what you're going through unless they've been through it themselves. I felt like I was in a bit of a haze, work, hospital, home, and sleep. Like some sort of cycle that wasn't really going anywhere.

A month later dad was finally home and on the mend and initially was doing really well, attending his radiotherapy appointments at the Velindre Cancer Centre and re-gaining his independence. Despite this, my anxiety was still at an all time high constantly wondering whether he was okay, what was the future to hold? Did I need to start looking at funeral arrangements? The constant stream of thoughts was endless. Then Covid-19 hit! Understandably, my dad was shielding and with me working in a hospital I was unable to see him for 2 months. This made me feel angry & frustrated, yet I knew I needed to keep my dad safe so the best thing for me to do was to stay home and speak to him over the phone. Little did I know that the longer we were apart the less help dad was getting, and the cancer had come back and began to spread aggressively to his throat and lungs.

Shortly after this, my dad's battle with cancer ended suddenly. We were attending a hospital appointment one day after an accidental fall during the night, the next day he was gone. I actually couldn't believe it and I was in shock for a long time. Nothing seemed real and I didn't sleep properly for days, each day blurring into the next. My eating habits became very erratic and I kept myself busy by sorting out funeral arrangements. I didn't give myself time to grieve as I had convinced myself that by doing so, I was saying goodbye to him, which I wasn't ready to do. I received many messages from family, friends & work colleagues with their condolences as well as flowers and other thoughtful gifts, but I struggled to link the feeling with the reality going on around me. I remember being so angry, I was angry at the lack of support my dad had received during the pandemic, the doctors for not recognising the cancer soon enough and I was looking for someone to blame. I blamed myself for not being more persistent in getting the help he needed and for not answering my phone the night he fell; I went through an intense state of self-loathing.

Four days after the funeral and a month since I'd been off work, I decided to return. I knew I needed some normality back and needed to get on with things. The first few weeks were really difficult, I would be having conversations with people but couldn't quite grasp what they were telling me, I just smiled and nodded. Being at work was such a challenging environment; working with individuals with mental health conditions who were attempting to self-harm was something I struggled to cope with. I spoke to my manager and explained my concerns and she appeared to understand without me having to say how I really felt. This was so reassuring; I felt heard without having to say anything and somehow things got easier from there. We spoke about how my grief was different to what my patients were experiencing and finding a way to separate these emotions really helped for me.

Now, 2 months on I am finally starting to feel a bit more like myself. I have allowed myself to let go of the blame and self-loathing and understand that even if I had done more for my dad I couldn't have prevented the inevitable. Even if I had answered my phone the night of the fall, I wouldn't have been able to change the outcome; this would have just been more painful. This was a hard battle at first, but eventually it is getting easier. I have days where the feelings of bereavement are completely overwhelming and I struggle to figure out how I am supposed to move forward. Yet I know I have the strength in me to do so. My dad provided me with his wisdom, strength, determination and courage to be able to battle everyday like he did and for that I will always make him proud and do so. I find death easier not to talk about, and convince myself that if I don't discuss it, then I don't have to face the reality.

However, I am looking into getting counselling and bereavement support and I feel this may help. Some days things still do not seem clear about his death but its getting easier to talk about and those that I do discuss it with have been attentive, and empathetic and I have been very lucky to have such a close support network who have allowed me to deal with things how I need to.

I hope in the future it becomes easier to approach discussions of bereavement for individuals experiencing it. I have been very lucky to have such a kind and caring partner by my side, and my sister regularly checks in on my mental health & wellbeing. However, I know other people find it a difficult topic to raise in case I become upset. I want to tell them that sometimes, I'm not okay and I would like to discuss it, but I don't want to make them uncomfortable by raising the topic in conversation, which I'm sure many people understand. But, if I become upset that's also okay because it's ok to not be ok and whilst taking one day at a time, eventually things will get easier.

> Email from: Dr Marianne Trent
> To: Chelsea
> Re: Your Story
>
> Dear Chelsea,
>
> You've done such a wonderful job. Thank you for sharing it with me. I'm so sorry for the loss of your Dad. It's so recent and honestly, it sounds like you're doing superbly. I struggled very much so for at least the first 10 months.
>
> Be kind to yourself, it takes time but also compassion. I'd recommend reading the Chris Irons Difficult emotions book. It's CFT and this, along with EMDR has been so helpful to me. I was first inducted into CFT by reading Paul Gilbert and Deborah Lee but in terms of accessibility, I really like the Chris Irons book.
>
> Thanks again,
> Marianne

18

Katie & Sam's Story

Sam was the first baby to be born in the family and I doted on him completely. I loved him coming for the weekend, spoiling him and going to theme parks. He had no fear and was always looking for the next big thrill ride he could go on. I adored being his Aunt.

Sam was just 14 when he chose to take his own life. He was a good-looking lad, the jokester of the class, always centre of attention, always happy outgoing and popular. No one knows what went through his mind the night he chose to end it all. Moments before his death he had been laughing and joking with his friends on the Xbox, told them he'd be two minutes, then half-way through making himself nachos decided to hang himself from his bedroom door.

My sister, Sam's mum, walked in the next morning with tea and toast to discover the terrible scene. Once she called 999, she called me, and I was on the scene not long after the police had arrived.

The shock and pain have been so hard to bear. Sam left no note, and no indication he had been depressed or struggling at all. The next few weeks passed in a blur, spending every waking minute with my sister, going over and over again the timeline of events, trying to make any sense of it.

We have so many unanswered questions:

- Did you plan it?
- Did something happen we don't know about?
- Did it hurt? Were you scared?
- Why didn't you leave us a note?
- Where are you now? Are you happy?
- Do you miss us? Have you been visiting us?
- Do you regret leaving us? Do you wish you could take it back?

We spent weeks wondering "if only". "If only" his phone wasn't smashed, maybe he would have called me. "If only" someone had come into his room that night. However, we can only act knowing what we know at the time and I know it's a dangerous road to start thinking about the what ifs and the could have, would have, should haves.

The death of someone you love deeply reshapes you. I will never be the same again. I love harder and care less about the small things in life. I have re-evaluated relationships, and my own faith. I have thought more about the death of other loved ones, and my own death when it comes. Where there has been deep love, there will be deep loss, and I loved Sam so very much, how can I come away from a loss like that and not change?

I lost my mum at 25, when I was pregnant with her first granddaughter, so I have known pain and loss before, but there is something different about losing someone so young and so unnecessarily. I always knew I'd outlive my mum, although I never expected her to die so young, but Sam was only 14, and I will spend the rest of my life thinking about the things he's missing out on. Every family celebration will have the thought of him, and the celebrations he is missing.

As I write this in September 2020, it's only been 4 months since we lost him, and we're still picking up the pieces and trying to find our new normal as a family.

> We miss him every day and if you or someone you know is struggling with thoughts of suicide, please reach out for help, know you are loved, and those who love you will never be the same without you.

19

Marianne's Story:

The Man who inspired the Collective

Growing up, my friend Vickie and I were always terrified of the idea that one day our Dads would die. We didn't believe we'd be able to carry on breathing if our Fathers were not. We would openly discuss our affection for our Fathers; Bob and Norm, who also happened to best friends with each other. The irony was not lost on us that as their stories turned out, they died 3 weeks apart from one another. Whilst breathing and other important functions have felt hard for both of us at times; they have however persisted in us. An exquisitely painful fact remains; that whilst carrying on without them has been incredibly difficult, it has not been physically impossible.

Before my Dad died in December 2017, I just don't recall there having been too much made about the death of a parent. I knew friends who had lost their parents whilst they were still children but because they were already adults by the time I met them it was a little harder to relate to. All 4 my Grandparents died across my childhood and early adulthood. I think perhaps there's something about the freedom and innocence of youth which didn't ever really allow me to be able to equate the loss of one of my Grandparents as also being the loss of one of my parent's parents! It perhaps sounds selfish to admit that now, but I just didn't get it. I couldn't I guess; children and young people are uniquely self-centred, not yet having the ability to consider things fully from another person's perspective.

What I have learned so far along my journey into Dad-lessness and beyond, is that I have found it to be an entirely de-stabilising process. It feels a bit like I previously had great structure and natural scaffolding. It was only after he passed that I was fully able to realise just what a wonderful reassurance he was and had been my whole life. Whatever I did, be it moving away to University, backpacking around the world or striding forwards in my career as a Clinical Psychologist, I was able to do because I knew that if times got hard, Dad would be there. If times went well, then Dad would be there. If times were middling, then you've guessed it, Dad would be there. So, what now? Dad's not in my present anymore. I can't call him to tell him about my highs and lows. I can't talk to him about writing this book or the latest funny things his Grandkids have said or done. So how exactly do I go about doing anything exactly? In the first 18 months or so, even playing with my own children, concentrating on things and cooking for my family somehow seemed to have lost the focus and effortlessness I'd previously enjoyed. My Dad was no longer breathing and suddenly the whole world felt different.

He was diagnosed with terminal cancer two years before he passed. So, I had a reasonable amount of warning, I knew it was going to happen. What I naively assumed was that the 'worst bit' would be his ill health and watching him falter and fade. I was wrong. The worst bit was still to come. The worst bit was learning to navigate my life without him being just a phone call away. All of my previously comforting and stabilising thoughts of Dad, those which kept my feet on the ground and allowed me to go forth and have the most incredible life, were now tarred with the memories that he was no longer with us. For example, I've always loved listening to music and I still get a buzz when I hear a song I've not heard in a long time. When I hear more unusual 90's songs these days I now have the surreal connection that the last time I heard that song my dad was fit and healthy and likely tinkering away in his garage as I sung away in my bedroom 1 floor above him. Most recently this happened when 'Oooh baby I love your way! Came on the radio unexpectedly as I was driving to the supermarket.' It reminded me of my Dad even though I'm confident that he'd never heard the song and would have hated it if he had! Music being a trigger to thoughts about my Dad is just one example, there are many.

I have 2 children; when my Dad was diagnosed, I was pregnant with my second child and my son was almost 2 and ½ years old. It meant that my second pregnancy was so far removed from the relaxed, joyful, exciting experience that was my first pregnancy. To this day, my youngest is a high needs kind of child. Determined and not terrifically easy to soothe – although Dad loved his wilful, roguish character. He was born requiring bowel surgery which was diagnosed when he was a day old and performed at 11 weeks of age. Whilst pregnant, I was working 4 days a week, supervising a trainee psychologist, seeing clients daily, alongside juggling family life and a poorly Father. I did, therefore find myself wondering whether the acute and enduring episodes of stress I experienced whilst pregnant somehow made him stressed too; meaning he's just a little clingier and a bit moanier and that his bowel didn't close up correctly at the point it should have. I know from my work experiences that it's not uncommon for Mothers to look to blame themselves for aspects of how their children are born or develop. I also know what I say to them: "It's not your fault, these things happen and blaming yourself punishes you but still doesn't change the outcome."

So, my youngest son's 1st birthday party was scheduled for a Sunday in June. Mum and Dad had been to my house on that Thursday and I said I would see them on Sunday. As it turned out though, that Thursday was the very last day my Dad would ever be in my house. Even to write that, causes me deep and painful emotion; my head swims, my eyes mist and my chest feels funny. I've often wondered what I would have done if I had known that would be the last day he'd be in my home. I just can't imagine. Growing up, I used to watch Home & Away and I recall this really cheesy episode where 2 characters were saying goodbye to one another and they did this really slow motion, cringe worthy close up shot of their 2 hands gradually letting go of each other before they then got into their own cars and drove into the sunset. I kind of imagine it would have been like that only with some wailing and a lot more snot. Truth be told, I'm not sure I would have been able to let him go. What I do know is that if I had known it would have been the last time, I would have cherished it more. I would have spent more time with him; just enjoying the sight of him just sitting on my sofa having a cup of tea or playing with the boys. It sounds bizarre but I miss the way he used to sit with one leg hooked over the other and the way his foot would just hang in mid-air. Instead of soaking all of this up and taking a million photos and recording the joyful sound of his laughter, what I actually did was lay down and chill out on my sofa all by myself whilst my parents took my eldest, then 3 years old, to the supermarket with them and my youngest napped in his cot. The compassionate part of me knows that I did that because I didn't know and couldn't have known. The compassionate part of me knows that I did that because my youngest used to wake so many times a night and get up super early; I was exhausted. The compassionate part of my Dad likely recognised that I needed some time by myself without being prodded and poked by my children.

So, back to June, my son's party was the first family occasion that my dad wasn't there. My husband makes incredible films of holidays, birthdays and Christmasses and I was really looking forward to getting some more footage of Dad at the party 'just in case.' Well, it never happened and by the time my son turned 2, sadly dad had been dead for 6 months. At the time though, I still didn't know it was the end.

Dad had oesophageal cancer and secondaries in his lungs. His first symptom had been that he seemed to be struggling to swallow stuff. Once they'd diagnosed the problem they inserted a stent and then suddenly he was able to eat normally. So, when he started to struggle with swallowing again, I assumed it was a case of just needing a new stent; they'd sort something out and then he would carry on as he always had. Dad was the kind of guy who didn't moan about being unwell. He just got on with it. So, this was different, because he didn't seem to be just getting on with it. When they checked, it turned out the old stent had slipped. Perhaps if he had gone to the hospital right away they might have been able to replace it. But he didn't. He waited, not telling anyone he was struggling to swallow again, not wanting to bother anyone. Mum had been researching alternative therapies and apparently bitter apricot kernels are quite the cancer busting drug. Who knew? But you have to chew them. But Dad found them so and laborious to chew on that he used to get bored and was probably fed up and just taking them to humour Mum, so he would so would just swallow them. Figured his stomach would do what it needed to and save him the bother of munching up the miserable stones. Which it might have done had they reached his stomach instead of getting lodged in his stent. Apparently when they removed it to try and change it 13 of these apricot kernels tumbled out! Kind of amusing if it weren't for the fact that in the time since the stent had slipped, the cancer had grown enough that they struggled to get a new stent to fit properly. It meant that it never allowed him to eat with ease again. The soft diet commenced, which yielded to the softer diet, which yielded to the mashed diet and then, over time, the pureed one followed by those god awful fortisips which appear to be universally hated by all. Food had always been such a pleasure for Dad and eating together as a family such a lovely, inclusive activity. The countless roast dinners and chippy teas and Thursday lunch time dates we enjoyed. Well, oesophageal cancer puts an end to all of that I'm afraid. Eating becomes something lengthy, self-conscious making and fearful. The meals out and cooking for my dad, something we had always enjoyed, ceased. Thankfully he was still able to enjoy his beloved cups of tea.

The 4th of July 2017 was the day I returned to work after my maternity leave. On the 5th of July, my Dad was admitted to hospital for the first time, he'd not been able to eat for days. My manager, Kyle, was amazing and said 'they'd coped without me for 14 months; they could cope without me for an afternoon' and so off I went to hospital. It was the start of an exceedingly difficult, stressful and exquisitely painful 6 months. By this time Dad had been diagnosed for 18 months and to be honest, I had been lulled into a false sense of security by how well he had been throughout. I have a photo of him whizzing down a giant slide in the village where he and Mum lived. I was pregnant at the time and it wasn't safe for me to go up that high. In this photo Dad is entirely bald because he was in the middle of his chemo! That's the kind of cancer patient he was - you can believe that I cherish that photo now. So it was hard to comprehend that Dad, who was still doing all the stuff he'd always done – tinkering in his garage, going to the pub with his mates on a Thursday evening and eating cheese and crackers in the kitchen of an evening, was dying. So, in July 2017 when his health really began to falter for the first time, it came as a big shock. I recall crying in my yearly appraisal meeting with my supervisor and my manager. It all just felt so terrifying, so unpredictable and so unknown. My manager is a lovely guy, but he really didn't know what to do with this strong, independent self-assured psychologist who was suddenly a blubbering wreck. Yep. Grief will do that to you.

Dad was toing and froing between home and the hospital a fair bit between July and November. In the past it had always been Mum suggesting they go to the Dr and Dad insisting he'd be okay. However, in November, Dad said to Mum: "Take me to hospital." He never came home again. I have found myself wondering if he knew that would be the last time he would be in his home. The home he had lived in since 1988, where he had moved in with a 9-year-old son and a 7-year-old daughter. The home they had extended twice and where he had started his business, tinkered with countless vintage motorbikes and raised their children into young adults. Where he welcomed 3 Grandchildren. Perhaps he did realise, but he was certainly too unwell to be overly sentimental about it. Mum started a pattern of visiting Dad daily and I would visit at weekends as I was working 3 days a week and looking after my almost 18-month on my days off. I decided not to take my children into hospital with me because I knew full well hospitals are boring to young children. So, I would get childcare when available and visit when I could. I lived 40 miles away from the hospital, so it wasn't an easy juggle with work and a young family. During November and December I continued to go to work. I was experiencing acute stress. I was tearful and experiencing poor short-term memory. I was terrified of him dying and what it would be like when he did – I was imagining all these dreadful outcomes involving painful screaming and terror, or my worst case scenario – that I would miss it or he would be alone when he died. I carried on going to work because we had no idea 'how long it would all take.' As it turned out I went to work on the 8th of December, but I didn't go back. That evening I was eating dinner around the table with my husband and 2 children and my mobile rang. It was Mum. "They've decided to withdraw IV fluids she said." The sound of the hollowed-out keening 'Noooooooo!' I responded with still haunts me to this day. To me you can live 3 weeks without food, 3 days without water and 3 minutes without air. He'd already gone a few weeks without food and so I thought I was being given just 3 days left with my wonderful dad being on planet earth with me. It felt like I'd been ripped into pieces.

Grief starts early when someone has a terminal illness. Since he'd been palliatively diagnosed in December 2016, it was not uncommon to find me sobbing by myself with tears coursing down my face or collapsed in a heap on the office floor as my husband cuddled me, or me crying myself to sleep. Well, after that phone call all of those behaviours sky-rocketed. I was just a mess. I would visit Dad daily; my car was drinking diesel like it was going out of fashion and I was mentally and physically exhausted. I wish I'd stopped work sooner, whilst Dad was still able to walk and to talk freely without him having to nap so often. By the time I stopped work, Dad was stuck in the hospital bed and spent a great deal of my visits asleep whilst I held his hand. I've long hated my weird little wrists – if you ever meet me you'll now see my wrists and conclude for yourself that they are indeed strangely knobbly. It was when I was sitting holding his hand in his final days that I realised that my wrists are a carbon copy of my Dad's. So, now, almost 3 years on, I get a strange sense of connectedness and of life going on from my own knobbly wrists! Anyway, I've digressed; I wish I'd thought to take his old childhood and family photos into hospital to share with him one last time when he was still well enough to enjoy them and reminisce for the last time. I am however grateful that I was able to be honest with my dad about my feelings around his imminent departure. I cried a fair bit in front of him and I don't regret that at all. I needed him to know that this was a big deal. I know from my work that it's okay to talk about feelings. So it was that a few days before he passed Dad was talking to me and he said: "I wish I'd tried harder in school!" My poor Dad was laying preparing to die and was clearly running through his life and thinking what life would have been like if things had been different. I think I'm actually pretty pleased that's all he could come up with in terms of regret! To me at the time though it was a surprise, I'd always been incredibly proud of the self-employed business man he was and to think he was thinking he hadn't achieved his full potential was a shock. He did also seem sad though when he said: "My Dad died at 73, I'm 71, I thought with modern medicine I'd get a bit longer!" I have to confess that I'd also hoped the same. I was 7 when my Grampy died and I was gutted. I continued to be throughout my life but never really shared it with anyone and I didn't want to worry my Granny. Growing up, I'd often compare my Dad's age to 73 and try to reassure myself that I still had ages of 'Dad time' left. I think now how much I would have loved those 2 years; 2 years where he could have enjoyed his Grandchildren, some more holidays and many, many more cups of tea. In contrast, 73 would have been great.

Dad had decided that he wanted to die in a hospice and not in the hospital or at home. With hindsight I'm glad it wasn't the family home because I think I might have struggled to adjust thereafter. Who knew that December is such a popular time to die though? It meant that the hospices were all full. So every day for a couple of weeks I would telephone the admissions department of our preferred lakeside hospice and ask if there was space for my Dad; there wasn't. I'm pretty sure that the Macmillan Nursing team and hospital team were also calling the hospice too; but I felt like it was something I could control in a mad situation which felt out of control. On the 18th of December we were notified that our second favourite hospice – honestly who knew you could have a favourite hospice? Had a space for Dad and he would be transferred that day. We waited. We waited some more. We waited some more. In the end Dad told us to go home; he would be okay and we would see him tomorrow. So it was that my Dad took a trip through the Northamptonshire countryside lanes alone in the back of a patient transport ambulance. What I didn't know was that this poor, sweet, terminally ill man who hadn't been out of bed for weeks hadn't been booked a bed transfer by the hospital. Instead, he was transferred 45 minutes in the back of a dark ambulance in an upright wheelchair feeling scared that he was going to fall out, not having the strength to hold himself upright and feeling every bump in the road from his now very slim frame. After he passed, I made a complaint to the hospital and they investigated and got back to me to apologise, that should never have happened; they shouldn't have allowed him to be transferred in a wheelchair. They said they would ensure it didn't happen again but I found it hard to shift the image of my Dad being scared and alone in the back of an ambulance on his last ever trip anywhere.

Dad arrived in the hospice shortly before the 18th of December ticked over into the 19th. He had been raised a Christian, however, throughout his ill health, much disturbed by the terror and persecution, genocide and atrocities happening across the globe he had decided that there just couldn't be a God. By the time I got to the Hospice on the morning of the 19th he said that the kindness and compassion he had been shown by the hospice staff since his arrival had restored his faith in God. I asked if he wanted me to arrange for my in-laws to come and pray with him and for the Hospice minister to visit too. He did and so we did. My in-laws brought with them a wonderfully tactile, smooth, carved wooden cross. I'd never seen anything quite like it before; but it was the perfect size to clasp in a fist. And there it stayed in his hand until the very end. I was very grateful for the comfort he was able to take from that. I'm getting ahead of myself though.

I recall the 19th of December being a pretty good day – Dad seemed to have perked right up and was awake for what seemed like most of the day. He did tell me he was scared about being on his own though and so I promised that he wouldn't be. We were careful to stagger canteen and toilet trips among us so that he didn't have to be alone. It lulled me into a total false sense of optimism with just how well he was that day. Some of Mum and Dad's long-term friends also wanted to visited as did Dad's brother so it wasn't a quiet hospice room by any means! It was so close to Christmas and as any parent can tell you, December means a seemingly endless list of school dates for performances and 'come and share' sessions. One was scheduled for that very afternoon. I felt I was weighing up spending more time with my dad or racing to be with my eldest son. Dad wanted me to go and be at school and so off I went. I recall it being a hectic and rushed goodbye with the promise that I would see him bright and early tomorrow. He seemed so well compared to how he had been for the week or so before he got to the hospice. So about 50 minutes later I was sitting in a tiny chair sticking glitter to a snowman with a dried up pritt-stick. I was trying to adjust my mental state from 'terminal hospice mode' to 'joyful time with a room full of 4-year-olds' mode; it wasn't easy. It was almost 3 years later when I was back in that very same chair in that very same classroom for my youngest child's 1ˢᵗ day of school that I realised I'd made the wrong decision; I should have chosen longer with Dad. My eldest might have been disappointed that day if Mummy didn't show up, but I could have asked my now dear friend Linzie to spend some time with my son in my absence and within a few days he wouldn't have remembered. I still remember and imagine the minutes and hours I missed with Dad and it hurts my heart and burns my eyes.

Mum stayed at the hospice with him that night for what turned out to be their last night together after 42 years of marriage. I got to hospice the following morning. Mum said that 10 minutes before I had arrived Dad had been very agitated, it has a name apparently 'terminal agitation' so you know, there's a cheery fact for you. In response to this agitation they had put him to sleep. I'm kind of grateful that I didn't have to see him suffer like that but also gutted I had missed saying a mindful and conscious goodbye by a measly 10 minutes. Believe me when I say that I've replayed that morning to see how I could have gained an extra 15 minutes back to get there sooner. But the fact remains, I didn't know and I couldn't have done. He had been so well the day before which had lulled me into thinking that maybe we still had longer together than we did. Maybe he was also imagining I'd go all 'Home & Away' on him so me missing the goodbye was for the best. That day that he died it was just my Mum, me and my brother and his fiancée. They'd recently got engaged in New York and shared a little secret with Dad: they were expecting their second child! Except for Dad forgot it was a secret and told everyone! Still, I'm glad that Dad knew about baby and that the Grandchild he would never meet was in the room with him when he passed. That very baby ended up being a boy and is named after my dad which was just the loveliest thing. They're also now expecting their 3rd child; so the family continues to grow! I'm so grateful to my sister in law for being there, not only for her emotional support at the time and since but because it somehow seemed, to me anyway, significant.

   We all spent the day there with Dad; doing our little relay if we needed to pop to the toilets or the café, to ensure that dad was never alone. I won't go into the details of his death, save to say that I recall it being very peaceful and that I was so massively grateful that my worst fear hadn't come true; not only was I there with him holding his hand but my Mum and my brother and his fiancée (now wife) were there too. My husband was home putting our kids to bed and I'm also incredibly grateful to him for that too. I was breastfeeding at the time and I was so worried about being away from our youngest and I didn't want him being distressed at bed-time in the arms of hurriedly assembled babysitters who wouldn't know the bed time routine. It seemed kinder to allow him to be distressed in his Daddy's arms than wonder where both of his parents were.

The hospice staff at Danetre were just wonderful. I shall be forever grateful and thankful for their kindness, compassion and discretion. Pretty soon after Dad died, I just felt like I wanted to go home though. I just didn't feel his connection or his presence in the room anymore. It might have looked like we all made a mass exodus from the room shortly after; perhaps we did. He didn't look like Dad to me though. He had become so thin in the latter stages of his illness that even my iPhone had stopped recognising him in photos. So I said I was going to go and I'd see Mum and my brother for lunch tomorrow. I got into the car park and went to start my car engine and an alert light flashed on 'warning fuel level is too low!' I couldn't believe it; all of those visiting miles seemed to have caught up with me. The irony also wasn't lost on me that the person I usually would have called for technical advice with my car in the event of a break down had just died! Similarly to that, my Mum's boiler packed up a couple of days after he died. Dad had been a boiler man since before I was born – you couldn't make this stuff up! Luckily, I managed to start my car and so it was that within an hour of my dad dying I was found myself filling up with car with diesel! So much had changed that day and already I was having to play by the rules of a life, a life which already seemed tilted off axis.

My Dad died on the 20th of December 2017. Ever the considerate person, he was careful to pass after his birthday but before Christmas. And at the thoroughly decent time of 6:20pm. What I craved most after his passing was time. Time to myself. Time to lay in bed and to grieve and to work out who I was without my Dad. However, it was the Christmas holidays and so what I got was an 18-month-old and a 4-year-old around ALL of the time. It really wasn't an easy time at all. I know it can't have been an easy time for my husband or my children either. Suddenly, the usually carefree and optimistic Mummy / Wife they were used to knowing was sitting with tears sliding down her face for what seemed like a really long time and with little to no notice. My youngest child was also waking 3 – 4 times a night at this stage and still liked to get up for the day at 6am or earlier so I was exhausted. What I have learned is that grief needs sleep in order to stand a chance of healing. In fact in terms of ability to process and recover from trauma, sleep is essential.

We had his funeral in the January and I am so thankful for that day. I recall it with bittersweet emotion; the church was packed with hundreds of people; everyone loved Norman. I gave a eulogy at the Church service and whilst it was emotional I'm so pleased I was able to do this. Many of my friends came, those who had known Dad growing up but also some who had never met him. One of my fondest memories is giving my friend a big hug after he'd driven from Essex to Milton Keynes to come to his funeral just so he could support me. I won't lie, I also liked the buffet at the wake and Dad would have loved it too!

I had some time off work when the kids went back to school and to distract myself from crying I mostly did unusual stuff like

The Man who inspired the Collective

make soap, when that didn't work I brought on the tears purposefully by binge watching 'This is Us.' I went back to work in early March; I'll always be thankful to my manager Kyle for how compassionate he made my return to work after Dad's passing. I was very fortunate that I could have been paid on full pay for up to 6 months of ill health. I was also allowed a phased return over 4 weeks. I am so thankful for this. I may have been back at work, but I really wasn't okay personally or professionally for quite a long time. I had a sense that I couldn't imagine wanting things for myself anymore. I didn't want to be getting myself involved in things that Dad would never know about. I had a sense that if I allowed myself to get on with my life that it would be somehow disrespectful. I also juggled this alongside the knowledge that Dad wouldn't have wanted this for me. He would have said he wasn't worth my tears. But I felt like I'd lost a lot. It felt like, I had lost the only person in the world who had unconditional positive regard for me. To my Dad I could do no wrong and he never had a bad word to say about me, he was always pleased to hear from me and would open the door for me when I visited, welcome me in, help me with my bags and make me a cup of tea. Without him I was irritable, short with my kids and I felt like the light behind my eyes had dimmed. I said to one of the fellow collective, that I felt like I couldn't recognise myself in photographs from 'before.' I had a sense that I didn't know who this young, care-free, smiling woman was anymore. How could she have smiled so easily and with such exuberance and warmth? Who was she and did she know how lucky she was? I kind of envied her. I missed her too; I'm sure everyone did. I kind of feel sorry for the patients I was working with in my first few months back at work, goodness only knows what they got from me. Fortunately, I was surrounded by some wonderful friends, family and colleagues and of course my 'Dead Dad Club' for support.

In the year after he died I did a number of 'physical things' in memory of his passing which I'm now able to take comfort from; somehow having these physical things in my house which

The Man who inspired the Collective

didn't exist before he died have helped me to mindfully accept that he is no longer alive. This, along with time have allowed me to piece my life together again. These things included:

- One of my best friends and her Mum made me a beautiful cushion from my very favourite 3 jumpers of his. They also stitched a tiny blue heart on one side which they made from a part of one of his much-worn and boiler suit trousers. The cushion sits on a chair in my kitchen. The chair wasn't there when Dad was alive but if he was here still I know he would have liked sitting in it and enjoying one of his much loved cups of tea.

- We gave the rest of his clothes away to charity. I hope that people bought them and they've gone on to have new and happy stories of their own.

- I had a piece of art commissioned by a wonderful artist called Mumma's Doodles. It's a poem which resonated with Mum and I and around the outside are drawings of things which were important to Dad along with our names. It now lives in our kitchen on the windowsill.

- I had some of his ashes made into an ashes paperweight. A friend also sent me a photo frame shortly after Dad died. I've put a picture of him walking me down the aisle on my wedding day. The photo lives on a shelf in my living room next to the paperweight. It gives me comfort.

- At some stage when he was unwell I bought a hardbacked notebook. I printed out photos to represent aspects of him I loved and memories and stories I wanted to remember with him. I called the book 'all the reasons I love you'. Dad said he liked it, but did also comment on how bad my handwriting had become!

Sorry Dad. That made me laugh to even type it! I now have this book and I read it and look at the photos when I need a good cry. I like knowing that it was once his book and that he knew I made it for him and because of him.

- My youngest child was too young to remember my Dad. About 18 months ago he began to ask for the 'Grampy Norm' movie at bed time; sometimes he would ask for it twice! I've got an iPhone and there's a feature where you can make a little movie of people you've got lots of photos of on your phone. This is what he began to ask for and so then twice a day I'd watch 3 minutes of my Dad playing out on my phone. I actually think that very much like flooding and Acceptance and Commitment Therapy (ACT) it helped knock the barbs off my grief and polish it up like a lovely shiny stone. I actually now recommend this as an approach to people I work with. It does take bravery and it is painful but I promise you'll get to the stage where you enjoy that lovely film rather than just look at it and think about how much you miss them!

- I think what made the biggest difference to my grief was actually something that was indirectly provided by Dad. He had left me some money in his will. I decided that since he had been so supportive of my career to date that he would fully approve of me using the money to further my development. And so it was that 10 months after he died, I found myself in Leicester on a course by Sandi Richman to learn Eye Movement Desensitisation and Reprocessing, (EMDR). The first stage was only 3 days but the training involves practicing on one another. By the end of the 3 days when I got home I just felt different, better, more energised and more like my old self. I'd somehow processed some of the trauma of losing him from my life. I would recommend it as an approach to anyone and I have received more of this since then. Thereafter I discovered Compassion Focused Therapy (CFT) and I feel like this, combined with EMDR has totally changed me as a person and a professional. I love that it's having these skills which then empowered me to start my private practice and that now lots of other people have benefitted from my doing these approaches with them too. It's the gift that keeps on giving.

Since then I have been able to move forwards in small steps. I've allowed myself to be involved in many exciting things. I'm proud of myself and I know Dad would have been thrilled too. I feel strong and resilient in both physical and mental health terms. I still use CFT and ACT on an almost daily basis to help myself. I started exercising, initially by joining a gym; then when lockdown struck by doing yoga and running. In July 2019 I challenged myself to eat 10 x 80g portions of fruit and veg per day for a whole year – I told you I liked a challenge! I definitely felt that by focusing on nourishing myself and by doing better meal prep and planning that my body and mind were in a far better state.

I write this in September 2020, just a few short months away from what will be 3 years since Dad died. The other day my husband got home as I was working on this very book that you hold in your hands. "What are you wearing he asked?" I was wearing an oversized grey zip up fleece. Earlier that day I'd been out with the kids and my sister in law, niece, nephew and their dog. Still adjusting to the new normal of Summer 2020; we met in a forest. It was a chillier day than expected and I hadn't taken a jumper. Luckily, rather than shiver, I remembered my emergency kit stashed with the spare wheel of my car! In my emergency kit was one of Dad's warm fleeces. Dad was a fan of a quality M&S jumper and when I had been helping sort Dad's clothes in early 2018, I was struck by how new and lovely many of them were. Even now, the sight of a jumper that Dad might have liked, or a man in socks or sandals or a nice pair of functional leather shoes can still move me to the point of tears but also makes me thankful I had him in my life for 36 years.

Anyway, I decided to keep one of Dad's jumpers for me to wear in emergencies. Much like I would have called him in a breakdown situation, now I could somehow keep part of him with me if I ever broke down or wasn't wearing warm enough clothes. When my husband mentioned it, I'd forgotten I was wearing it but I went and had a mindful look at myself in a mirror and then packed it away in my boot until the next time I need it.

> I think, for me, that's what learning to live with grief is like, once the pain wears off a bit, you learn to look in the mirror again and find comfort and strength from that person even though they're absent.

20
Liz's Story:
A reply to Marianne

> Email from: Marianne
> To: Liz
> Re: Dad Story
>
> Hey Liz,
> Thanks for saying it's okay for me to send you the stuff I wrote on Dad. I didn't want to send it without checking first as it's potentially pretty emotive. Have a read and let me know what you think. I won't be offended if you'd like anything changing but would welcome your opinion.
>
> M x

Oh! Lots and lots of tears when I read that! I think it will be helpful for so many people though. Grief is awful and I know that everyone suffers differently, I think everyone who has experienced grief has so many regrets and 'what ifs?' Trying to run a house/ two kids a job when losing someone is such a difficult thing to do. I don't think anyone truly looks after themselves when trying to let themselves heal.

I loved that you wore your Dad's jacket when we went out and have it for emergencies; I think that's just so lovely. I can't imagine what it must be like to lose someone so close.

I haven't experienced any deaths in anyone close to me or family so when your Dad was ill I experienced something that I had never before. I cried most nights while he was really ill, while he was in hospital and when he was at home. knowing what he was going to be missing and also the pain of him knowing that himself. I couldn't help but get upset thinking about how he must be feeling going through it all.

I felt awful for your brother because the same as what you had described a glint in his eye had gone. When I meet people now who are in an awful situation, I just remember how traumatising it was to see your dad ill with cancer and the suffering he went through. It was so inhumane.

I also had bouts of unpredictable crying. But seems it was during rather than after your dad died. I took Mollie (2 at the time) with me to the hospital one day to deliver a newspaper and the nurse wouldn't let me on the ward as it wasn't visiting times. I turned round, sat on a bench outside the ward doors and I just couldn't stop myself from crying, I was literally wailing! Then the nurse came back to tell me I could come in as they had let someone else in and she found me in a complete mess. She was so apologetic and even sat with me for ten minutes while I could calm myself down and get myself in order; I didn't want your Dad to know I had been crying. She explained that because he was palliatively unwell on a general ward that really visiting times shouldn't apply.

I think it helped your brother knowing we had another on the way to take his mind off the loss of your dad. He doesn't grieve the same way you do, but I can see that it does affect him. We continue to grieve for your Dad and I also recently experienced a more recent grief too. You'll remember that my

A reply to Marianne

brother split up with his girlfriend and due to the circumstances of the split I felt that in order to support my brother that we could no longer be friends. Even though I know she hadn't died and occasionally messages me still, I tried to brush it off, not let my brother know it really affected me too. I felt similar grief although I know nothing like losing a parent; I couldn't listen to music, I'm even crying now thinking about how I miss her so much! She was one of my best friends / like a sister. I spoke to her nearly daily and she saw so much of Mollie. The circumstances which led to their split just hurt me so much. I could feel the pain for my brother too. The worst is that even now, Mollie asks why we can't see Sarah and where she's gone; they're hard concepts to convey to a 5-year-old. My anxiety built up so much from grief.
The aftermath seems to hurt me so much more than the initial shock of it.

I'm always here for chats, I'm not good at words but very good at listening.

Lots of love, xx

Email from: Marianne
To: Liz
Re: Dad Story

Oh Liz! So well put. Thank you. Would it be okay to include your reply in the book? I think it's wonderful. M x

---

Email from: Liz
To: Marianne
Re: Dad Story

Yes! Happy for you to! Hope it all goes well! Keep me posted!
Liz, x

21
Joanna's Story

In April 2006 I woke to the sound of my best friend and flatmate Jane's alarm persistently going off. I went into her room and found her unresponsive in her bed. I called an ambulance and whilst waiting was told to try and resuscitate her. I knew from the minute I saw her that she was dead, however I did my best knowing there was nothing I could do. When the ambulance arrived, they confirmed my worst fears that she had passed away some hours before. It took weeks for the autopsy which was inconclusive and the cause of death was noted as sudden adult death syndrome. Death is hard enough to deal with when there is a reason they died but this was such a shock........a 26 year old (same age as me at the time), gorgeous and very fit girl doesn't just die......but Jane did and I'm not sure if this made it harder to process! I had experienced grief losing a grandparent before, but I think it's more expected with age! My worst nightmare came true, a young friend dying and seeing her lifeless body that didn't even seem to resemble her.

Immediately, on the day Jane died, I left my beloved flat in London that we shared and went home to my parents' house to try to come to terms with the events that had occurred that horrendous morning. I was in bits and kept seeing images of her dead and going over what had happened in my head. I couldn't sleep and was petrified of anyone near me sleeping in case they died too.

Days later Jane's parents flew over from overseas and met me at the flat and wanted to know everything about the days before her death, I happily told them everything as I don't think I had ever seen her so at ease and comfortable with life.

About a month later I tried to put a brave face on things and go back to my flat and go back to work. I found living in the flat hard and I hated myself for not being able to look at photos of her without making me retch, I couldn't understand why I couldn't remember her as my friend but could only visualise her dead. I couldn't remember nice times together and I most certainly couldn't look forward to life without her. I beat myself up about it and couldn't understand why I felt like this? It was difficult because I wanted people around me but couldn't deal with them sleeping near me as I worried the same would happen to them. If anyone stayed, I kept checking their pulse in the night. Every time I walked past her room all I could see was the image of her dead on the floor where I'd put her in the recovery position.

My attempt at returning to normal life lasted a few days, I sat at work and burst into uncontrollable tears! I think I had slightly been in denial about how hard it had hit me. It all came flooding out and I broke down, life seemed pointless. I could not focus on anything, fell into an absolute pit of trauma and grief. Looking back, it was a breakdown but I never admitted it. My mum came and collected me, they packed up my flat and I moved home, work gave me time off. I am so grateful I had that support otherwise I don't think I could have ever got over it.

At home my parents gave me space but tried to talk to me about it but I couldn't speak to them it was so raw and I hated myself for the way I envisaged Jane, not remembering her gorgeous smiley persona but all I saw was death and it freaked me out. I hated the way people looked at me and gave me pity, everyone spoke to me in a different manner than ever before or they completely ignored me. To this day one 'friend' has never spoken to me since, perhaps it was left too long and he had no idea what to say to me or how to cope with me, but I have seen a pattern in his behaviour over the years and I think it's a coping mechanism from him, when the tough gets going he just walks away.

Grief totally overtook my life and I split up with my boyfriend. I hated myself for not being able to look at photos of her, being afraid and all my thoughts were consumed by mortality and why did this have to happen? could I have done anything and why wasn't it me? I begged her to communicate with me, if ghosts did exist why didn't she visit me? I lost all perspective of my life and everything around me, I didn't care about anything, couldn't sleep, eat or focus on anything.

I stayed at home in a blur for about a month, didn't see anyone. I couldn't speak to anyone, no one understood what I had experienced on my own. At this point my mother thankfully arranged that I should do something to get out of the house and arranged that I went to ride for a horse racing yard close to the family home. I arrived there on the first morning feeling anxious and afraid of people's reactions towards me, I didn't want pity but I also felt so alone as no one understood what I had experienced. It was perfect as I think Mum had briefed Lisa, the yard owner. On arrival she told me to hug the horse if I felt sad and it was time to go riding. I felt comfortable with her as she didn't ask any questions about it. I love riding horses and fell at ease doing so, this I am sure was a great healer for me.

At the same time my mum got me to see a grief counsellor, so I started seeing her. I remember arriving for the first session not knowing what to expect but I basically spent the whole session in tears explaining the situation. It felt good talking to someone who didn't judge me or speak to me like I was a victim. Over the next six months I saw my counsellor at least once a week, twice to begin with. She asked me questions about my fears and pain. I talked to her about everything and

Joanna's Story

she explained to me my feelings were normal and it would ease as time heals. It does but only if you address your grief. For months we talked and talked and slowly I began to feel slightly better and the tears began to dry up. I changed so much as a person and lost a great deal of confidence. I am not the same person as I was before Jane died, I'm not better or worse, just think differently and have learnt to live with my grief.

After six months or so I was feeling stronger but not yet ready to try and shoehorn myself back into my old life. I was still finding I'd crumple at the slightest thing and people's reactions towards me were odd. I loved being at home with Mum and Dad but knew I had to do something to help myself recover. I got a job working in a safari lodge in South Africa, they knew nothing about my experiences and I felt anxious but got on a flight not knowing what to expect. It was so refreshing being in Africa, no one knew my story and slowly as I got to know the other workers I opened up. Being in South Africa put life into perspective for me, we would sit under the big African sky talking late into the night by the fire. I was there for seven months and came home feeling different, but stronger.

I gradually rebuilt my life, we sold the flat and things became easier day by day but I took it very slowly. I was fortunate that I was able to take time out of my usual life, I was able to gradually come to terms with my grief and trauma. I'm aware that not everyone is able to do this as not everyone has such great support and the financial help to put your life on pause while you confront your problems.

14 years later and I am married and happy but still have pain and will never forget Jane, she changed my life and I now live for both of us. I miss her every day, I have lovely framed photos of her in pride of place in my house, now I look at them a smile recalling happy times we spent together. On the anniversary of her death I always raise a glass to her and send her family a message.

I don't think grief ever goes away, it gets easier over time and manageable but its always there. I am so glad I confronted it and dealt with it head on with seeing a counsellor, otherwise I fear I would never have moved on.

22
Mia's Story

No one but me understands my relationship with my Dad. Even if family or friends saw our arguments, saw either of us boil into a rage or heard me complaining of how incredibly annoying he was, they'd still never fully be able to understand what that feels like for me. It's even more confusing when these are quite a few of the experiences I have to look back on now he's dead.

Throughout my childhood and teenage years my Dad took us many places – camping and caravanning trips across the U.K. He also took us on loads of bike rides and mountain walks (too many if you'd asked my opinion back then!) Starting from when I was about 11, we'd go on a family holiday abroad each year starting – France, Spain, Holland, Greece. He taught me the importance of experiencing other cultures when abroad. He was very artistic and was once in a band. He could play any tune on guitar and as a child I often enjoyed performing a guitar and singing duet with him. He often took me to art galleries, museums, the cinema and many concerts that we both thoroughly enjoyed as we shared a passion for music.

Through my mid-teens, I often said how my Dad and I were extremely similar. It was his way or the highway just as it was for me. He could sometimes find it funny to wind people up in the same way I do. But it always felt because we were so similar, we clashed, and his mere presence could annoy me. Our last camping trip and walk together was in August of 2018. We stayed at a camp site in the Lake District for a couple of nights. Of course, he had walks planned for us both. He took me to a large hill and pointed to the top. He was used to walking and had sped off. When I got to the top I realised there was a valley and two more large hills to climb. I remember feeling so angry and holding back tears for the mere fact he had blatantly lied, probably so I would be quicker! I sat on the first hill for a good 15 minutes before setting off again to calm down and to ensure I took as long as I wished.

All this is why in the last year before he was diagnosed with terminal cancer, I'd see him, on average, once a month. Please don't get me wrong, I loved my Dad and I know he loved me (even though I sometimes overthink myself in to feeling he didn't!) We were just both sometimes the stubborn argumentative type, which means I have a fair few negative memories of our relationship. In those times I did spend with him, we would drink together, listen to music, always watch a film (often La La land which we both came obsessed with due to the music and story!) We'd listen to the new jokes he'd found on the internet and sometimes go for a mountain walk or camping trip (often much to my disapproval!)

At Christmas 2018, we had our usual Christmas dinner at my Dad's. He was a really good cook and I wish I knew his recipes now. My Dad wasn't able to stomach much of his dinner and he'd lost a lot of weight, but since I'd barely saw him that year I was unaware that he had been ill for a while. I went to my brother's whilst my Dad decided to have a rest. As Christmas and holidays often seem to do, we ended up having a few laughs but also a few deep conversations. My brother (actually my half-brother) told me that he in some ways wishes he had a Dad like mine because he would take me and my sister everywhere, always want to do things with us and cared for us a lot. He said that the reason I was probably getting so angry at my Dad all the time was because of how I felt about him and my Mum splitting up back in 2014. In a nutshell, my brother was telling me that just because my Dad acted the way he did with my Mum, it never meant his love or care changed for us. I went home thinking to myself how I was going to try and be nicer and act different because that may have some truth. But 2 days later, my Dad gave us the news that he had just been diagnosed with pancreatic cancer. He got ill really quickly and died 2 months later on the 2nd of March 2019.

In those 2 months he became extremely ill, I was very confused. I tried to be busy and keep it to the back of my mind. I never spoke about it much with my Dad because I didn't know what to say to someone who knew that he was dying. I did go to a couple of counselling sessions whilst he was ill. The issue I brought up was that my Dad had a bad relationship with his parents and didn't want to tell them he was ill or dying. But they were still my Nan and Grandad and part of me felt wrong for keeping it from them. I tried to explain this to my Dad, he got angry; ordinarily I'd have been able to get angry and argue back. But instead I burst into tears and left the room. On reflection, I'd let any dying person have their death however they wish; I regret having that last argument with him.

I don't think I cried as often as I'd have liked as I tended to keep myself occupied. But I do remember a positive dance worthy song coming on the radio (Rude, by Magic) and it broke me to tears as the lyrics reminded me that although my Dad was just about alive; he soon wouldn't be and death is forever. Through weddings, my graduation, my future children. It also sort of hit me in that moment that my Dad had practically died already, since I didn't feel I could discuss these thoughts with him or discuss pretty much anything with him whilst he was so ill.

A more positive memory from that time was one of the last times we watched TV together – Dragon's den and also a documentary he'd recorded for me that was about some of my favourite rappers he knew I liked. He also said: "when he got better" we would go for an Indian together again; that comment was bittersweet although I'd have loved it, I think we both knew that wouldn't be happening.

I didn't react much initially when I was told that my Dad had died. I think I might have said 'okay'. I went in to see him. He looked as he did the day before and to my surprise, he didn't even feel cold like I'd expected. I said what I wanted to say quietly and once I'd left I didn't see his body again. Other members of my family did but I felt I'd said my piece.

I remember feeling the worst mental pain I'd ever experienced when some of the more extreme emotions of my grief came out. It truly felt physically and mentally painful to the core and literally crippled me. I curled into a ball when I thought about what had happened – it sometimes, although less frequently, still does.

I also feel a lot of guilt for the lack of time spent with my Dad and the way I was with him. I have to remind myself that despite our squabbles, Dad loved me. Someone's wise words helped me. They said that 'this happens with most adult / child relationships; we fight and rebel from our parents, especially as teenagers – it's just most people get the time to resolve those issues and build the relationship again', which, unfortunately, I didn't.

I was also in a bit of denial. It's all a sick joke isn't it? It's not real, I've just not seen him in a while? After he died we went on a commemorative walk on his birthday. There was a man who looked like him and was dressed just like him sat on the top of the hill we were climbing. I felt as though it might really be him, waiting for us to say it was all a big prank. Unfortunately, that wasn't the case. My partner also has my Dad's car. I sometimes look away from my partner driving and imagine that it is my Dad driving me round as usual. That all sounds really weird I suppose but I think the brain does whatever it can to not let go and to make things bearable.

Early on, everyone was extremely supportive in checking up on me, but I suppose that had to stop somewhere; it pretty much did after the funeral. I felt and still feel, sort of bewildered by that, everyone is there and almost being too overbearing but then they're gone! 'Oh - it's time for me to face it all alone!' It also still makes me question if what happened was really that bad? Is it normal for a parent to die when you're 19? 18 months on, I'm still confused whether my feelings are valid because 18 months have passed. Aren't you meant to 'get over it'?

I don't think you ever really do. You would've loved them eternally and you'll miss them eternally too. It's the price of love I suppose. But my grief still affects me, I suppose it just does so more quietly now. When I bring it up to people who don't understand, they try to give me the 'other people have it worse' argument - I know they mean well but that doesn't help anyone. I wish people were comfortable with just letting people vent their emotions - no matter how distressing, instead of trying to fix what in my situation feels like a completely unsolvable problem.

We re-painted my Dad's house and we had a Romanian couple move in to do it. The wife (who knew nothing about us) asked my Mum if someone living there had died. My mum said yes why? The woman told my mum how she'd found a dead bird in the chimney breast and that it was a sign of death where she was from. She did the usual ritual she traditionally did at home and said that whoever it was who had passed was peaceful now. I've never met a more atheist person than my Dad and I know full well what he'd have thought of that, but for me personally it did provide some comfort. Another comfort was getting a teddy made from one of my Dad's shirts as a Christmas gift and it still smelling of him. It still sits pride of place in my room. We are going to make it tradition to go for a walk on each of his future birthdays. I'd like to do the last walk we went on together again one day too. The one I complained about. I hope that will bring me some comfort also.

Overall, I suppose the feeling of grief hasn't gone away. It stays with me throughout my day to day life and many thing,s both happy and sad, remind me of my Dad. I can still feel the extreme feeling of grief if I allow myself. But I often feel I don't have time to do it justice.

> I also think that if death wasn't such a taboo subject for others, I'd feel a lot more in touch with my emotions and less like a robot who should keep it all in.

23

Losing Mum:

Jane's Story

Few of us would admit to having a 'favourite' parent. So, when mine was diagnosed with cancer in October 2014, it felt like falling off a cliff. Parents will often say "when I'm gone..." and the words are met with an anxious laugh, the conversation turning quickly to other things. But this was real.

My Mum was, and I still consider her to be, the bravest and most beautiful person I have ever known. But this time, it wasn't just me navigating this uncharted territory; as well as my Dad, my brother and all her friends, she had three granddaughters who adored her, and she them. I wasn't just losing my Mum: I also had to watch them lose her, and her being robbed of watching them grow into the beautiful women they have become. It was undoubtedly the most painful thing I've ever experienced in my life.

Grief is not an emotion that can be tied up in a neat little package. Grief, for me, is many things: it is fear, it is rage, it is confusing, it is sad, it can be strangely humorous, it is physically and emotional painful, it can make you feel that you will never catch your breath again. On Valentine's Day that year which was seven weeks before she died, with her permission, we held a gathering at her home, twenty of her nearest and dearest. All they had to bring that day was a memory of Mum they were prepared to share with her and us. Everyone accepted the invitation - some travelling very long distances. Everyone shared their memory. We all knew this would be the last time. There were tears of absolute sadness but also much laughter, mostly led by Mum, glass of wine in hand, who that day put on a dress and her favourite lippy for the last time. And she sat in the midst of everyone, laughing and drinking it all in. Because she knew too.

So, for the last few months of her life, I went to all her appointments and kept everyone up to date with information. I'd drive an hour there and an hour back, fuelled by fear and adrenaline, wine gums and Abba. Sitting in the small windowless hospital room at the end of January 2015, to be told that she had seen her last Christmas and she wouldn't see the summer ahead, broke me. But she guided me, she consoled me, and she comforted me. I asked her how she could remain so calm and she answered "because I knew".

Telling my girls this devastating news broke my heart, and theirs. But, on reflection, I realise Mum had taught us all well and we found strength for her and for ourselves, strength I believe we carry to this day.

We all spent days leading up to the final one, sitting with her and, eventually, lying with her. I asked her what scared her the most. She replied "dying alone". I reassured her that wouldn't happen. And it didn't, Mum. We were with you at the end, holding you lovingly, whilst you slipped peacefully away.

Mum didn't want a religious funeral. When we asked her who she wanted to speak that day she said "my Jane." So that day, I stood in a small chapel full of all the people who liked, loved and respected her and, with a heart full of pride, told them about my Mum. There were a lot of tears that day, because only I knew that, before we all left her in that chapel, I would read out five loving and farewell messages from her, in her own words, one each to her two best friends, one to her beloved granddaughters, one to my brother and lastly, one to my Dad. People asked how

I could do it. It was an easy reply. Because she was my Mum, and I loved her. Who else knew her like I did?

All these years later, my girls and I still talk a lot about her - and I don't think that will ever change. And the word I miss saying the most? Mum.

Five months after Mum died, my girls and I took her down to Cornwall, where my brother lives. As darkness fell over her favourite beach, we went down to the water's edge and "let her go". It was both painful and uplifting and something she'd have loved.

She's also in a small wooden box in my knicker drawer. She'd love that too.

24

Jody's Story

The definition of grief is the intense sorrow of losing something important to you. I hope to share my experiences of losing my Dad in the hope that my story may resonate and help others experiencing similar losses.

I'd like to start by telling you a bit about my Dad. Growing up, my dad was fun, loving and generous. I am extremely grateful for all the happy memories I have from my childhood. When I think of my childhood, I see smiling faces, contentment and togetherness. My Dad lived a full life working hard and pursuing many interests; having completed the London marathon a number of times, being an accomplished runner was one of them. As I grew older, he welcomed my then boyfriend (now husband) into our family like a son. He was frankly THE best Grandad to my sisters' children and my own son; I appreciate everyone thinks this, but he really was.

In my teens, I was told there was a 50/50 chance that my dad could inherit Huntington's Chorea (HD). My parents reassured us that we had not inherited the gene, and therefore we were safe. Still, I lived with a shadow over me, not knowing what the future would hold for my Dad. It was something that wasn't really talked about, so I silently watched him like a hawk. I could sense what was coming. His diagnosis was confirmed around the time he was forced to take retirement early.

He was a chef and dropping sharp knives was not ideal! He found his movements were harder to coordinate, suggesting signs of deterioration. His neurologist reassured him that the way he had inherited the HD it would be nothing more than a slight inconvenience. I would regularly search for this 'mild' form of HD, but never found any evidence. What I did find was how the age of onset could vary, from teenage years onwards; regardless of the onset age the trajectory was the same. I still struggle with anger towards that neurologist who was out of his depth. I have wanted to confront him so many times. Professionals should know their limits and not practice outside them. During Dad's retirement he relished more time with his grandchildren and enjoyed growing vegetables in the garden. Over this time the progression of the disease was very slow, I think for me I could see it more noticeably as I lived further away. I can see now that I had already started grieving for him all those years ago. He was slowly not able to do all the things he loved and I was sure that he could see this too. I could see him fading away and knew it was a matter of time. It was awful to watch, and looking back I can see how I passed through various stages of grief a number of times. All these emotions where perhaps less intense, but they were present all the same.

Dad had been on a slow downward slope for a number of years, but there was sharp turning point. It seemed this had been triggered by a drug which should never have been prescribed. I recognise the unresolved aggression I have towards that neurologist. This time, the deterioration manifested in dark thoughts. I won't disclose the nature of these in order to respect him and my family. Needless to say, they were the stuff of nightmares. The thing is with HD is that once he started thinking them, he was unable to switch them off. It was truly the most stressful time of my life. In the first few days after the sudden downturn I would leave my son and husband to drive home to support my family as much as I could. I was working in the care profession and I would switch into work mode and use low arousal techniques to manage challenging situations. We were screaming out for help, but the HD meant that he fell between services. During this time, I had a conversation with him that made me realise how much I had lost. He spoke to me as if I were a stranger. He talked about his daughter Jody. He failed to recognise that it was me sat there with him. I am fortunate that we had many more conversations after this where he did know who I was. I can only imagine the sadness for those relatives with dementia where this becomes a permanent reality.

At the same time, I was pregnant with my second child. I began to fear that the stress was going to bring on early labour. With the cocktail of stress we were already enduring, this was something we really didn't need. Taking a break and laying on the bed at my parent's I could feel strong tightenings; I knew I needed to go home. I felt awful leaving my family in crisis, a horrible feeling that became quite familiar over the years. Shortly after began a long journey between mental health services and a care home. Living far away with a newborn made this journey incredibly frustrating. I wanted to be able to support at meetings or liaise with the teams supporting him, but it just wasn't feasible.

At the end of my Dad's life it was another sharp decline. No one had suspected anything was wrong, yet we had a call in the middle of the night saying he had collapsed and was in ICU. They thought it was a lung infection and it was serious. The events are a whirlwind in my memories. I recall an emotional conversation with a compassionate doctor, speaking to us about how 'if the worst happened', they weren't going to resuscitate him. Over the next week we were on a rollercoaster, but Dad was stable and able to communicate with us. There were conversations about PEG feeding tubes and oxygen supplies. I couldn't bear to think of him suffering more and losing more and more function. It made me question what was the point in all those supports for him to lie in a bed rotting. I still wrestle with the guilt that I pushed for him to die sooner. He had never made it clear what his wishes were, and I could only apply what I would want for me. When he was still in the hospital having the oxygen gradually reduced it was the day of the London Marathon. We had a wonderful day watching all the runners together, in awe of my dad for taking part so many times. It is a memory I will hold dear forever.

We managed to get him transferred to his care home, and spent the week waiting for the inevitable. Sitting in that room day after day listening to the rasping breaths was exhausting. It was impossible to sustain the emotional poignancy which seemed appropriate. Over the years, I had come to terms with living far away and accepted that I was unlikely to be there when he passed. I was ok with that. In all honesty, I would have preferred not to see his dead body. Life had a different path, and shortly after arriving to see him one morning I was putting on his favourite music and chatting to him when I realised that he was going. My mum and sister walked in at the exact moment he let out his last breath.

There is so much emotion wrapped up in that moment, and the moments that followed. I know it felt different for my Mum and sister, but the experience solidified it for me. I felt very little attachment to the dead body lying there. It may have been his blood and bones, but it wasn't him. But my sister wanted to stay with the body until the funeral directors arrived, so we all sat with him. Those moments have frankly haunted me for some time. But now I am more able to move on when I feel them building in my mind. Perhaps if she hadn't wanted to stay I would be full of regret that I had left.

Immediately after the passing there is a strange limbo preparing for the funeral. At the time, I recall it feeling extremely important that I speak at the funeral. Looking back I'm not really sure why. When it came time to say the words I had put together the emotions I felt were so intense. The memory is such a blur, but I'm pleased I did it. The day of the funeral felt like such a positive event, a time to celebrate his life.

It had so many personal touches, and so many family and friends were there. It is a truly treasured memory.

It was really important for me to find something creative to involve my children in the process. I decided to do rock painting. We sat in my Mum's garden together and all had the chance to draw things that were meaningful to us. We had quite a collection of images; all drew on happy memories we shared. It may sound strange, but for me it was a lovely experience. The stones are now split between my garden and his tombstone. I love having a reminder of him in my garden, and I have found that I focus more on the photos and memories that are tucked around my home.

For me, the grief of losing my Dad is countered with great comfort knowing that he is no longer trapped in a state of distress. Which at times perhaps makes the grief lighter and easier to accept, however it brings with it guilt for feeling that way. I also feel that his death has given me permission to grieve, something that I 'shouldn't' have been doing when he was still alive.

I miss him so much. I miss his hugs. I miss how proud he was of us. I miss him being the best Grandad to my kids. I often 'talk' to him, and I feel his presence around me, and watching over us all. My youngest has no idea who he was. She met him only a couple of times, which naturally brings huge waves of sadness. The idea of tides and waves really resonates with me as a lovely analogy for grief. I can feel fine one day and overwhelmed the next.

As I reflect on my journey I can recognise the different stages of grief, but for me these were spread over a longer time. I was grieving my dad for years, to-ing and fro-ing through the different stages. The fact that each of my family has experienced this differently reminds me that everyone's journey is their own. It is important to respect and be sensitive to that. At times this was a source of frustration for me, although I can see we just had different points of view. Through it all, my husband was incredibly supportive. As I sit here and reflect, I can see how much he held and listened to my ramblings and guided me to more reasonable ways of thinking. When I was in denial, he would remind me the importance of my visits. When I was sad, he comforted me. I want to take this chance to thank him, he was a guiding light in stormy seas.

I also feel that the process of writing this down has been really helpful, so thank you to Marianne for the opportunity. This form of free reflection has helped me to revisit the narrative from over a year ago and make sense of all those emotions and experiences. This might not be the case for everyone, but the process of writing down your own journey might be something you find helpful. It doesn't have to be something to share; it can be something entirely private, but it might help to make sense of the intense emotions you may experience.

25
Amber's Story

In my first year of university I worked in a very well-known restaurant part time where I made loads of friends. One late shift, one of my colleagues came into the store crying as if something terrible had happened. He wanted to speak to the shift manager. I carried on with my duties; I remember mopping the floor and I saw them both leave the office. Before I could even ask the manager if everything was ok, he just gave me a look as if to say, 'don't ask.' I continued with closing up and wiping things down, but I just had this horrible feeling but couldn't put my finger on what was wrong. In my mind I was thinking my friend crying surely isn't going to affect me that much? Clearly something has happened in his life and maybe he just wanted to come in to tell the manager why he won't be in tomorrow?

We all came to the end of our shift and the manager asked us to sit in the lobby and he needed to chat to us, so at this point we were all a bit on edge but also thinking 'its 1am, we have all had a long shift we are all tired we just want to go home! What is so important he wants us to wait and chat at this time of the morning after a long shift?'

We all sat down, and he says:

Amber's Story

"I know you've seen Ian come in earlier very upset, I have some sad news for you all......Owain has passed away this afternoon, he had a motorcycle accident and he didn't make it".

We were all in shock, Owain wasn't just another work colleague he was a friend, and the most smiley, happiest person you would ever meet. Owain was only 24 when he passed away. He had been on 2 weeks annual leave and was a massive motorbike fanatic and for weeks he was so excited to spend his leave riding around Brecon on his new bike.

I think that the friends I had made while working together were the only reason we all got through the death of someone so young in our lives. We all pulled together and had regular gatherings where we would drink plenty, share stories and cry while comforting each other. Since the restaurant that we worked for is such a big company we were all worried that we wouldn't all be able to go to the funeral however, they let us all go and got staff from another store to cover.

Even though we'd had his funeral, because Owain had gone on annual leave we were all kind of still just waiting for him to return from holiday, which never happened. We got a plaque made for him for our store which is still hanging there today. His family still go there to visit and have coffee and I think they find comfort in being somewhere where so many people adored their son. Without the support of my work family I don't think we would have gotten over the loss of such a young person in all our lives.

I was incredibly sad about my friend's passing, I felt his loss more keenly around my other colleagues and at work and of course when I saw people on motorbikes. However, the worst bereavement and grief reaction I have yet experienced in my life was one very much close to my home and my memories of home. It was when I lost my very first best friend and family pet, my cat named Fluffy Jay. I had Fluffy when I was five years old and he passed away when I was twenty-one years old, making Fluffy seventeen when he passed. I feel like this was the worst loss I have ever experienced because as I said previously he was my first best friend, I used to see him every day of my life, cwtch him, kiss him, play with him and from a little kid I always used to tell him my thoughts, feelings and secrets and after telling him these things I would always feel better. As Fluff was getting older I always dreaded the day he would die thinking how would I survive without my best friend? Who am I going to cwtch when I've had a bad day and have a little cry to, even though he couldn't answer back (for obvious reasons), I always felt comfort from him as though he understood and that I would be ok, as silly as that sounds. Fluff always had an active life, he was a major hunter and loved going outdoors and laying in the sun. Before his death I couldn't remember a day without him and that just added to the intense bereavement I experienced once he had passed away.

Seventeen years old for a cat is quite old, and as Fluff was getting older his kidneys started to fail, as a result he become weaker and weaker and it was the worst thing to see him in so much pain. The vet kept giving him pain relief but said that with the pain relief he was receiving although it was helping with his pain, it was also adding to his kidney failure as that is just how that pain relief worked over time. She said, 'if he gets any worse within the next week, we need to start thinking of putting him to sleep.' In my mind I was never going to put my best friend to sleep and, he was going to pull through because he couldn't die. Not only was I not ready for him to die, but I didn't know what I would do without him as selfish as that sounds. After bringing him home from the vets the next day my mam had found Fluffy laying in his own urine as he was in too much pain to move and did not make it to the litter tray; when we saw this we knew the kindest thing we could do was take him to vets and get ready to say goodbye. I got his favourite blanket, wrapped him up and we got in the car as Fluff laid on my lap and I sat there cwtching him and breaking my heart the whole way to the vets. When we pulled up, the vet had come out to see us as my mam had pre-phoned them. It was the most beautiful early evening, the sun was blazing and since the vet met us in the car park she asked if we wanted to do the procedure here, which we agreed to because the sun was Fluff's favourite thing. I held fluff in his blanket as the vet injected him and I literally saw his little life leave his body. As you can imagine, I was inconsolable and I couldn't let his little body go to give to the vet, so the vet left him with me for 10/15 mins even though this felt like 2 mins while I cwtched him and just continued to break my heart. No one could have made this better, no kind words, nothing. I had lost my life long best friend and I had no idea what I would now do without him. The vet came back and took Fluff off me even though I still wasn't ready, I remember seeing the vet give me back the blanket that he was wrapped up in and started walking away with fluff in her arms.

Fluff passed away when I was 21 years old and I am now 25. Still to this day I am not able to talk about him for long periods without breaking into tears. When he initially passed away, I would cry with every song that came on the radio that reminded me of him even if I was driving, which meant I spent many car rides breaking down in tears and sometime having to pull over because I was crying so much. My boyfriend took me to an ASDA where we printed out all the pictures I owned of Fluffy (which was a lot) bought a beautiful photo album and put them all in the album I could always keep safe. We decided to have Fluff's body cremated which took a couple of weeks. I remember going to pick up the tiniest box from the vets and when the receptionist passed me over this little box I again broke down in the middle of reception area where all the clients were just staring at me. On the way home from the vets I sat in the car cwtching this box and just continued to cry.

For weeks after Fluff's death the house was just so empty without his presence, so me and Mam decided even though it was probably too soon, that we could go down to cat's protection and adopt a cat in need of an owner. When we got there, we were shown all these beautiful little cats who all needed love and a home, and even though we were open minded to adopting any age cat when we got to the kitten section there was this little black and white cat (which was the same colour as Fluff) who caught my attention. They opened up the cage and this beautiful little kitten came right to me and wouldn't leave me alone and demanded attention off me; his brother was doing the same thing to my mam and we knew we just had to adopt these two little babies. That day we ended up leaving cat's protection with two little black and white cats called Troy and Theo. Even though they will never replace Fluff, they helped me focus my attention in caring for another little creature who needed love and a home.

Sadly, Fluff's passing wasn't the last of my significant constant figures disappearing from my life. A few years after Fluff's passing, I lost my grandad. My grandad was such a gentle, loving and funny man. He loved Disney and soppy love stories and cheesy Christmas films that you would only find on that Christmas 24/7 channel. I would often sit there, watch amazing films with him while he made us hot chocolate or really milky coffee and eat too many biscuits. My grandad just reminded me of a big kid who always believed we could do whatever we wanted and always had great advice and always cared and provided for our family.

He owned his own fruit and veg business which included both shops and market stalls. He was such a unique character; he was cheeky and was always cracking jokes on the market. Sometimes he would say something with such a serious look some people didn't know if he was joking until he would deliver the punch line. He was such an amazing business man; his engagement with his customers is what kept them coming back. Even though he would make a joke, he would also be very caring which allowed some of his regular customers to open up to him, making them become not only customers but lifelong friends. I remember my gran telling me this story once about how there was a homeless man who used to hang around near one of his stalls and at the end of the day Grandad used to see him go through bins for food. My grandad decided to buy him food and this became a daily thing, he bought this man food every day for weeks, he bought him warm clothes and because this man wanted to remain in his tent, provided him with a sleeping bag. The man was so grateful for his kindness. One day he approached my grandad with this little china boot and told my grandad that he had spent his last 50p on it and that he wanted my grandad to keep it as a thank you present. He was now moving from the area to camp somewhere else and he wanted to show him his gratitude. To this day, my gran still has that boot in their home. This is one of the reasons why his funeral was absolutely jam packed with people; some people I knew and some I didn't, but every single person had nothing but kind words and funny stories to say about him.

Overall, my grandad's health was pretty normal for a gentleman in his 70's, however he did develop Parkinson's a few years back which was getting worse as the years went on. At the end of May 2019, due to his Parkinson's, he had a massive fall which hospitalized him. It was so bad he bruised all his face and shattered his knee meaning he would need a knee replacement. At this time, I hadn't long started a new job as a support worker for a homeless charity. This brought its own stresses as I was mostly working long 12-hour night shifts. It meant I would hardly ever get time off to visit and when I did have a day off, I was so tired from working nights I would usually just sleep all day. This meant I never actually got to visit my grandad in hospital in the time between the fall and the operation. He finally had his operation on the Tuesday that week and I actually had 2 days off in a row, so for the first day I used it to sleep and planned on going to visit my grandad on my second day off.

But around 9pm I was in bed worrying because I had this gut feeling that I should have gone today, but I knew I was too tired to drive. I had a phone call and when I answered, my dad was on the phone crying saying that my grandad has passed away. Along with the instant upset I felt this overpowering sense of guilt because I hadn't seen him. I just kept thinking 'I'm the worst grandchild alive!' My dad told me that after my grandad's operation they offered him this injection in order to stop blood clots, but he refused to accept it, and it was later discovered that he died of a blood clot. Me and Dad later got talking, saying because his Parkinson's was getting worse he started to hate how his body was betraying him. It seemed that he'd had enough with life, not only because his condition was getting worse but because he had also lived through seeing two of his own children die and we all knew how much he ached for them both and how the bereavement he experienced every day of his life never went away. My dad and I felt like he made that conscious decision to decline that injection maybe to be reunited with his children.

Even though I was very upset over losing my grandad, during the funeral and the wake I felt like I had to be strong for my gran and for my dad. My gran was married to this wonderful man for 60+ years and all through their life they had experienced everything together. They had developed a very successful business together, bought luxurious houses and holiday homes all over Europe, been able to raise three children and see eight grandchildren grow up. They also went through the loss and the mourning of two of their own children; their son who was 33 years of age and their daughter who was 30. My dad was now the only son left and I could see how heartbroken both my gran and Dad were as we watched the coffin being cremated. I felt like my own needs must take a back seat compared to my Gran and my Dad. The only thing that helped me through the loss was being around my family and sharing amazing stories such as the one I spoke about earlier with the homeless gentleman, the stories about his life and all the silly jokes that my grandad used to love telling us helped us keep his memory alive.

These are 3 very different losses; but I wanted to share them with you because they are significant and because I hope that my story might help so you with your own grief processes.

I'm so sorry you're having a hard time right now.

Email from: Dr Marianne Trent
To: Amber
Re: Your Story

Dear Amber,

Thank you for sharing your story with us. Your Grandfather sounds like he was a wonderfully compassionate man. The idea of that little boot ornament will stay with me.

I'm glad that the restaurant kept Owain's plaque and that his family can still find comfort and connection from being there, one of the places where he was well loved and known.

It sounds like Fluff had really been a constant presence in your life and that you'd always felt comfort and acceptance from him. It's understandable why the idea of him not being there felt so derailing. I'm pleased you've been able to find more joy from the arrival of the kittens who are now I'm sure fully grown cats!

Thanks again,
Marianne

26
Lindsay's Story

It's inevitable, as we journey through life - we experience loss. The longer we live, the more losses we encounter. My first experiences of losing someone dear to me, was as a child when my great-grandma died, having suffered a massive stroke in her sleep. I still remember seeing my dad with tears in his eyes, sobbing and wiping the tears from his face as he explained to us that his dear grandmother had died. My dad, who I have only ever seen cry a handful of times. I remember feeling sad and wishing I could make him feel better. I thought a lot about how much I had enjoyed going to her house every time we visited. I had really fond memories of visiting her. The crayons and colouring books she got out for us, the old nutcracker and packet of walnuts she always had tucked away. Her smell, I can still remember her smell.

Throughout my childhood, I remember attending lots of funerals of older family members, as the natural course of life took place. I even remember my younger brother (who was aged about four at the time) announcing at the top of his voice: 'Can I have Aunt Polly's teeth', as my dear old Aunt Polly was lowered into the ground – I suppose false teeth are a novelty in the mind of a four year old!

My mum worked as a manager of sheltered housing, and my brother and I often spent time with the older people she supported, attending the social events and outings- it was a big part of our life growing up, and we felt part of a lovely huge extended family. Inevitably, we also experienced the loss of a lot of the individuals we grew close to. We attended a lot of funerals and wakes as children!

The next memory that I have was as a pallbearer at my gran's funeral. I stood next to my dad, siblings and close relatives and lowered her into the earth. I remember feeling a sense of relief. My gran had suffered for years with Alzheimer's and years before her death had lost her speech, movement and ability to swallow. She was a shadow of her former self. I was grateful I had been able to sit with her in her final weeks and days, hold her hand and speak to her, telling her how much I loved her. I remember singing to her, and thinking 'my God, if she could speak, she would probably be screaming at me to stop!' I was relieved her suffering and pain was finally over and she was once again reunited with my grandad who had died when their children were young. She was a strong and serious woman and I will always remember staying with her and sleeping over in her room; completing puzzle books together into the early hours. I also remember her coming to stay with us for Christmas, just before her Alzheimer's got really bad and sleeping in the room with her in case she got confused in the middle of the night!

I have also lost several friends and old school mates over the years too. I think the difficulty with losing a friend, the same age is that it reminds you how fragile life is. It doesn't feel right, someone so young should be taken from the world and their loved ones so early. It didn't follow my picture of the natural course of life, painted by my early experiences of death. Their chance to experience the richness of life, gone. Again, I found recollecting fond memories of these wonderful people and great times shared was my way of dealing with the sudden news they were no longer here.

Given my experiences of death throughout my life, you would think I had developed helpful coping strategies to deal with loss and grief. To some extent I have, like reminiscing and talking to others and sharing experiences. Yet, nothing could have prepared me for the loss of my unborn baby. I fell pregnant with my first child at the age of 24. It was a huge shock at the time, and not a planned pregnancy. He was our surprise baby! It therefore came as a great shock to me and my partner, years later when we decided the time was right to try for a second baby that it actually was not that easy to get pregnant! We had tried for over a year without success. Then finally, the two blue lines I had been waiting for appeared; I was pregnant - and overjoyed! This state of sheer happiness was short-lived; eight weeks later, I was at work and I started bleeding. I went straight to the early pregnancy unit at my local hospital. They did a test and took some bloods. They told me my pregnancy hormones were starting to decrease and it was likely I was in the process of a miscarriage. I would have to wait for the process to complete and then was advised to take another pregnancy test later on to check it was no longer positive and my body had managed to 'terminate the pregnancy successfully'. It was an agonising wait. I had so much false hope that my body would pull through and give this precious life all that it needed to survive and thrive, despite being told it would not. I spent the time thinking about anything I might have done to cause this, anything I could have done differently. I prayed and hoped all would be ok, I had bled throughout my entire first pregnancy with my son (who was now a fit and healthy five-year-old), maybe all would be ok. It was not to be. My body finally gave in four days later and I fully bled, losing my pregnancy. I was in complete shock. I sat there, completely numb with pain. It was all encompassing. As it happened, I was away with close family at the time on a trip that had been booked for months. I didn't want to be there, I wanted to be in my bed at home, on my own. I didn't get that time on my own to sit and really feel the loss as it happened. I had to get up and carry on, as I didn't want to upset others. Everyone around me carried on as normal, like nothing was happening. I remember feeling so angry. Angry at having to carry on and get up and go about my day. Angry that no one seemed to understand how I might be feeling.

When I think back, I remember people around me responding with reassurances such as 'you can always try again', 'miscarriage is really common you know, you will be able to have another baby'. Someone close to me commented 'it wasn't a baby; it was too early- don't worry'. These responses made me feel so disconnected from the real world and others. I felt no one understood my pain or loss. I may have been in the early stages of pregnancy, but this was not just a 'foetus' or 'cells', this was my baby. When a woman becomes pregnant, her body starts responding immediately. When I found out I was pregnant, my love and attachment started straight away. I was picturing my son as a big brother, and the family adventures we would all have together. I was excited to find out whether we would have a boy or girl, and what our lives would be like. I remember feeling so weak and so vulnerable. That aching pain was like no other I have experienced. I remember having to phone up and cancel my 12-week scan, absolutely heartbroken.

Now, although the physical pain of losing my baby has passed, there are moments often when I think about it. This loss differed from all other experiences of loss in my life. I had no fond memories to comfort myself with, just pure loss of all that could have been, but never was. When I think of how people around me responded, I can see that they wanted to make me feel better. They said the things they did, to try and ease the suffering at the time.

If I was giving advice to someone or thinking about how to support someone with a similar experience, it would be that there is often no 'right' thing to say. What is important, is to sit with someone and allow them to feel what they feel. No matter how awful it is, it's ok to feel numb with pain when you lose someone that means so much to you. It is a normal and appropriate way to feel. I would argue it is an important part of the process of healing too. As humans I think we struggle to see others in pain and distress and understandably try all we can to 'fix' this. I would say, allow yourself to acknowledge the loss and feel it. Be kind to yourself. We don't have to 'fix' things right there and then. All too often I was guilty of telling myself I was being pathetic, or I needed to 'pull myself together'. Something I found difficult with losing my baby, was that I didn't have memories, or a formal ceremony saying goodbye, all things that have soothed me in the past. I have since decided to plant a tree in memory, so that I ensure my loss is not forgotten. It is a part of me and my story. The thought of something physical to mark my baby's presence in my life was hugely important to me and one that provides me great comfort.

> After suffering two miscarriages, I am happy to say we are now a family of four, and I am mum to two beautiful boys, who fill my life with chaos, laughter and lots of love.

27

Claire's Story

"My Nan died. My kind, wise, beautiful Nan. You know, somewhere in the back of your mind, that your grandparents, if you're lucky enough to know them at all, will at some point pass away. And it is absolutely the rightful order of things. But when it happens, you feel a huge sense of injustice. I'm lucky enough to have known my Nan for nearly 36 years, and the happy memories will prevail, but at the moment I feel jolted by her passing and can't quite come to terms with it. In the days following her death I woke every day and remembered that she was no longer here, it felt like I was being retold the news every morning. I feel guilty about not seeing her in the weeks before she died, particularly because I had been thinking about her for about a week, "I really must go and see Nan, it's been a few weeks". Now I'll never get to see her again, and that thought makes me so very sad.

As well as your own grief you are consumed with concern for others that have been left behind. My grandad, at 84 years old, is completely and utterly heartbroken. He is trying to keep busy, and is, in fact, coping with the day to day chores like washing and cooking with amazing strength and resilience. But spend more than 5 minutes with him and you can see him realising all over again that Nan is no longer here. It passes over his face like a cloud. And my Mum, who has lost her Mum, is being so very brave, but she is haunted by the idea that she will never see her Mum again. She looks sad and tired, and her life will never be quite the same as it was. She is joined in her grief by her three brothers, my uncles, who are each dealing with it in their own ways but are all absolutely devastated. My sister and cousins alongside me have lost their beloved Nan, and my gorgeous babies and niece have lost their Great Nanny. What is it all about?

As the days go on, we will start to feel better and we will laugh and we will remember the good times, of which there were many. But we have all suffered a great loss and her passing will leave a hole in each and every life that she touched. She was a wonderfully kind lady, never a bad word to say about anyone, and the church full of people at her funeral is testament to how much she will be missed. Rest in peace Nan, thank you for everything, and I'm so very sorry that I didn't spend more time with you."

It's September 2020 and I wrote this letter above in the weeks after my Nan passed away, four and half years ago now. Reading it through again, it still makes me cry. I don't carry that grief on a daily basis anymore, but every so often, when least expected, she will appear in my thoughts, and I can still feel desperately sad that she is no longer here. My Grandad rallied, and created a life for himself, but he never really recovered from losing the love of his life, and sadly passed away a couple of years later. This hit us all just as hard, we had all spent more time with him since Nan had died, and so the inevitable hole that was left when he passed away felt all the bigger. My wonderful son, only 8 years old at the time, cried with me when we found out, and this both broke my heart and brought me comfort. My beautiful Mum, who tries so hard to be strong, lost both of her parents within a few years, and the trauma of this is still evident.

I vividly remember where I was and how I felt when I found out that Nan, and then Grandad, had died. These locations will, I suspect, be committed to memory forever. But also now, I am able to find the happy memories, and talk about them with my children, with my parents, with my sister, my niece, cousins, uncles and aunts. My children remember them, particularly my Grandad, and this makes me incredibly happy. I love that they talk about them and have memories of their own: of my Nan's 'bits box' and my Grandad's mints and £2 coin every time they visited. We go on, and we remember them happily and fondly.

Email from: Dr Marianne Trent
To: Claire
Re: Your Story

Dear Claire,

I am so struck by your Grandad's £2 coins and I can practically taste the polo mints although I realise now I've said that, that you only actually said mints and I've conjured the polos up all by myself! Words can be so powerful and evocative. Thanks once again for your story and your words with us.

Marianne

28

Vicky's Story:

Bonfire Night

As I child I loved bonfire night, the smells in the air, the crackling of the fire, the skies being lit up like a rainbow in darkness and as a family we would eat jacket potatoes and sausages, while visiting our local fire station to watch the display. The air filled with excitement and dad holding my hand when I got scared of the loud noises from time to time, he made me feel safe, he was my protector.

Fast Forward to Monday 5th November 2018, this day is no longer filled with happy memories but with sadness and fear. This is the day I lost my dad forever, the person who I looked up to, talked to and made plans had gone forever.

I remember during the days leading up to his passing I had people telling me: 'don't worry, he will be going soon, he will just slip away peacefully, you will not notice'.

How could people be so wrong? How can they promise these things when they have no control at the end? My dad was a fighter right from the diagnoses in December 2017 until his passing in November 2018.

Watching someone you love in so much pain just lying there is one of the hardest things I have ever done, during his final 4 days I did not leave his side. I talked to him, letting him know I would keep my promises I made in our final conversation a week before. I sat and held his hand even though I could tell his body was shutting down, and to me the only thing that mattered was letting him know I was there for him and it did not matter how I was feeling.

At 7:45pm on Monday 5th November, my dad took his final breath. I had heard about the death rattle; but I never thought I would experience it first-hand. It is something that I would wish no one to experience. I said goodbye and told him I loved him one final time, my mum put her hand on his chest as he fought so hard to stay with us and she said: ' it's time to be with your Mum now' and then silence; it was over. After months of hospital visits, treatments, operations and pain and suffering he was finally at peace.

The next few hours were a blur, with visits from the doctor, Macmillan nurses - who were amazing, to the undertakers. I don't remember crying when he first passed, I just felt numb. I remember sitting in the living room with my mum holding a cup of sweet tea, as people say things always look better when you have a cuppa; but they didn't, it just made the realisation of what had happened a little easier.

For the next few months, I just remember being on autopilot, blocking out my grief, making sure my mum and family were ok, as I promised my dad I had to be strong for them. I showed little emotion over the coming months just trying to adjust to a whole new life without my dad. On the 27th November 2018 we had my brother's wedding; originally Dad was going to be best man. Instead, we had his funeral on the 3rd December 2018; there was no time to show weakness.

I could not be more wrong, the more I ignored the grief, anxiety and depression the worse the symptoms were increasing. As each month was passing, I ended up becoming a shadow of my former self. I refused to go out, I was suffering from severe insomnia and functioning on less than 2 days sleep a day. I was suffering from severe panic attacks, while also having flashbacks;

most often at random moments. I was also having nightmares which were usually of my dad's final moment.

As everything around me was spiralling out of control, the one thing I knew I could control was my food. I would go for days or weeks without eating properly, I was so exhausted, but when I did eat, I'd end up eating a meal only to be sick straight afterwards. But for once this made me feel better, like it was the one thing I could take control of. However, I was not in control, not by a long way. The grief was controlling me, the anger and emotion that was building up inside was eating me away. All I wanted to do was scream and shout, who was I angry at you ask? The doctors for their misdiagnosis, the nurses for promising me he would not suffer and my dad for leaving me (which I know he did not want to do). But if I am being truly honest with myself, I was angry with **Me**!

When I was overwhelmed with grief I had so many questions I was asking myself:

- Why did I not believe him when he said he thought he had cancer many years ago before the diagnosis?
- If he'd had treatment would it have been better to have 3 months of a better quality of life rather than months of suffering and pain?
- Could I have done more to help him?
- Did he know I loved him, even though we would argue about things that did not matter?
- Did he know I didn't mean the things I said when we were both scared and angry?

There where so many 'what if's' and when grief overcomes you, you become obsessed with them, making you feel lost, alone and most importantly, afraid.

One of the biggest questions I asked myself was: "what do I do now? How do I move on without him?" My dad was my life, my go to person when I needed help and guidance, the person who just got me - we got each other.

I have to say that on the day my dad passed a piece of me passed with him; I lost my personality and identity, everything about me had changed and I hated I was no longer the happy and bubbly person I was before, I was a shadow of my former self.

There is no time limit on grief or a manual to say how people should grieve as we each have our own process. Unfortunately, mine did not work and ignoring it and hoping it will go away was no longer an option.

Now, after a long and hard struggle I am finally starting to feel like me again. I'm doing the things that I used to love like baking! I'm even setting up my own baking business, something Dad and me were always planning to do together! I'm now sleeping 8 hours+ a day, having sessions with a personal trainer 3 times a week, he is amazing by keeping me on track with my meals making sure I am eating properly and most importantly talking to experts through the use of trauma and grief therapy.

During the course of my therapy my psychologist helped my process my grief through the use of EMDR. At first I was scared and sceptical about this process as I did not know what to expect because it allows you to face your grief and trauma head on with the movement of hand and arm actions. It was really scary at times as it brought up all kinds of emotions and feelings and flashbacks that I had ignored for so long but I am really glad that I used this method as it allowed me to process my grief and trauma in a safe environment and I would definitely recommend this for people considering help in the future. I am now also more open with friends and families about how I'm feeling and being able to acknowledge my emotions by embracing them and not being fearful of them.

I now feel like I've finally passed the storm and I'm just riding the waves. But I know that there will be moments where I feel overwhelmed and I just want a big bear hug from him. I know I can't have that; so I do what I can to face my fears head on and embrace the moment by letting my emotions flow, after all I am only human. However, if there is one thing that grief has taught me, is that it's ok to live in the present and not the past, as I know my dad would want me to be happy.

By the time the 3-year anniversary comes I will have been to: Kenya on a safari which will be my first trip away by myself without my family, climbed Kilimanjaro with my mum and completed a skydive.

But as for now, it's September 2020 and as the 2-year anniversary approaches, I no longer fear the 5th November. Although of course, it is a day filled with mixed emotion, it will also allow us to remember the good times. Even though I know he is no longer here in person, he is with me with spirit, giving me the guidance when I need it most. Just little signs like a robin in the garden just checking in to make sure we are ok, and we are, or at least we are learning to be.

29
Marina's Story

My Dad died at aged 76 years, which I know can be looked at as quite a good 'innings'. In the height of my grief I would think to myself that some people's loss is worse than mine. However, I think I was trying to make myself feel better and somehow put my dad's death into perspective. Unfortunately, deep down this did not help relieve my grief or my other emotions such as guilt, blame, and anger which I experienced due to the circumstances surrounding his death.

My dad died the day after Mothering Sunday. Over that weekend he had deteriorated and became weak. We called 111 and had a doctor visit Dad on both the Saturday and Sunday. On the Sunday, things took a turn for the worst and Dad was struggling to urinate despite needing to go to the toilet. The doctor that saw him that day advised us to ring a non-emergency ambulance as he said it appeared dad had a urine infection so would need his bladder draining. I always dreaded my dad going into hospital due to his vascular dementia which he had been diagnosed with following a quadruple bypass a few years prior to his death. We waited about 3 hours for the ambulance. I went into the ambulance with dad and showed the paramedic dad's urine sample and he responded saying it was the worst sample he had seen in 15 years.

At the hospital in A&E dad was still awake and responsive. One of the doctors took us to one side and spoke to us about them not wanting to resuscitate Dad if he went into cardiac arrest. We weren't too sure why they were saying this because as far as we were concerned Dad would be coming home once his infection was resolved. The doctor said they had put Dad on some antibiotics and if it was our that he could go home tomorrow. He said it would be best to see how the antibiotics reacted over the next 24 hours though. At this point myself, mum, and 3 siblings were sitting in A&E at Dad's bedside. Eventually, he got a catheter inserted, but to my dismay there was no fluid in his bladder despite being given several litres of IV fluid along with his antibiotics. I overheard one of the doctors mention palliative care for dad, naively I didn't fully understand the terminology and severity of the situation. I left dad about 3am the following morning once he had been admitted onto a ward and he appeared more settled.

I returned to the hospital at approximately 8.30am. Dad was awake when I got there however was in discomfort. I gave him a drink and some yoghurt that I had taken to the hospital with me. Not long after my brother arrived and the staff said they would give Dad a small amount of morphine to make him more comfortable. Shortly after this the doctor came in and broke the worst news to us we could imagine, 'all the numbers from your dad's tests were going the wrong way and that there was nothing more we could do'. The doctor then mentioned my Dad had sepsis and his organs were shutting down. Dad never woke up again and passed away later that day.

I felt that the sepsis may have been treatable if diagnosed earlier. I blamed myself for not knowing the signs, and I blamed the two doctors who visited Dad the that weekend. I blamed the A&E doctors for not telling us the day previously that he had sepsis and how poorly he was.

We visited Dad in the chapel of rest at the hospital and also at the funeral parlour. I felt a comfort being with him where I could see him, it was leaving him that was always hard. Talking to the vicar was also comforting prior to the funeral.

I had so many unanswered questions swirling around in my head, so I contacted Patient Advice and Liaison Service (PALS) who arranged for a meeting with the doctor from the ward. I wrote down everything I needed answers to and the doctor answered my questions honestly. It turns out the sepsis was diagnosed when in A&E so I felt angry. Angry that the A&E staff did not inform us of Dad's diagnosis and the likely outcome, as we still had high hopes he would be leaving the hospital the next day. I am glad that my dad had his whole immediate family around him when he passed away.

I think what shocked me the most when my dad died was how quick it happened. I just couldn't process that he had died. The last 24 hours of Dad's life kept repeating itself in my head and I had a horrendous amount of blame and guilt aimed at myself for not being able to save him which led to a constant sick feeling in the pit of my stomach. For the first year after Dad's death I honestly don't think he was ever out of my mind, not even for a second.

I think being able to accept that somebody close to you has died and the way in which they have died was the obstacle I had to overcome to try and move my thought process on. I tried to go back to work after 3 weeks but to my surprise, when somebody spoke to me, I started to cry and was not able to stop. I found it hard to admit that I wasn't ready for work and my grief was still too raw to focus on something else other than my dad's passing. I went to my doctors and had a further 2 weeks off work.

When it was approaching a year following my dad's death, I still didn't feel I had moved forward in learning to accept what had happened. I decided to message a counselling organisation through my employer. I felt nervous at the first counselling session, however she soon put me at ease and I felt comfortable to open up about my dad's situation. I think I cried for the whole hour. I found there were particular trigger points when discussing Dad that I struggled to talk about. I feel that openly talking about his last 24 hours really helped confront and rationalise these aspects that I would have otherwise avoided.

It has taken a long time to accept that in reality there was nothing that I could do to prevent my dad's death as we sought the appropriate medical help. If the medical professionals did not spot the signs of sepsis leading up to his hospitalisation, then how could I? Nevertheless, it still doesn't take away the wanting to go back in time so I could have asked different questions knowing what I know now.

There are certain things that I have kept of dad's in a box such as his bus pass, photos, scarf and a comb. Sometimes I think I should get rid of these items and just keep the photos, however having actual items that Dad touched and used somehow still lets me keep part of him with me.

I am glad that my children have fond memories of their Grandad, and we talk about him often.

What I have learnt is that you can never be prepared for the feeling of loss when someone you love passes, and I think whatever the circumstances it will always be hard to accept as we want to be with our loved ones forever.

30

Joanne's Story

So, I've been trying to get down some things about my experience of grief. It's actually quite difficult to know where to start. So I'll probably start at the beginning and go with the flow.

I've lost many loved ones over the years, grandparents, aunts, uncles, close family friends but the grief I consider as my own is that for my parents.

This is my grief.
This is the grief I live with every day.
This is the grief I struggle with every day.
This is the grief that broke my heart.

My mum died at the end of July 2008, so 12 years ago now. My first son was due to start reception in the September and my middle son was 15 months old. She never knew I'd go on to have another son.

She had battled with cancer for around 9 months. Been through 2 major surgeries, one at a specialist hospital, gone through radiotherapy and chemotherapy; just as we thought we were clear, it had come back with a vengeance. We knew it was aggressive but thought it had been dealt with.

I think my grief started from the day we were told she was terminally ill and we only had a few months left. We started to plan nice things to do, she laughed and joked. She planned her own funeral. She spent time with her loved ones and her sister came over from Australia. The emotional whirlwind is quite horrendous and not only do you have that battle to cope with the emotions of grief, anger, upset, jealousy etc. You have another battle - the one with yourself for having these feelings because, for example, you shouldn't be jealous that your mum is seeing her family and friends but that is how I felt. You have a sense of loss and the numb emptiness and dread inside grows with each day while you get closer to an unknown deadline.

The day it started, I really didn't expect it would be the time. The previous day she'd had a wonderful day with her sisters. I was due to see her the next day for my eldest son's 'graduation' from preschool but unfortunately, she was having difficulty breathing and was taken to hospital. I met her there, she was in resus but was otherwise fine; normal and chatting. I went off to preschool with my Aunty instead. We went back to see mum and she couldn't talk. She knew we were there, she could understand and I told her about the ceremony and showed her the pictures. Early evening, I went home, things seemed to be the same but I was called back to the hospital in the early hours of the morning as she was unlikely to make it through the night. I am haunted by the memory of finding myself at her bedside trying to wake her up, shaking her and repeatedly calling 'Mum!' I was just so desperate for a sign that she knew I was there. At the time I wasn't really aware of my actions, my family had to calm me down as she was in a ward with others with just a curtain round her bed so it must have been upsetting for everyone. She hung on until the morning until she was in a side room alone! In the 5 minutes we weren't with her, she went.

I had heard of the terms 'heartbreak' and 'heartache', but I just thought they were words to describe immense upset a person may feel. It's actually real. My actual heart hurt, it ached all the time to begin with.
My heart and chest feel heavy still now, but not as often. Not because it's less upsetting but I've learnt to live with it. These days I feel it when I get upset about it, for example as I write

this, I have tears while relieving the moments, my chest is hurting, my heart aching.

The time after was quite strange there was a physical ache but emotionally, I was numb. It was a blur. I struggled to function and truly believe if I didn't have the kids, I would not have made it through as well as I did. I couldn't do anything; I didn't want to do anything (housework/washing/showering) but needed to do 'something'. I dumped all my thoughts on paper and wrote a poem (of sorts) that I read out at her funeral. One last thing that I could do for her. This poem is at the end of my story.

For the months and years following, you end up in a state of going through the motions; I don't think I really got to grips with living without her for a good 5 years. To get to a point where I didn't feel guilty for being happy and enjoying life.

She was so loved by everyone, but I didn't feel that anyone knew how I felt. My grief was not like anyone's else's. I felt alone and that no one truly understood how heartbroken I was. I've now come to believe that no two people's grief is the same. It's no more or less. It's just different because our love for the person who has died is different.

A lot had happened during that time. I'd nearly split up with the father of my children, we had been separated for a year and continued to struggle. Part of our problem was my grief. Not that he ever blamed me or used it as his excuse, but it definitely impacted and contributed to our issues. I recognise now that when I'm struggling emotionally, I'm not a nice person to be around. These days I'll take myself off to my bedroom away from anyone. We worked through our difficulties and we're now married, if I'm upset he'll come up and give me a hug then leaves me to it.

Back then, I had shut down and stopped talking to him about it, pushed him away. He couldn't bear to see me so heart broken. Whenever I spoke about how I felt he tried to 'make it better'. That frustrated me because nothing could make it better. Nothing could bring her back and that was the only thing which could make it all ok. All I wanted him to do was listen, let me pour it out, let me wallow in self-pity for that moment or day, dry my tears and give me a hug.

Later on, when things came to a head, we spoke about this and we understood each other better. Sometimes, even now, he'll start and I have to say - stop, you can't make it better, I just need you to listen.

I had finally got to a good place, it felt like the darkness had started to pass by. It didn't happen overnight, it was a gradual thing but it kinda hit me one day and suddenly I thought "oh, I'm happy!"

We had decided to have another child, we were in a much better place as a couple. Maybe that's what helped me come to terms with my grief too.

Then my dad became ill in 2012. They had separated when I was nine and they both remarried. My dad had gone on to have twins. I had always been close to them all, took comfort in the fact that my children still had my dad. His journey was different, he had cancer too, but he was told in his very first appointment there was nothing they could do. My grief rose again with a vengeance, but this time I felt more prepared, in that I had done this before so I knew I could survive it again. It was going to be tough, but I could do it. I kind of knew what emotions would come and rather than fight myself, I let them. I was also expecting our 3rd child, so we had something positive to focus on as well. Sadly, he never got to meet him. After 3 months, my dad died in July, exactly a week before my mum's anniversary. I didn't have the time to go to pieces in the same way I did when my mum died. The children were older, life was busier. My support network had grown, my relationship was stronger, I had siblings that had similar childhood memories.

In the years that have followed, the grief is very much there. I'm left living with it, but I understand it more. I have bad days, before it may have been months, weeks now it more like a day or maybe two. I allow myself that time to wallow and be miserable, I cry and allow the darkness to take hold. Then I know I have to get back up and brush it off. It's like it builds up inside and just gets too much. Reminding me it's still there and will never go away, I've accepted it now. The emotions that go with grief are so strange and I have been left with a few things that continue to bother me. Even though deep down I know it's daft; I can't help it.

1) I feel guilty that I complained to my mum about my relationship issues, causing her to worry, when she was coming to terms with being told she would die. People have said, she wouldn't have minded, you probably took her mind of it, made life feel normal etc. To a point I guess it's true, as a mother, regardless of what I could be going through I will always want my children to be able to talk to me.

2) I feel guilty that sometimes I feel like I miss my mum more than my dad. Deep down I know that's not true. It's just that a mother's love is different. We had been through a lot together. We lost each other when I was in my late teens. I was a victim of domestic violence and coercive control with an ex-partner and as a result, didn't see my family for 3 years. So we were never going to lose each other again. We did everything together. I spoke to her everyday and told her I loved her everyday. I worry

she didn't know how much I appreciated all that she did for me and ask myself did I show her enough?

3) I feel guilty that I convinced my dad to go into Myton Hospice when he was having lots of falls. I thought he could go and get his medication changed and be home again within a few days. He died within 5 days. Deep down I think he knew. As I helped him with his socks and shoes, he looked at me and said: "Are you ready for this?" I replied: "Yes Dad, you'll be home before you know it! Now, looking back, I wonder whether he was he trying to pre-warn me. I also feel guilty for telling him off for not eating and drinking. He had lung cancer and I now know that when it's so far advanced, the food and drink can go into your lungs and not down the gullet. Deep down he knew it was just because I cared and because he never told us how bad he really felt.

The anger and upset of losing them from our lives is intensified in grief. The anger is more than just limited to grief too - you just feel angry about everything, more than normal. Over time, the anger subsided; it became upset and a sense of loss. I feel anger that they were taken from my children. The boy's dad's parents aren't around and although they have step-grandparents from my side who love them dearly, I can't help but feel my sons have lost something so very special - my mum and dad both idolised them.

Time is not a healer. I get annoyed at this saying and ones like it. I also get annoyed at people who don't understand grief in a similar way to me. Or those who say their grief is the same as mine. No - mine is my own and yours is your own. Time is tough - the more time that goes by, means we've been living without them for longer. We all feel the loss, with every occasion, birthday, Christmas, achievements. I have a hard time on these special occasions, some years I cope better than others. I know the struggle is coming and I'm open about my 'off days' with those around me.

I have regrets, that I didn't record their voices telling the stories they told me all my life. I didn't get things written down, I've lost family history with their passing. Especially with my dad as he was an only child and his parents have both passed away too. I think it's part of the grief that makes you want to cling on to anything that you can to preserve their being and to feel tethered to something somehow.

I try and take comfort in my belief in spirits living on and that as such they are always with us. I have searched for a reputable medium and I've had private readings. Looking for that message that includes information only my parents can give me. I've not heard it yet. I'm not sure if the search is helpful or a hinderance to my coping?

My coping strategies are not anything special. Just what suits me at the time:

- I allow myself to continue to grieve for them. I cry if I need to, sometimes in front of the children, I'm open about this with them. My youngest often gets upset that he didn't meet them - that's a tough one.

- I talk about them, try and remember them and hold on to our memories. I love to hear other people's memories of them both, to hear their stories.

- I have memory boxes with trinkets and things in.

- I have pictures around the house of them.

- I listen to the music they liked, the music that has a memory for me.

- I remember them by doing something for those in my life now. For example, on my mum's anniversary, I will take her sister flowers or a gift; it makes me feel happy to do this and we have a moment to remember her together and wipe away the tears. I think my mum would approve of that.

- I have found great comfort in my Aunty too. She makes me feel loved in that maternal way, she loves me and my children almost as much as my mum did. If I'm really struggling a chat or visit with her eases my aching heart.

- I try and appreciate the times we had, remind myself that I had great parents who were not perfect but loved my and my boys unconditionally. Although I feel alone in this, I'm not. I remind myself how much they were loved by the rest of our families; husband, wife, children, step children, grandchildren, son in law, sister, nieces and nephews. They have their own grief and while we may not experience it in the same way, our love for my mum and dad and the loss that we feel will always connect us together.

In all honesty though; I am forever heartbroken. Some days it feels heavier than others. Those 'whirlwind moments' of intense emotions and painful memories, that are so long ago, yet feel like yesterday.

I often say and believe it's true – "my boys are my saviour."

Joanne's Story

The poem on the following page is the one I mentioned in my story. It's about how I was feeling at the time after my Mum died and about the gaps she would leave in our lives.

> Email from: Dr Marianne Trent
> To: Joanne
> Re: Your Story & Poem
>
> Dear Joanne,
>
> Thank you for sharing your story and poem with us. It's such a powerful story and the idea of you being by your Mum's bedside trying to wake her is so emotive.
>
> Your story also demonstrates how grief can affect the other relationships in our life too. I like the idea of you and your husband having been able to find a way to respect what you both need – his desire to help and your desire for time to hurt and to be heard.
>
> Thanks again,
> Marianne

Joanne's Story

"Sprinkle of Sue"

You were slowly being taken away,
Then snatched in a moment,
Just in a day.

We ran out of time,
But we had our plan.
To see Mary Poppins,
A week in a caravan.

Heartbroken, alone,
Angry and sad.
Scared I'll forget
The stories you had.

A little girl inside,
Who once sucked her thumb.
Sobs very loudly,
I just want my mum!!

The shock starts to fade,
Grief taking it's place.
Just to hear your voice,
See the smile on your face.

Closing my eyes,
I take a deep breath.
Memories of you,
Rush into my head.

Barry is out with the band,
We spin around in the chair,
So many memories,
So many to share.

Culture Club, Madness,
Posh crisps, dip and wine.
Sweet peas, Fuchia's,
A diary and the hot line.

Shines earrings, a gold locket,
Brackets, sparkling diamonds in a ring.
"Susan if you want it, have it..."
You loved your bling!

A night in with the girls,
Fridays at Nan's.
A day with the boys,
They are your cutest fans!

Maybe out with the band,
Or a family doo,
We loved the time we spent with you.

I'll always remember
the love we shared.
Not just with the words,
But the way you cared.

I had to be near you,
Talk to you everyday.
You know you always,
Took my blues away.

I knew I'd miss you,
as much I do.
This last song I chose,
Just for you.

Ours unconditional,
Nothing more, Nothing less.
Your love, our love,
Is just the best.

I look around the church today,
Together we wipe out tears away.
Each one here with a special memory you,
All here to remember my lovely mum Sue.

An amazing woman,
So brave and so strong.
One hell of a battle,
you fought for so long.

Always caring,
Sharing your words of wisdom.
Gentle, kind, loving and loyal,
That was my mum.

We'll chat and remember,
Our memories of you.
Leaving her today,
With a "Sprinkle of Sue

31

Rebecca's Story

15 years ago, when I was only 12-years-old, my Grandma passed away in her sleep. Despite being young at the time, my memories of her and our relationship remain strong. I think this is testament to the kind of woman she was. My Grandma was the matriarch of the family. Like most Grandmas, her house became the hub which united an ever-expanding family, yet despite the heavy foot traffic within the house, Grandma always had a way of making you feel special. Thinking back to my childhood, I have two categories of memories; those with Grandma and those tainted with grief at times that I wished she was there.

My Grandma used to run her own playschool and this is where my memories of her begin. Throughout all of my early education, with both of my parents working, I spent a lot of time at her house. Running a playschool gave my Grandma lots of ideas of games, and I'm not talking about manufactured board games, I'm talking about the ability to turn newspaper into a game called "Fish & Chip Shop". For a long time when I was younger, I simply wanted to work in a shop on a till, not because the idea of filling shelves filled me with joy but the association of that activity with my Grandma. She had such a unique ability to make everything and anything appear fun and exciting. I think back to those times and there is so much that I could write about; those times fill me with so much joy. She was not only my Grandma, but also my best friend, my sous chef, my teacher, my guardian and my biggest support.

I have no memories of ever thinking about her dying, despite my Grandfather passing away a few years prior, the idea that my Grandma would die never entered my mind; and if it did I don't think I ever would have paid it too much attention. Thinking back I can pinpoint the moment things changed for my Grandma, from her perspective that is. I assume it was a Sunday, because she taught me to make a Sunday Dinner when I was around 10/11-years-old. "When the roasts are done, you need to pour the lard into the dish on the window." Soon after that, I was making Sunday Dinners nearly every weekend for her; reheating any leftovers during the week for me to eat when I came back from school. The taste of a reheated Sunday Dinner brings back so many memories, that sometimes I think I prefer it that way. Making Sunday dinners developed into changing her bed, setting up her nebuliser, disinfecting her commode and walking to the local Post Office to pay her bills. Even now I pride myself on my ability to do a three-point turn in her living room on her electric scooter. Like I said she had a unique ability to make things fun. I never questioned, I never refused, she was my Grandma and I wanted to do those things for her. I love my Grandma and I wouldn't change our relationship for the world. I live in regret for not recognising that this symbolised deterioration in her health and for not having the opportunity to say goodbye.

The day of her passing was a blur, I believe that I saw her the day before, but I cannot be sure. What I do remember is being told by my Dad, her eldest son. We sat, we cried and my heart sank. A piece of me, which I will never get back left the day she died.

Her funeral was emotional; our family was ripped apart and broken with no one to bring it back together. My Grandma played that role, who was supposed to do that now? Till this day, our family remain both separated and united by grief.

Rebecca's Story

The past 15 years have been spent within my own grief cycle. I live every moment in the hope that what I achieve will make her proud. She has made me who I am today; driven, caring, and creative. I'm also a pretty decent baker and still bake cakes using her mixing bowl! I still have lots of her trinkets, endless collection of salt & pepper shakers and most importantly, her crochet flowers. They still smell of her, they provide comfort and give me strength. One of my most favourite possessions is a notebook where she has written down homemade remedies for everyday ailments. I cannot count the number of times that I've looked through it but when I did a few months ago, I found on the back page lyrics for songs that I can only assume she heard on the radio. I searched the lyrics and found the songs. I had never felt closer to her than I did that night. I used one of the songs as one of the recessional pieces of music at my wedding in February 2020; another special moment in my life where I couldn't celebrate with her and where the moment was tinged with an element of sadness and anger.

Life continues on, memories fade and my grief for my Grandma will always remain. I hope she is proud of me, of who I have become.

> The greatest achievement in my life will be becoming even half the Grandma that she was.

32

Kara's story:

My Darling Angel Baby Jessica Lou

After three early miscarriages, I was delighted to finally be pregnant with my second child. I had always wanted a daughter and my 20 week scan revealed that I was indeed carrying a girl. I already had a healthy three-year-old son. I felt wonderful and so, so lucky to be completing my family with a daughter.

On 20th October 2017, my world was turned upside down when I heard the words "I'm sorry there's no heartbeat". Two of my miscarriages had been missed miscarriages and so I had needed scans to confirm the end of those pregnancies. At those scans, that awful sentence was uttered too. This time I was 33 weeks pregnant though. In my mind, I had naively assumed that baby was 'safe' at this point in my pregnancy. How could this happen?? I had watched in awe as she smiled at me on a 4D scan just four days before she died. Everything was looking perfect and there were no complications in the pregnancy. How could she just die? At that time, I honestly believed that healthy babies in a 'normal', low risk pregnancy did not just die. I now know all too well that that just isn't true though and it can happen to anyone and does happen daily. The baby loss support groups that I went to after Jessica died had lots of bereaved families telling similar stories of suddenly losing their healthy baby with no known reason for their death.

My Darling Angel Baby Jessica Lou

The night I found out that Jessica had died was a Friday evening. I had dashed to the hospital to check on her because I hadn't felt her move throughout the day and I suddenly couldn't shake the feeling that something was wrong. I actually assumed that she was just hiding behind the placenta but I knew I had to check given the lack of movements and the strong panicky feeling, which I couldn't shake. I had an anterior placenta in her pregnancy and I had been checked for reduced movements once before. Jessica was found to be happily kicking my placenta that time. I never felt her movements as much as my son's pregnancy in all honesty but she was growing well and everyone believed her to be healthy. So I reasoned that it was just the position that she and the placenta were in, which prevented me from feeling her move very often.

I went to the hospital alone that night, while my husband put our son to bed. Finding out alone was awful in so many ways. My husband was texting to ask if I had been seen yet and was everything ok? I couldn't say tell him over text, especially while he was putting our son to bed. I asked him to call me when he'd done bedtime. When he called me after our son was asleep, I had to tell him over the phone that she had died. I felt so cruel. I also feared that he would blame me for not going into hospital sooner- he never has blamed me though. He too assumed she was fine and that I was being over-anxious. After all, we had just seen her happily smiling at us at the 4D scan!

I then had to call my mum and tell her that my baby had died. Immediately after, I had to ask her to drive 45 minutes to my house and look after our son, so that my husband could come to the hospital. I recognise that this couldn't have been easy for her. On the phone, my mum just kept saying "there must be a mistake, are they sure?" The thing is although I never contemplated that Jessica had died as I rushed to the hospital, as soon as I saw them scanning me and struggling to find her heartbeat I knew she had died. All of a sudden that panicky feeling I'd had that 'something was wrong' made sense. I had the same feeling with the early miscarriages and it prompted me to request early scans to find out. However, this time I had dismissed the feeling as me being over-anxious because of the previous miscarriages and because a close friend had lost her daughter to neonatal death three months previously.

Thinking back, as I drove to the hospital to be checked, I did cry in panic and I did consider that Jessica may be poorly and/or that medical intervention might be needed. However, I didn't consider that it would already be too late to save her. The hospital scanned me three times and various members and grades of staff had to verify that there definitely wasn't a heartbeat. Throughout all these scans, I just stayed silent, willing the process to be over quickly, as I knew no-one would find a heartbeat. I was staring at the static screen, I'm not sure why because the screen was compounding my agony. I knew all too well that her little heart would be flickering if she were alive. It was hard to tear my eyes away from her though.

I will always wish that I had listened to my 'anxious' feeling and gone into hospital sooner. Perhaps going in sooner would have saved her life. Perhaps it wouldn't too though? I'm painfully aware that I can never bring Jessica back now. So as much as I wish more than anything that I had acted on her lack of movements sooner, I have learnt not to dwell on my feelings of guilt. Like Marianne, I too am a Clinical Psychologist. I know through my profession, that ruminating on such guilt, would negatively impact my emotional wellbeing and would not actually benefit Jessica or anyone else. It took me time to get to this acceptance of my guilt though. It was definitely a process to get to where I am now. Now I tell myself that 'I did what I could with the information that I had at the time'. If I had of known she was unwell, then I would have course have acted differently.

The hospital were wonderfully supportive that evening. The staff seemed really concerned about me having no-one with me for emotional support, both when I found out and immediately after. One of the midwives kept asking when someone would come to join me and if I wanted her to stay with me. She also keep popping back into the side room to check whether I wanted a hot drink or a cuddle. I remember thinking how British it was to be offered tea as a comfort at such an awful time. Ironically, I hate tea and coffee; but I really appreciated her compassion and the offers of things that might possibly have brought me comfort. In reality, I just wanted to be alone I spoke to some close friends over text/ whats app and I just cried. That was my way of beginning to process the news.

When my husband arrived at the hospital about an hour later, I was having swabs and sterile blood tests taken. The hospital were trying to ascertain if I had an infections or anything medically unusual occurring that might explain Jessica's sudden death. A male consultant came and explained that I would need to be induced, he warned me that labour would be more painful than usual and advised me to utilise full pain relief to cope. He said my 'feel good' hormones were obviously not going to work, which in turn would slow labour and cause the extra pain. Another consultant informed my husband and I that we needed to decide if we wanted a post-mortem for Jessica and if so to complete the necessary paperwork. My mind was spinning. So much was happening, which was difficult to comprehend and all the decisions and paperwork seemed to need to be done immediately. I still just wanted to be alone to process it all and cry. I did not want to think about someone potentially cutting open my baby girl, especially given that I hadn't even birth to her yet. However, my husband and I both agreed that we had to at least attempt to find out why she had died. So we did complete the paperwork that night.

About three hours after first going into the hospital, they advised me to "go home, try to get some sleep, then pack your hospital bags in the morning and return at 10am for induction". Of course, neither of us really slept that night. The hospital gave us a folder of bereavement leaflets to read. Included in the folder was a story to read to explain infant death to siblings. We tried to read it but neither of us couldn't get past the first page without hysterically crying. I was so desperate to hug my son but of course he was asleep. So after checking on him, I just went to bed and tried to think more about how I would tell him. I didn't feel I could physically say the words baby has died aloud without being in floods of tears yet. Our son had excitedly watched Jessica on the big TV screen at the 4D scan the week before too. He spoke about her loads. I worried about the impact of her death on him. I was also worried about going into hospital to be induced straight after. I didn't want to leave him to think over what I had said without his parents to support him or answer his questions. We contemplated not telling him until I was back home but actually we ended up telling him because the first thing he said in the morning was "can we see Jessica on the big TV screen again today". It was clear he needed the truth to understand why we were so sad after he said that and why we both needed to go back to the hospital. We kept details minimal at this point as we simply weren't ready to talk about it in any depth and we didn't know how to phrase everything mindfully. We also didn't have answers to the many of the questions that a three-year-old would naturally ask yet. I promised my son that we could talk more when I got back from hospital though. I made it clear that mummy and daddy were ok and that we both loved him lots and that it was nobody's fault. We told him that nanny was going to take him to his usual football lesson and that we hope they had a great time together and I couldn't wait to see him again soon.

Choosing the one outfit that Jessica would ever wear was agonising. Hubbie told me just grab anything but I wanted it to be perfect for her. I didn't consider that actually she would get blood on that outfit and so it wouldn't be the outfit that she was buried in anyway. Instead the hospital would change her into knitted outfits that had been donated and by the time I realised she had been changed, her body had become too fragile to change her again.

The induction and labour process was incredibly lengthy. It was definitely more difficult than my son's birth too. I won't go into detail about it here. However, in some ways it wasn't as bad as I was warned too. I was determined to have a water birth and I will be forever grateful to my bereavement midwife Shelley. She advocated for me and helped me refuse pain and induction medications that would have prevented such a birth being medically allowed. Jessica was born using gas and air in the birthing pool, which was important to me. In retrospect, I think partly because I needed to feel in control over something that was happening. We had planned a home birth previously. The hardest bit of Jessica's birth for me was the silence that seemed to echo in the room throughout the night as I was birthing. There was no guidance on when or how to push during labour. I interpreted this at the time as a lack of emotional support because the midwife who was present didn't need to ensure that baby arrived safely. I later learnt that actually it was the first stillbirth labour that that midwife had attended and she didn't know what to say and felt it may be more helpful to just stay quiet.

In the early hours of 23.10.2017, Jessica was finally born, she looked so perfect. She was just like a sleeping newborn. Again I couldn't stop thinking how could this happen and why oh why did she die?!!! To say I was devastated just doesn't even come close to portraying the heartbreak of those early days, weeks and months.

The hospital had a 'cold cot' which preserved Jessica's body and enabled us to see her until we were 'ready to say goodbye'. As if anyone can ever be ready to say goodbye to their child. Jessica was born at 4.12am on the Monday and at 10am that day my mum informed me that my son had been admitted to the local children's hospital (an hour's drive away). So I had to discharge myself almost immediately and rush to him, rather than spending the time I felt I needed with Jessica. He was very poorly when I arrived and I felt so guilty that I hadn't been there to take him to hospital myself. He'd never been away from me for three consecutive nights before either. I feared he would feel neglected and like we didn't care. Luckily, he only had severe tonsillitis and with steroids his breathing finally stabilised and he was discharged home the same day. As a result, I returned to visit Jessica again was once my son was asleep for the night. I cuddled Jessica. I took books with me and I read bedtime stories to her. I was amazed how natural it felt despite her being as cold as ice, due to the cold cot.

I ended up going to see Jessica at bedtime for four nights in total. My mum and a friend also came to meet Jessica on two of the nights. I would say goodbye to them, then stay longer with Jessica on my own and read her our 'goodnight' stories. Reading this, I realise it may seem like I was in denial that she was dead at this point. I was of course painfully aware that she was dead. But I wanted/ needed some memories with her. Despite the sadness, those nights with her were special too. On the Friday, my husband and I decided we needed to say our 'final goodbye' together. I literally couldn't understand how I would ever say goodbye and not see her again. However, the hospital had told us that she needed to be sent for post-mortem and that leaving it longer may affect the accuracy of the results so we had to somehow let her go. We included a family photo with a handwritten message to her on it. We placed a heart in her tiny fingers and arranged her cuddling a teddy. We also included my son's comforter in the cold cot. Saying goodbye was so devastating. But eventually we kissed her goodbye, took photos of her and forced ourselves to leave the bereavement suite without her. That was the last time my husband ever saw Jessica.

I visited Jessica again four weeks later when she returned from post-mortem at the funeral directors though. I was warned that she wouldn't look the same because so much time had passed and she hadn't always been in a cold cot during that time. However, as her Mummy, I had a need to arrange her tiny baby coffin or 'forever bed' myself. I wanted it exactly the way we'd arranged the cold cot together that day. There was no doubt in my mind that I had to talk to her one last time too. I will be forever grateful for the time I spent with Jessica and for the experiences that we shared together over that week.

As a Clinical Psychologist and a mum, I wanted to protect my son from the magnitude of the devastation that I felt whilst grieving but I also knew that it was important to talk to him about what had happened at a developmentally appropriate level. I would explain that I was sad that baby Jessica died on the occasions that he noticed my tears. I would answer his questions however painful I found them. In addition, I knew that I needed to allow myself time to cry and grieve openly too. I seemed to quickly and quite unconsciously learn to let the grief flow most heavily when my son was asleep or at nursery. Shelley, my lovely bereavement midwife was often on the end of the phone to me on Fridays. She would listen to me howl as the week's grief poured out. Shelley really is one of the warmest and most empathic people I know and I will forever be grateful that it was her supporting me through those early days and weeks of my grief. I will also always be grateful to Oscar's Wish Foundation, a Sussex based baby loss charity who had just opened the maternity bereavement suite where we stayed for the three days that I was induced. This suite was also where I saw Jessica when I visited in the evenings. The room was so cosy and the perfect place to make precious memories with my precious baby girl.

One of the feelings that I found the hardest in those early days of grieving was the intense longing/ need to be with Jessica. This caused an unease in myself, which nothing seemed to reduce. I knew the feeling was literally my body screaming 'there is something missing, you need to be with your baby'. As I couldn't be with her though, I couldn't seem to ease that feeling. I felt like part of me was missing, which of course it was and I was just incomplete without her. I saw no way that that this feeling would or could ever change. I think it was partly why the time I spent with her in the bereavement suite was so comforting. Even though she was obviously unresponsive when I laid and read to her, I felt almost at peace and whole again while I was there, because we were together. When I left the hospital I just felt that intense 'need' to be with her again so strongly.

It was a month after Jessica was born before we were able to hold her funeral. I spent those few weeks painstakingly trying to find the 'perfect' songs for the funeral, create the most loving and fitting order of service, pick the 'perfect' funeral car and moses basket style coffin, pick the most fitting flowers etc. My husband and I both wrote personalised letters to Jessica. We printed copies and I put them in her forever bed with her on the morning of the funeral. We also read copies out to her at the funeral. The funeral felt like the only thing I could do for her now and so in my head it had to be completely perfect. In reality, her funeral wasn't perfect though. Three things went disastrously wrong. Firstly, we had a beautiful wicker basket style coffin for Jessica. We also had a lovely idea that we would invite any guests who would like to, to light a candle for Jessica in the service. Unfortunately, we hadn't considered that every guest would want to do just that and that the table for Jessica's basket and the candles for memoriam was actually quite small. So as I read out my heartfelt letter to Jessica, I saw my dad run to that table blowing at the coffin, which had caught fire! Although I was initially horrified by this, family members and friends helped me to reframe it in ways that I now look back on this almost fondly and with a smile. There was also an issue with the music. The song that will always consider to be 'Jessica's song' wouldn't play. I ended up playing it via my phone, which wasn't ideal but I felt I needed it to be played somehow. Finally, Jessica's coffin was lowered in the ground with the feet end in the direction that all of the headstones were. I really struggled with this and begged the funeral directors to turn her round so that she was facing the 'right' way. Apparently once a body is lowered into the ground, it is illegal to remove the coffin again or tamper with it in anyway though. The funeral was of course emotionally incredibly difficult. It is true no-one should ever have to bury their baby. So many people came to support us, which was touching though. I hadn't anticipated that I wouldn't really be able to speak to anyone at the wake though. My brain just didn't seem to work. I couldn't force myself to be my usual sociable self. I found it hard to even express my gratitude to the friends and family who travelled from far and wide to support me that day.

Jessica's death was my first ever real experience of grief. I had lost a couple of family members who I wasn't very close to but no immediate family or friends. Through my work, I knew about grief theoretically. I knew the stages of grief model, I knew grief provokes a complex range of emotions. I knew the saying the more you love someone, the harder you grieve. But I honestly don't think I ever 'really' understood grief until I experienced it first-hand.

Coping with Jessica's death whilst parenting a lively three-year-old was the most difficult thing that I have ever had to do. I could not stop the biological longing to be tending to my gorgeous baby girl. Instead I was going to soft play and toddler groups, which seemed to be brimming with healthy newborns. I would forcibly hold back the tears and try hard to focus instead on giving my son the normality and fun he needed. My need to be Jessica's mum and to mourn her seemed in direct conflict to my need to be a good mum to my son. Somehow my son and I got through that time and actually made some nice memories on days out together, despite the pain I was feeling. In retrospect, 'keeping going for my son', really helped me too. My gratitude for him grew stronger and stronger. I also didn't feel guilty if we had moments of laughter together, which perhaps I might have done if Jessica had been my only child and I had of laughed with someone else when the world seemed so dark to me. My son gave me a reason to get up each day. Parenting him gave me purpose. Likewise, I did a lot of fundraising for Oscar's

Wish Foundation (OWF) in those early months. I campaigned for a maternity bereavement suite at another local hospital, where I was also working at the time. I joined the renovation team alongside OWF, Abigail's Footsteps and the bereavement midwives and we opened that maternity bereavement suite, partly in Jessica's memory, in June 2018. My son, the fundraising and the renovation project, alongside returning to work four months after Jessica's died all gave me purpose and helped me 'live', despite feeling so hopeless and bereft. In my head, I felt like I was doing a lot of these things to help others and hopefully they did help other people but they definitely helped me to cope too.

Other things that helped me cope were: talking with family and friends; keeping a diary; visiting her grave each day and keeping it tidy and pretty; talking with other loss mums; making an Instagram account for Jessica which included her photos and memories- I only shared this account with other loss mums doing the same; spending time with another loss mum who lived locally and had a similar experience to me; making a Jessica photo album, buying little Jessica mementos for her memory box- named candles etc; writing her name in the snow or sand, paying for a beautiful Jessica sunset picture; making her first birthday special via a dove release and gardening each day (I've never been a gardener but I found that nurturing a memory garden for Jessica helped direct my natural urge to nurture her in a useful way).

Jessica's grief has forever changed me as a person in both positive and negative ways. I don't feel like I have the same capacity to multi-task as I did and I definitely feel like I'm more easily affected by stress and anxiety since she died. I need more self-care than I used to manage the busy demands of being a working mum. I also think I will forever carry some guilt for her death. However, Jessica's death has probably made me a more empathic Psychologist too. I understand trauma, loss and grief whole heartedly now. At the time of Jessica's death I was working in an NHS major trauma service. In this role, I frequently heard people say to me that as a person they felt broken following the trauma they had experienced. I remember thinking and telling a couple of people that I too felt broken in the months after Jessica's death. In the six years that I worked in that trauma service, I frequently saw people move to a more positive place in terms of their self-identity as they processed what had happened to them and/or grieved for what they had lost though. In my own grief, I recalled many of the patients I had worked with and each of their life stories gave me hope that one day I too would no longer feel broken.

For me it was true that the first year and all the first's which followed were by far the hardest emotionally. It was also true for me that grief came in waves. Initially, the waves came so hard and fast that I could hardly get a breath between each grief wave but now the sea of grief is much calmer. I can still be bowled over by a huge grief wave, where the emotion feels intense again like in the early days but usually this is in response to a direct trigger such as the anniversary of her death and her birthday. I will always love and miss Jessica. Jessica will always be missing from my life but I live with my grief and still have a full life now too.

It is important to me that Jessica's memory will always be a driver for me to do good and help others. My husband and I vowed to each other that we want to better people because of Jessica's tiny but incredibly important little life. I now volunteer with Oscar's Wish Foundation. We run free monthly emotional support groups for other loss parents and for parents pregnant with or trying to conceive a baby after loss. A pregnancy after a miscarriage, stillbirth or neonatal death is commonly known as a 'rainbow pregnancy'. I have written a book to support children/ siblings in understanding and coping with rainbow pregnancies. I also help loss parents in my work. I have slowly managed to put the pieces of my life back together. The birth of my incredible rainbow baby has definitely helped bring further hope and joy to my life again too. Although, she is obviously no replacement for Jessica and I would never want her to be a replacement either. She is equally perfect as she is. I would describe myself as different now and my priorities have changed but I no longer feel broken.

I will never be able to thank my friends and family enough for their support as I grieved and as I anxiously awaited the safe arrival of my rainbow. A rainbow pregnancy is also an incredibly difficult experience due to the fear of another stillbirth potentially happening again. Marianne was one of four psychologist friends who has been there for me day and night, whenever I needed them. Thank you so much Marianne and to all my other friends too- you all know who you are. I hope you all know how much I love you too. Having the level of support and empathy I did really helped me so much in surviving my grief.

I wrote this case study because I found reading similar loss stories to mine, helped me when I was grieving. So if you are grieving and want to feel like someone else understands too, then I hope this helps you. If you have experienced grief the loss of an infant and feel that psychological support from someone with their own loss experience could benefit you, then please feel free to get in contact with me. My details are listed in the Chapter 'Helpful Resources and Ideas', which is towards the end of this book.

My Darling Angel Baby Jessica Lou

Email from: Marianne
To: Kara
Re: Your Story

To my lovely friend Kara,

Thank you so much for sharing your story with us. I still remember exactly where I was when you first told me what you were going through; I was sitting on my sofa in the kitchen and my blood just ran cold. I was devastated for you and just couldn't believe what I was reading. I am so desperately sorry for what happened and that we never got to know your lovely Jessica.

There is no one else in the world I have ever sent crying photos of myself to in order to demonstrate which funeral songs upset me the most. There is also no-one else in the world who would have responded without missing a beat by sending me photos of them crying in return! You are a wonderful friend and I'm so lucky to have you.

Much love, speak to you in about ten minutes and then about twenty minutes after that probably,

Marianne x

P.s Well done on your book 'There's a rainbow baby in my Mummy's Tummy.' It's beautiful, I'm so proud of you, x

33

Samantha's Story

My Nan and Grandad were called Gill and John Sims, both aged 73 when they passed away within 4 months of each other. They met when they were 14, married at 20 and had been inseparable ever since. They were kind and generous people and with three daughters and four grandchildren, both so proud of their family. You could always hear Grandad boasting to anyone who was willing to listen! You only needed to walk into Nanny and Grandad's bungalow to see how their walls were littered with photos of all of us, to see how they were bursting with pride. Nanny was the matriarch of the family and the strongest lady that I've ever known. Although she was assertive and headstrong (you wouldn't want to get into an argument with her!) With her social work background, she was also one of the kindest people and always looking after the vulnerable. My Grandad was a hugely respected man, he spent most of his life in the Army and working as a civil servant. Both my Nan and Grandad were young grandparents as they were in their 40's when I was born; they felt like second parents to me and I couldn't imagine life without them.

In March 2017, my Nan was diagnosed with terminal breast cancer. On the day I found out I remember walking the dog on the beach with my Mum and just feeling so sorry for her that she was losing her own Mum. I remember saying 'I can't imagine if it were you'. My Mum took my Nan to the breast centre regularly for her appointments and they would both comment on the number of young women in the waiting room. This encouraged us to check ourselves more regularly; it's weird that you almost feel invincible to cancer until if affects one of your family.

A month later, my Mum found the smallest of lumps in her own breast. She invited me round for dinner one evening and sat me and my brother down to tell us that she had also been diagnosed with breast cancer. I remember everything suddenly felt like it went into slow motion; I was in a state of shock, it didn't feel real. My brother broke down crying, but I just kept asking questions, trying to make sense of what I was hearing. My world felt like it was falling apart. I remember going for a run and screaming on the top of a hill. I felt so angry.

My Mum's biopsy came back and it was positive news; the cancer was caught early; the lump could be removed and with a course of radiotherapy her prognosis was looking good. This meant everything to my grandparents as my Nan had saved my Mum's life, without her diagnosis my Mum would definitely not have checked as thoroughly and probably wouldn't have gone to the doctor as quickly. As a family we spent the next 2 years creating memories with my Nan whilst we had the time. We had a family photoshoot done which was something my Nan really wanted and this gave us some lovely photos to cherish. My Mum and her partner got married and my Nan was well enough to attend the ceremony. We also went on a family holiday to Dorset which we all thoroughly enjoyed.

In the Autumn of 2019, my Nan started to deteriorate and she was taken to the hospice around the end of November. We felt lucky that she was able to spend time there as it took the pressure off my grandad to look after my Nan at home. One of my Nan's wishes was to make it to Christmas; this was always a really special day for our family as we spent it together every single year. I put together a Christmas present in the form of a 'memory jar' and asked my brother and my two cousins to also contribute to it too. I wanted my nan to read all of her grandchildren's favourite memories. I remember asking myself- 'what Christmas present do you buy someone that's dying?' which was quite painful for me to think about. It became a likelihood, rather than a possibility, that my Nan wouldn't make Christmas. So, I decided to give the jar to her straight away. The week before she passed away, we all gathered in her room at the Hospice as she read out some of the memories one by one. There was a mixture of laughter and tears, but I remember her saying it was the nicest present she'd ever received which meant just everything to me.

During her final days and hours as she became more unwell, we read more of the memories to her and sang her favourite songs. She wasn't able to respond to us, but we all knew she could hear us and the slightest squeeze of her hand or change in facial expression told us that. Like the strong and stubborn woman she was, she continued to live for 2 more days, despite the hospice staff continually telling us she was in her final hours. She passed away on 6th December 2019, with her husband, three daughters and two eldest grandchildren at her side and I am certain that she knew how very loved she was.

I took a week of compassionate leave off work which came before two weeks of planned annual leave over the Christmas period. Christmas without her was difficult, but she still had her place at the table as she'd always done. My partner and I went to Venice for a short break and knowing how much my grandparents loved travelling, I knew she would have been happy for me to go and have some time away.

I returned to work in January, and at this time, our family concerns fell to my grandad who had not known a life without my Nan since he was 14. My Mum and her sisters would stay overnight with him and encourage him to look forward to things including a family holiday to Malta that they had booked as a surprise Christmas present. This meant a lot to my Grandad as him and my Nan spent many years living there during the early part of their retirement.

It was around the same time, my partner's dad was having some health problems and stomach pains. It was after coming back from India in October 2019 and so the GP initially put it down to 'Delhi-Belly'. In the January, just after Nan passed, when this hadn't subsided, further tests were carried out and it was found he had stage 4 oesophageal cancer which had spread to his liver. I still have vivid memories of my partner coming home from his Mum's house after receiving the news and breaking down in the living room. The following month was a completely overwhelming. He had been admitted to hospital with Sepsis just weeks after his diagnosis and it was touch and go as to whether he would make it out of hospital. However, he was discharged from hospital to receive palliative care at home and he was there for another week before passing away, with all of us around him.

I struggled a lot during this time. The knowledge that I had around cancer, the jargon used by health professionals and having just seen my nan in the final weeks of her life meant that I knew soon after his diagnosis that he was very poorly. At no point did anyone tell him he was going to die in a matter of weeks. With the sepsis taking hold so quickly, he didn't even make it to the consultant appointment to discuss his prognosis. I felt like a spectator as another family around me fell apart with grief. I was spending most of my time in my partner's family home to be with them and was aware that the grief for my Nan was being postponed.

It became really clear to me how people cope in very different ways. My partner was completing his teacher training at the time and continued to go to his placement during the final weeks of his dad's life, whilst I was signed off work by my GP due to stress and bereavement. In a weird way I felt guilty for taking that time, like I was a fraud because it wasn't my Dad. I tried to return to work and my manager encouraged me to stay off and suggested that I was trying to come back too quickly. I became frustrated and tearful, I just wanted life to return to some sort of normality.

COVID-19 hit a month after my partner's dad passed away and added another dynamic to both of family's grieving processes. Not being able to spend time with each other meant that we couldn't process our loss. We stuck to the restrictions exactly as we should, for the fear of losing anyone else in the family to the virus. My grandad and my partner's mum were both living on their own and not able to see their children or grandchildren for comfort.

My grandad was shielding and in April, my aunty visited him with his shopping. He had been unwell for some time, and we had put his symptoms and weight loss down to grief. He looked so unwell that day though that she immediately took him to A&E where a scan revealed a blockage in his bowel which needed to be operated on. The blockage turned out to be cancer. After two unsuccessful operations he went in for a third which the surgeon described as a 'last ditch attempt' to remove the whole bowel. My Grandad never recovered from this and the decision was made to take him off the ventilator. We weren't allowed to visit him because of COVID-19 restrictions. But my Mum and my aunty were permitted to attend his bed side during the last 30 seconds of his life. During these last seconds, the rest of the family and I facetimed to say goodbye to him. The image of my grandad at this time will never leave me. When Mum got back from hospital I visited her in her garden because the government advice was we weren't to be in each other's homes. Having to sit opposite her from the other end of the garden whilst we both sobbed, not being able to share a hug was awful. The COVID-19 pandemic has taken so much from so many.

I still feel devastated that I never got to say goodbye to my grandad and that he never got the send-off he deserved. His funeral consisted of close family and two or three friends which did not represent how loved and respected he was. We were so proud of how grandad looked after my Nan whilst she was so unwell over the past few years. He ensured that she felt loved right to the end, and we were unable to do the same for him.

When my grandad died, this accumulated grief seemed to hit me like a tonne of bricks. He passed away the day before my 30th Birthday and everything felt so surreal. I had nothing to celebrate. My grandad had written my birthday card whilst he was well and given it to my mum to hold on to. Opening that card was so difficult, I nearly didn't open it at all. I kept calling my Mum just crying hysterically down the phone. It suddenly dawned on me that my Grandad had been keeping my Nan's memory alive. He represented both of them and a whole generation. Before lockdown I used to go round to his bungalow and it felt like she was still there somehow. Within the space of four months, I went from having both of my grandparents to not having any.

I took a week off work after he passed. Working from home seemed to help and having a reduced caseload at work meant I could pace myself. I am a psychological wellbeing practitioner for the NHS, so my day job means that I deliver therapy to patients who have anxiety or depression and have long-term health conditions. I knew I wasn't going to be able to do patient work for a while, as awful as it sounds; at that time I genuinely struggled to care for anyone else's problems.

Samantha's Story

I would like to say the summer became easier, but it didn't. My mum experienced some pain in her neck and there were concerns that her breast cancer had become metastatic and spread to the bones. Bone scans reveals hot spots which then needed further MRI's and this process took over a month. This genuinely was the worst month of my life and I'd whole heartedly convinced myself that my Mum was going to die too. The results came back and showed significant trauma which was musculoskeletal and unrelated to cancer. The relief that we experienced as a family was like nothing else. My aunty also had a health scare shortly after with one of her mammograms showing up abnormalities. Biopsies were taken which also gave good news that she did not have cancerous cells. Both of these results helped me to restore the positive outlook and the hope that I seemed to have lost so much of recently.

I am also a Trainee Health Psychologist in my second year of my doctorate; so I found myself throwing myself into uni work to keep distracted. My partner and I spent time renovating the garden and once lockdown eased we booked a trip to Wales. We also decided to get a puppy which we felt would focus our attention and give us a sense of purpose. What we have come to realise is that none of this can fix anything. We still cried whilst we were in Wales, we actually felt tired with how much energy the puppy required, and although we love him, he couldn't take the grief away!

The biggest impact I noticed was on how relationships changed; my partner responded to loss through withdrawing and taking time to himself. However, I needed to be in company, talk things through and to feel close to people. This put a strain on the relationship which was exacerbated by lock down and only being able to see each other! I have to admit I found myself feeling quite isolated at times; when lock down eased my partner quite rightly would prioritise his Mum who lives very close by, whilst my family do not live close enough just to 'pop round'. I also struggled to open up to family or my partner about how I was feeling with the awareness that everyone around me was in a state of grief too. I found that going running would help, and I would often have a cry as I ran and thought of my grandparents. Certain friends have also been amazing and really validating of what an awful year I've been through, someone on the outside of the family can really help give this perspective.

I've considered what I've learnt about myself and the nature of grief from this year so far. A huge thing I've realised is that grief does not start at the point that someone dies. Grief can kick in even at the thought of someone dying. I genuinely believe that I started to grieve for my Mum when we believed the cancer had spread to her bones. I would lay in bed at night and imagine life without her as if it were a reality.

I've also learnt that grief doesn't just start and stop. I experienced four rounds of grief for my Nan; at the point of diagnosis, when she deteriorated in the autumn, when she died and again when my Grandad passed away. There were moments in between these stages when things started to feel better and then it hits you again. There are still triggers that are unexpected, particularly in my line of work I find myself feeling very tearful after sessions that I have with patients when their stories strike a chord with mine. Sometimes, it's also hard to tell who you're grieving for when you experience so much loss in such a short space of time.

I've experienced first-hand the impact that a pandemic can have on the process of grief. Part of accepting your loss involves the need to return to some sort of 'new normal'. Unfortunately, because of COVID-19 my grief has been complicated; we couldn't mourn as a family, meet up and share memories or have a 'normal' funeral for my Grandad. We even had to scatter his ashes in secret because of the COVID-19 regulations! My family still need time to find our 'new normal' but we know this will come in time. One positive thing that has come out of this experience is my ability to gain perspective on things that would have previously caused me stress. I can let go of day to day worries as nothing feels significant anymore as long as those I love are healthy.

Everyone we have lost this year was taken too soon and under difficult circumstances, but the one thing they have in common is they loved life, loved their family and lived life to the full.

These values will live on through us as we'll all plan to do exactly the same.

34

Yvonne's Story

My son and I were with my mum for 2 hours on the day she passed. We'd managed to get her to eat something as she had lost her appetite, she was in full conversation with us both. I remember my dad arriving back home from his allotment and my mum's brother arriving a few minutes later. My son and I decided we would leave as mum had some company.

We arrived back home less then 20 minutes later and I remember my husband shouting "your dad is on the phone saying your mum's not breathing". I remember screaming and saying: "what do you mean she's not breathing I've only just left her!" My heart sunk, I remember trying to call my sisters, my brother and my children but I couldn't remember any phone numbers I couldn't remember how to use my phone I was just in a state of shock and I just needed to get to her.

When I arrived at my mum's house she just looked like she was fast asleep, she looked 20 years younger and just lying there looking so beautiful. I just couldn't believe she had passed away. All my brothers, sisters, nieces and nephews decided to stay with my dad for the next few days, just to keep him company and to support each other in our grief and to remember all the good times that we used to have with Mum. We laughed, we cried and I was up and down like I am now writing this and crying.

Yvonne's Story

My mum was my world and best friend, we did loads of things together, she was always there for me and my children. The best Mum and Nanny you could ever wish for.

My mum who, sometimes I called 'Mummy' when I wanted a hug and some love, was very well known in Coventry for her cooking. Everybody would always want to sample my mum's cooking so when it came to planning her funeral, we made sure we had the best people to cook the food she liked! She was so well liked that she had over 800 people at her funeral! We gave her the very best funeral because she deserved the best because she was the BEST...my mummy!

Text from: Marianne
To: Yvonne

Yvonne,

Thanks for your wonderful story.
Your Mum sounds wonderful, I'm so sorry for your loss.
I really wanted to include the lovely heart emoji you put at the end of your story, but I can't figure out how to get my laptop to do emoji's!

Much love and thanks again,
Marianne x

35

Eleri's Story

I've always been part of a close-knit family. Apart from parents, my cousins were one of the first relationships I had formed - my first friendships. I would look forward to the weekends as every Saturday was spent at our grandparent's together.

This all changed when I was 9. At nine years of age I understood the concept of death, but I never thought I would experience loss at such a young age. It was always something I thought 'would never happen to me'.

The day I lost my cousin is still so clear, it is unfortunately one of the clearest memories I have. It was just like a normal day, it was a Sunday morning, the phone rang and that feels like the moment that everything changed for me. There was nothing unusual about the phone ringing, but it was my Mum's reaction which sparked the feeling of uncertainty for me, the fear of the unknown. My mum went out of the room to talk and I could hear crying; I had never seen my mum cry before. I felt a wave of worry take over my body and it seemed like what was a short phone call lasted forever. Then my mum told us what had happened — my cousin had passed away suddenly from Meningitis.

My cousin was only a child himself and it was so unexpected which is what I struggled with in particular. I remember running into my garden and screaming. I screamed and cried and struggled to regulate any emotion I was feeling. I felt like everything around me was on pause and I was the only person in the world. My mum hugged me which finally helped me feel calm again, but the awful feeling was still there, I felt numb. It was from that moment onwards I held everything in; everything I felt, I masked so no one could tell what I was thinking. I was a quiet child growing up anyway, I was always the child who would get involved but would be happy with the attention being placed on someone else. So due to having an introverted personality this was easy to obtain.

As a child your job is to play and be carefree. I would switch between having these feelings of sadness and then feeling like nothing had happened and just getting on with life as normal, like a child should experience. When I felt these feelings of loss, I tried as hard as I could to not let them out and I did a good job of this. My brother dealt with the situation a lot differently than I did, he would come home from school with drawings of my cousin and would talk about him with my mum. I felt like there was something wrong with the way I was coping, I couldn't talk about my cousin and every time I heard the word 'meningitis' I would go into 'freeze mode' and everything would be a big blank to me. I did not go to the funeral as my parents did not think this was the right decision for me, but I attended a 'Memorial Day' at my cousin's school. There was a speech by the headteacher followed by a charity rugby match. The speech probably only lasted a few minutes, but it felt like a lifetime. I couldn't even hear the words, I can just remember concentrating so hard on trying not to cry, trying to keep a straight face which was exhausting. I had this worry that I didn't want to upset my mum by crying; I didn't want her to feel any worry around me as she had enough to deal with.

Time passed and I carried on with my life, burying my feelings further and further away. It was not until my teenage years where this unhealthy coping strategy became difficult for me. I could still not talk about my cousin without feeling a huge amount of pain. I felt out of control, I became so focused on sports, I spent most of my time around it, it was a way I felt I had some control.

It wasn't until I went to university where all these feelings came flooding back - the first week of fresher's week and my flat mate contracted Meningitis. I felt like I went back 10 years and I was in that 'freeze mode again'. I remembered all the feelings I had when I lost my cousin, the way I dealt with it and how it affected me for the years gone by.

I told myself this time things needed to be different - I let the people around me support me and I supported them. I talked about how I was feeling, the worry/the relived experience. As uncomfortable as it felt to start with, I felt like a weight had been lifted, I felt more resilient. This led to me talking about my previous experience of bereavement with the people close to me. I felt a lot of guilt at first, for not being able to talk about my cousin, for the pretending it didn't happen. I felt anger too - I was angry at why it happened to me, but also angry at myself for burying all this emotion. I was eventually able to feel happiness again, I was happy to talk about memories I shared with my cousin and was able to laugh without the guilt and sadness.

I always think back to how everything would have been different if I dealt with the grief in a different way but everyone experiences grief differently. Talking and accepting support from those around me and realising it is actually ok to feel sadness has helped me to become a more resilient and open person.

36

Diána's Story of Losing her Strong Pillar

I grew up in a broken but supportive family. My parents had been separated before my birth. However, I can wholeheartedly say that both of them actively took part in my upbringing and I could easily count on their support. Specifically looking back on my relationship with my father, it could be described as a deep, one of a kind emotional connection which was based on mutual respect, love and understanding. My father always used to be excessively optimistic about the future even in the most ruthless and burdening times. He looked at me as an adult, at least he made this impression by listening to me attentively and taking my problems and plans seriously. Our rituals included sitting down together, contemplating our lives and planning for the future. I remember one warm summer we were sitting on a bench at our farm and attempting to escape the reality of financial difficulties through our ever-lasting conversations and by making a mental journey into each other's plans and desires. We listened to each other as we hypothetically decorated our wooden house, the comfortable and colourful pieces of furniture we chose and toys that I filled my room with. As we let our imagination soar, the picturesque dream house became more vivid and the implementation of our plan got more sophisticated and fine-detailed, regardless of the ugly and saddening reality of constant hopelessness and financial distress. Looking back to those conversations, I can see that my father's approach to parenting was fantastic – His goal was to teach me to develop a sense of "I'm good enough", to form a core belief in myself and essentially see the light through goggles even when everything falls into darkness.

Receiving the news

I was 12 years old. I remember it was a Wednesday when I received a text message in the middle of my Math class that informed me of the devastating news: my father had passed away. From that moment, I only remember 2 things: which classroom I sat in and the sheer feeling of nothingness. Feeling like that text message injected me with a serum that made me incapable of showing any affection or reaction at that moment. I was just sitting in the classroom helplessly, listening to the teacher which sounded like indistinguishable voices, acting as nothing had happened, being emotionally and physically numb.

While I was walking home from school with my best friend, being in absolute denial, I bluntly shared with her my saddening news. As I got home, my mom sat down with me to talk everything through, but I still didn't quite realise what actually had happened. I remember asking her whether it is okay if I go to the cinema that evening as I had already made this plan days ago with my best friend. She encouraged me to go and switch off as much as I can. This is the story of how I saw a movie called Déjà vu while ironically, I cannot recall a single moment from the plot due to the state of shock.

Seeking meaning in incomprehensible death

I was aware that my father's health had deteriorated in the last six months before his death, but my mother never placed an emphasis on the severity of my father's condition. Since I normally only spent time with him during school breaks his worsening health just wasn't tangible to me. Reflecting back on my mother's reaction, in one aspect she just wanted to protect me from experiencing sadness but at the same time, I think she also wasn't quite ready to face the possibility of my father's death either. A few years back, my mother told me that my father hadn't wanted me to visit him and be remembered by his weakened state. From my point of view, all of this led to an experience of unexpected, inexplicable and ruthless death which provided no sense of closure. It made me angry at both of my parents for a while. This is the only thing I wish they would have done differently – more transparency probably would have gone a long way, shielding me with better endurance against this debilitating tragedy.

The approach of grief in my culture

The following period was emotionally very burdening. The first phase of the bereavement started by the combination of absolute denial and anger as I was shouting to my mom that my father hadn't passed away and she shouldn't dare to state such things. This was shortly followed by a familiar feeling of emptiness. I was just laying in bed alone all day and repetitively listening two songs and somehow the passage of time became palpable. That was the exact moment when my father's death broke into my consciousness and the pain that came with it transformed into sobs. Later, the funeral definitely helped me to bring some sense of closure as it authentically depicted my father's personality: his ashes were brought on a horse-drawn carriage to the cemetery while in the background gipsy music was playing, finally, we poured homemade Palinka (fruit brandy) on his grave in order to send him to the afterlife with his favourite drink. This farewell fully resonated with his personality and I could see him for the last time and say goodbye.

I returned to school soon after the funeral. By the time of my arrival, all my classmates and teachers knew about what had happened. To tell the truth, nobody in my environment knew how to approach me and handle grief. To give you one example: while the whole class, including me, was running around the gym hall, our physical education teacher called me aside to express her condolences and then sent me back to run right away. It seemed as if everything had to be in motion, others had to run "around us" to share her empathies with me. I instantly felt like she didn't know what to do with this situation and neither did I. I felt quite embarrassed and disturbed, to say the least. This taboo approach of mourning continued. It felt like everyone attempted to open Pandora's bereavement box and then abruptly tried to close it down avoid having to face any discomfort or sadness.

My family didn't want to forcibly delve into my feelings. I was simply trusted to eventually initiate the conversation when I was ready. That moment only came a year later. My teachers didn't want to interfere, however, they felt sorry for me which worsened my feelings. Due to all of this, I chose to close down my sorrow to the external world which distanced me further and further from my classmates as I couldn't be present. My interest was just lost, I became more and more isolated and this was followed by bullying which deteriorated over time. I got to experience the true and cruel colours of bullying, from creating questionnaires in the class about how much they don't want to see me, to finding out how much they hate me and want me dead by writing it on mirrors in the bathroom and blackboards. During this year, as I couldn't oppress my anxiety and sadness any longer, psoriasis plaques appeared for the first time throughout my entire body. The bereavement was devastating to my mom as well who encountered similar difficulties coping with grief and long-term unemployment that left us with unpaid bills and the fear of losing our home. Looking back, this is where I encountered the deepest point of my life. I knew that somehow I had to get out of this depressing and overwhelming phase. I just didn't know how.

The healing process
One weekend, I decided to watch a movie called 'Peaceful Warrior.' By the end of the movie, something just clicked, as if

I had a Eureka moment. I was engrossed in the plot right to the very end. This blockbuster was the most paramount material that could successfully bring my soul out of helplessness. The story is partly based on true events and covered topics such as grief, coping with mourning, restart, acceptance and provided a different so-called mindfulness approach to life. I could easily resonate with the main character which in return helped me to open up my feelings and illuminated my life from a different perspective. I was determined to spend the day by contemplating my thoughts and writing them down in a journal. This second act really helped: the power of writing.

I began to use the most powerful mental tool that my father taught me: I started to redirect my focus to all the positive things even if it was difficult. Suddenly I was thinking about my friends, who were there for me and supported me to the best of their ability throughout this experience. It felt like my mind just initiated a positive train of thought and brought up all the content memories of my father, all our lovely conversations, all the exciting events on the farm. This afternoon provided me with time to reflect on my fondest memories. Eventually, for the first time, I felt that I allowed myself to accept the death of my father as I knew that his memories and teachings would always be with me and be kept alive through my narratives. I truly believe the following quote from a movie called Coco couldn't capture this experience better: *"Our memories, they have to be passed down by those who knew us in life – in the stories they tell about us."*

A few days later, after finishing up dinner with my mom, I finally initiated a talk about my dad. I remember awkwardly trying to create a space to talk, but once it started, we shared each other's burdening emotions and then all the memories abruptly burst up that had been kept deep inside us. During our conversation, we gave room for both crying and laughter. It was an uplifting and liberating feeling for both of us. We talked for hours until there were no more words left. Through a collaborative effort, we gradually shifted both of our perspectives to become more optimistic about the challenges we have and then using my father's technique, we tried to make future plans, even in the face of adversity. Of course, it would be naïve to say that we believed in them at first. However, the more we talked boldly about our plans and supported each other with positive statements, the more we started to internalise them and believe that it could actually happen to us! It felt a paradox that my dead father's wisdom had a profound impact on us to overcome depression and save us. I will always be grateful for him for helping us to construct an ever-lasting optimistic attitude through his death.

Looking back now, as hard and saddening the grieving was, I am truly grateful for it. Similarly, to Alice in Wonderland, I went down the rabbit hole and went on a painful but magical journey that comprised an intense exploration of my beliefs, my true self and where I want to move forward in life. By the age of 16, I managed to support my mom financially and work as a baby-sitter alongside high school. In retrospect, grief truly helped me grow, form my sense of identity and find my purpose in life: becoming a Clinical Psychologist in order to support people surmounting difficulties and help normalising grief.

37

Laura's Story

I'm 39 now and I was 22 when my dad Terry died. He'd been ill for some years and for a plethora or reasons. He was warm, funny, short, he called himself an 'ugly little git' and was in no shortage of people who really loved him. But of course, as we all know he is now a 'saint' because he is dead and heaven forbid he was ever just a human.

I always used to say I was glad I got to know him as a man and not just my dad, that we'd said all we needed to say when he died. I think that just meant that I'd heard stories of other women he'd met previous to my mum and he'd told me things that he wouldn't have told me as a child (and I'd got pissed with him a few times!) But who knows if that's true now? Did I know him? Do any of us know someone so distinctly even after so many years?

Now I hold on to fragments; like the smell of engine oil, fags, or later on cigars and some kind of powerful roll on deodorant. Brute, my mum said.

The saddest thing sometimes about grief is that is doesn't hurt like it did. And you are left feeling disrespectful, like part of the way you honour someone was the pain it left you with. But you're more or less ok and you can't remember them like you did.

I wonder frequently if he would like me.

38

Mariella's Story

I lost my brother when I was 15 years old, weeks before I was due to sit my GCSE's at school which I didn't end up sitting. Living without him has been undoubtedly the most challenging and draining experience I've encountered. Growing up wasn't easy and I had more bad memories from my childhood than good, but knowing he was going through the same was a comfort blanket for me. We always had each other. I'd turn to him and he'd turn to me and that was it. I still remember the day he left vividly. I remember everything I did, what I ended up making us for lunch when I came home from school because he loved my omelettes, what I did after school and the conversations we had that day. I still hear my Mum's screams when he made it home that night after being stabbed. Still remember watching him gasp for air, change colour and begging for help as I watched him die helplessly. I called the ambulance and spoke to them as if I knew he'd be ok, even though I knew deep down he was slipping away. I've never been able to erase that memory or block out the sounds in my head. When he was taken in the ambulance I went to stay with my nan at the bottom of the street, I slept in the spare room but felt frozen cold so I asked if I could sleep with her with her electric blanket on. I was still freezing. I lay awake for hours and heard a knock at the door. My heart sank. I stayed put hoping it was all just a bad dream. My nan spoke to my dad out the window and asked me to go downstairs. I remember feeling like my legs weighed a tonne and found it hard to move forwards. I walked down the stairs and saw my dad's face and my legs gave way. He didn't need to tell me. I went to my dad's that night and decided to move in.

I went to visit my brother at the morgue three weeks after his passing and wish I never had, because it destroyed me all over again. That same year I tried to take my own life several times. Attempting overdoses, slicing my arms and wrists, starving myself, feeling guilty for smiling when my brother was lying six foot under. When I felt this physical pain it took away the emotional pain for a little while and gave me something else to focus on. I never imagined life without him. We went through so much together and then I literally had no one to turn to.

For a long time, I didn't go back to the area of the city where I grew up. I couldn't accept what had happened. I cut people off if they spoke about him in the past tense, disregarded sympathy. For years I never had a single picture of him around and never spoke about him to anyone at all. I now have my beautiful daughter and talk about Jack to her. We visit his resting place sometimes and she talks about him too. I never wanted children. I always thought if I had a child and lost it, I wouldn't be able to cope with that kind of pain again. My daughter wasn't planned and it terrified me but I eventually accepted that I just have to protect her the best I can. I still have my bad days. I went through this trauma and more in my younger days and feel like I carry a lot around with me but I manage it better now I have my daughter too.

39

Lockdown;
The Deaths of my Nanna & the family cat & How I came out the other side

My name is Paul. I'm 39 years old (38 at the time I'm writing about). I have two daughters one 16 who was living with me full time and an 8-year-old who I co-parent with my ex-partner. It was March 2020 and life was shaping up to be a really exciting year. Erin my eldest was in her final year at secondary school and was really starting to get ramped up for her final exams, her mock exams had put her in a really determined mindset with achieving her outcomes which was to get the grades she needed to get into college. Her plan was to move to Wales and live with my parents while studying at a welsh college for the next two years. Libby, my youngest, was at primary school and enjoying the simple life of year three. She was forming amazing relationships and growing into the life of a type 1 diabetic who was not prepared for this condition to get in the way of any of her outcomes in life. For me, 2020 was also setting up to be a really exciting year; in January I had just passed my life coaching qualification and this was moving forward at a really fast pace. I had several clients in the pipeline, had done my first public speaking event in front of 40 people and was planning to run my first local event. This was to be aimed at the parents of a local primary school as well as working with the school to enable and empower children with amazing life skills. I had spent the winter climbing several times a week at the local climbing wall and was stronger than I had been for several years. I had several outdoor routes I'd wanted to climb for several years and was now in a position to attempt them! I'd also met a lady whom I'd connected with and was at the start of a new exciting journey with her.

The first turn of events came in the first week of March when I damaged my shoulder at the climbing wall; I knew as soon as I had done it that it wasn't just a twinge but still tried to ignore the severity of it for several days. I was in denial for quite a few days and even went climbing to see if I could bear the pain enough to carry on climbing. I had work several days later and it was alongside my new lady so I didn't want to call in sick really . By the end of the shift it was clear that my shoulder was not up to my job, so I booked sick on the 6th march. I was feeling a little low as I knew that my injury was not going to be a quick fix. The next few weeks consisted of physio and GP appointments and an ever-increasing interest in the COVID-19 virus which was starting to look like a national lock down was coming.

On March 15th, I was sat on my sofa with both girls as we watched Boris johnson inform the U.K. people that there would be a national lockdown and that all schools would be closing; GCSE exams would not be happening this coming summer. This is where the biggest feeling of uncertainty I'd ever had ever had came over me; it was a feeling I didn't even understand.

The biggest struggle was trying to reassure my girls that amongst all of this uncertainty, that everything would turn out okay. All of a sudden, a year involving our planned music festivals, weeks away camping, climbing trips to the Shetland isles and a new chapter to my eldest daughter's education seemed a huge unknown.

The initial excitement of lockdown kept us upbeat, and enjoying so much family time together was glossing over all the stress from lockdown. We were queueing to get into supermarkets, home schooling, but also not being able to see my new lady, not being able to get a diagnosis on my shoulder injury or an idea when I would be returning to work; although admittedly with the virus being such an unknown I was in no rush for that.

On the 30th March we received a group message on WhatsApp, it was the international family group and the message was from my uncle: "Mum has gone to hospital with breathing difficulties, she is on high flow oxygen." After speaking to one of my ambulance colleagues, me, being the ever optimist, reassured everyone that she would be well looked after and that Nanna was taken into hospital for precautionary reasons. My Nanna was a hardy lady who would always bounce back, perhaps sometimes with a bit of moaning and groaning, but always with the persuasion of cake.

Her blood results had come back; she was positive for COVID-19. What did this mean to her chances of getting better? No-one knew. Only the worst could be imagined, she was elderly, with underlying health conditions. Top of the risk factors, 'she's a tough old bird,' I told myself. And chose not to think about the worst case scenario.

My Nanna was by far my favourite Grandparent; to me she was the perfect Nanna. Gave the best cuddles when I was little, filled me with sweets and then sent me back to my parents hyperactive and over-excited. But, most importantly would always give me good counsel in questions I had in life, although very old-fashioned with her views, would always tell me as it was in her eyes. I have a lifetime of memories with her and spent several years before she went into a care home doing her shopping and helping her several times a week, in between school runs and work. We were very close and the cuddle we had on a Tuesday before I did her weekly shop meant just as much to me as it did to her. The last time I saw my Nanna was on a night shift at work, I attended her care home in my ambulance to see one of the other residents. The staff on shift knew who I was and let me sneak down to her room and give her a kiss and a cuddle. She woke up and said "what are you doing here?" I kissed her and said "just looking after your neighbour, go back to sleep, I'll see you soon, love you!" My Nanna never told me she loved me or anyone in her family. To my knowledge it was the way she had been brought up but she loved me very much. I knew that.

On Friday the 3rd of April at 08:10am it was time for another group message from my Uncle:

'Mum just passed away'

And so she was gone; and a very strange time began.

My uncle had been to see her the day before she had passed away and spent most of the day and night with her. Due to COVID, no-one else was allowed to go and see her, so all communication was through him. The whole family asked for her to know we were thinking of her and to send 'get well soons etc...'

Dealing with death in my family had up until this day been a positive experience. I chose to speak at my Grandad's ceremony in 2013 and at my Nan's funeral in 2019. Death has always been openly talked about in my family and the general feeling was that the person who died should be celebrated not mourned.

So here we were, this family who'd found this great way to get emotional completion on people dying and we're in a national lockdown where funerals could not take place, no-one could meet up to hug or reassure each other through tears, body contact or just being together. I really struggled with all of it, the fact I hadn't seen her in the hospital, I couldn't see how my dad was feeling about his mum dying. A zoom call for me didn't show how someone was coping. A response tells you nothing as we can all say what we want people to hear, but a physical connection like a hug or a hand shake can tell you so much more. But none of this was available to me or any of the family. My parents lived in Wales, my uncle and Aunty in the USA and even my uncle and sister who lived a 15 minute drive from me were out of bounds.

Nanna was cremated and her ashes were collected by my uncle, from a logistical point of view that was it, nanna had died and life went on. But that was one of the huge problems, we were still in a national lockdown. I had no distractions of school runs, after school clubs, revision clubs and the usual busy time that came with having children. I didn't even have work to distract me as I was still off with my shoulder. I'd actually managed to get an MRI scan on it but was still for the result. My life was filled with so much uncertainty and lack of direction. I like to think I usually have a really good awareness of my state of mind and can tell when I'm not coping with things. This would usually be when I would make time to share how I'm feeling with friends or family; either at the climbing wall, over coffee somewhere, or even just stood at the park after school chewing the fat with some of the school run gang. None of this was an option and I started to internalise it all.

I wasn't at work so I didn't need to put a fake smile on there, I wasn't doing school runs so didn't have to interact with school Mums and Dads. The girls could get up whenever they wanted so there was no reason to keep a routine; breakfasts got later, lunches got later and dinners sometimes didn't happen. Once my youngest had gone to bed I spent a lot of time online gaming, it was a great distraction to turn my brain and my emotions off. The coaching work had all gone online and we were running weekly webinars with some great guests. One week I woke up in the morning and had no drive to go on the webinar and promote wellbeing and happiness whenI wasn't even feeling that myself. I told the two other people I wasn't going to be on it and withdrew from the only real thing giving me direction at that time. In my mind it was mission complete. I could now just float in the ether with just enough drive to sort the kids out and get by day to day. I couldn't even see my new lady as she worked for the ambulance service and we were from different households so there was never any time to isolate long enough before going back to work. I feel I need to add here that as low as I was, I still knew that I had to go through this period and that I would come out the other side. But lockdown had no real time frame, I was off work, I couldn't climb and schools were closed...... what could go wrong now?

The one thing I was still enjoying about lockdown was that I could finally get sorted some of those time consuming jobs around the house I'd been putting off for some time; one of those was washing everything washable in the house. Sofa cushion covers, curtains, duvets, pillows it was very satisfying. This was when I discovered Bobbob was not very well. Bobbob being a cat; one of two brothers we'd had since they were 8 weeks old. I was changing Libby's bed and picked him up and realised he was much thinner than normal. He was a night time cat so he slept all day and was out all night, a bit like me I suppose, usually working nights and sleeping in the day.

Suddenly a few things clicked, I noticed that the cat food had been lasting longer than usual, for the last few weeks the bowls were a lot fuller than normal. Being that Bobbob was the fatty of the house, that would explain a few things. A poorly cat wouldn't normally be an issue but being that we were still in lockdown this was a huge unknown. And it was a Sunday....

I left it till Monday morning to see how he would be over the next 24 hours but it was clear that he was really unwell;

he hadn't had any water or food for over 24 hrs that I knew of. Due to COVID, the vets had a telephone call back service, so it was mid-morning before I spoke to anyone, it didn't take much convincing to get the vets to want to see him and an appointment for 6pm that day was made.

Again being that we were in lockdown this was not the usual thing, Libby wanted to come with me as he was her cat, that couldn't happen. I had to sit in the car in the car park. They came and got him and I sat in the car for what felt like hours with a 5% battery so I couldn't even pointlessly scroll social media to distract myself.

He was really poorly, not a little bit poorly, a lot poorly they were keeping him in over-night and going to refer him to a specialist in the morning. I told Libby the truth, I never hide anything from the girls unless I really think they don't need to know, but this was carrying potential for him to not be coming home and I wanted to make sure this didn't give her false hope. The next morning I picked him up from the vets and drove him down to the specialists. When I got there I had to wait for someone to come out and pick him up, so I face timed the girls and they said good luck to him and I fussed with him. If I'm honest, I knew he probably wasn't coming home from what the vets had said but you can never say never. That was the last time the girls saw him and three days later after several days of tests and failed blood transfusions, I was stood around the side of the garage on my phone, far away from little ears, talking to the consultant about the next steps. She was amazing with me, everything was explained to the level I understood and we chatted for a good 20 minutes. I was dragging the call out as I knew what was going to be the outcome of the call. But she wasn't going to suggest it directly; it had to come from me. I was already crying before the words came out of my mouth." I think we've done all we can and it's best if we just let him die". I tried to tell her why I was crying but the words wouldn't even come out, I was just about to break my daughter's heart and there was nothing I could do about it. She reassured me he would be comfortable and in no pain the whole time whilst they put him to sleep. Writing that now has made me cry as I recall standing in the garden crying actually felt good - that was the first emotional release I'd had since my Nanna had died. I hadn't been able to cry until then and it was more because it involved someone else being upset not me.

  Both the girls were laying on Libby's bed waiting for me to finish the call and give the latest with Bobbob. No words were needed when I walked into the room, the tears already rolling down my face said enough and we all just hugged and cried on the bed. Llibby asked me: "when is he going to be put to sleep?" I managed to tell her "right now darling" and we just hugged and cried until Libby said to me "Daddy, I'm really sad, can I play on my iPad to take my mind off it for a little while?" We spent the next few days talking a lot about Bobbob and all the amazing happy memories we had of him. We spoke a lot about what we were going to do with his ashes, which Libby was going to keep by her bed.

  I believe that both my girls have a very good understanding of death and also how to connect emotionally with it. Erin had been to several funerals from a young age and Libby had been to my other Nan's funeral when she was 8, this taught them the importance of expressing sad emotions and how being sad can be a good thing.

  Arranging Bobbob's cremation was a really nice process. The lady on the phone was amazing and made the whole process easy, enjoyable even and even with still being in a lockdown went out of her way to ease the sad time for us. His ashes were dropped off to us with a card to me and a personalised card for Libby in a nice bag. His ashes were in a lovely box that is now on Libby's bedside table, just like she wanted, although he did spend the first 2-3 weeks snuggled up next to Libby in her bed; even bedtime bunny was kicked out of the bed in preference for Bobbob.

Before having the cats I was a dog person 100%, I thought cats were selfish and only wanted food and a cuddle on their terms; having the cats changed my mind completely. Bobbob was the biggest softy ever, had so much love to give and was the best living teddy bear you could have. I still expect him to be on Libby's bed most days when I go in her room. It takes me a little while to process that he now lives on the bedside table.

By the time I returned to work I'd been off for 11 weeks; even though I was going back I hadn't had my shoulder assessed by a medical professional due to the much discussed lockdown. However, we were now allowed to meet people in small bubbles and socialise in public. This was the start of an upward curve in my mindset that took until around September to get back to where it was before all of this. From the first week in June, a group of 5-8 of us socially distanced and went climbing to the Peak District every Tuesday. Prior to lockdown none of these people had really met before but they all knew me individually. We came together as a group and the difficulties of lockdown slowly started to unravel. Friendships were formed in this time, that without lockdown would never have happened. I believe that the reason the WhatsApp group that was setup is still pinging with energy is because, as many other people will have realised from lockdown, the importance of actual interaction is so important. Climbing involves so many different things, trust, confidence, motivation to name a few.

A huge turning point with regards to gaining closure on my Nanna dying was in August. We had managed to go camping in mid-wales near my parents for ten days with several of our friends coming up at different times. Whilst there, my uncle and his wife who had just sailed halfway round the British coast had made it to the coast near my parent's house. One afternoon they came up to where we were camping and me, my dad and my uncle stood and chatted about my Nanna's death and how we all felt. Both my dad and uncle don't show much emotion and were brief with how they felt, but for me it was enough that I could see for the first time how they were and that I could now share with someone how I felt about it and it was just what I needed. It was like I had taken off a weighted vest I'd been wearing for four months, carrying this emotional package around with me that I'd had no idea how to let go of. I had now gained that emotional completion on my Nanna's death. I didn't even recognise it at the time and reflecting back on it now gives me even more clarity that I gained a lot from the brief connection with my dad and my uncle.

There are many more emotional journeys that occurred through lockdown regarding many different things which, again, upon reflection were all completed with some form of connection. My youngest daughter returning to school was magical and the smiles on all the children's faces when they got to play in the playground as friends once again with no boundaries was magic.
The completion of the uncertainty of my eldest daughter's education was very intense, gaining her results, getting her college place and then waiting to hear whether her dream of living in Wales would be possible. Returning to work and knowing my shoulder injury hadn't ruined my climbing career.

Even though as I write this at the end of September 2020, COVID-19 is still here and lockdown number 2 is looking all the more likely, life is better and connections are stronger than they were before the first lockdown. I'm thankful that I got to experience that journey and have learnt so much about myself. I tell people that in lockdown we embraced it for the opportunities that were given to us. I'll cherish the fact I got to spend so much quality time with my children. From an emotional point of view the importance of knowing it's okay to not be okay and that a connection with someone is more important than a response from someone.

I'm now 39 years old, I'm still called Paul - and once again I have a very exciting year ahead of me! My eldest daughter is living in Wales with my parents studying B-TEC level three. She's very happy but misses her cuddle times with her dad so she's coming home next week for some. My youngest daughter is happily back in school with her friends although now in year 4; she even learnt to ride a horse this summer. I'm looking forward to a winter of indoor climbing and getting strong ready for next year. Work has taken a really exciting turn which for me connects several of my passions and is in an amazing place. And as for my lady, well, our connection continues to grow every day.

Email from: Paul
To: Marianne
Re: Your Book

Hi Marianne,

It's funny to think that when we were in GCSE Science Class together all those years ago that we were younger than my eldest is now! Also made me smile to think that now I'm writing in YOUR book rather than you writing ALL over mine in class!

Take care,

Paul

Lockdown;

> Email from: Marianne
> To: Paul
> Re: Your Science Book
>
> Hi Paul,
>
> Oh Yes! That's so funny, made me laugh out loud – I totally did used to do that!
> I bet that was terrifically annoying!
>
> Thanks again for your story and sorry to hear what a difficult time you had in lockdown; glad things are looking brighter now!
>
> Marianne

40
Nikki's Story

The morning after my birthday, we got the dreaded call, Dad had passed away. I had just turned 14, and I was 'Daddy's little princess.' Looking back, I remember dreading going to stay at his house as he was a stickler for the rules, and I was not, whereas now I'd give anything to be able to stay with him for one more night. He had brain tumours, and despite surgery, they could not be removed. Eventually he was moved to a home so he could receive support catered to his needs. Visiting him got harder and harder as he changed before our very eyes. His body began to wither and his memory began to fade, and he found it increasingly difficult to remember who I and my siblings were. Perhaps this is one of the most difficult things, to begin grieving for someone whilst they are still alive. They are physically still the same person, but mentally they are not. All those memories we had together were fading from his mind.

I had begged to see my Dad on my birthday, like I would have any other birthday before, but my family took the decision that it was best if I didn't visit him on that day. I think they knew he was getting worse, and they were trying to protect me from seeing him 'like that' and they didn't want that to be my last memory of him. Despite their best intentions, I am still somewhat resentful of this over 15 years later. I feel my last goodbye was taken from me, and I would do anything to have had that opportunity, no matter how difficult it would have been. I did get a 'goodbye' of sorts I suppose; I visited him in the funeral home, where he was so still and peaceful. That image of him lying there has only just left my mind, and it haunted me growing up, but now as an adult I am so glad I was able to have one last moment with him, knowing that it would be our last.

I remember sitting with my Mum and siblings, trying to choose music for his funeral. Dad was an avid Queen fan, so it felt only fitting to have this as his funeral songs. We discussed the song 'Invisible Man' and laughed that it would have been a funny choice to have had when he was being carried in to the crematorium to have that playing, as if it was Dad playing a practical joke. We felt others wouldn't appreciate this, so we went with other Queen songs instead. You'd be surprised by how often Queen songs are played, and I struggle to not be right back in the midst of grief every time I hear a Queen song. I think for many of us, funerals really mark the end of the 'denial' phase of grief, where you are forced to confront the reality of what has happened, the reality we all try so hard to refuse to believe, because we simply don't *want* to believe it.

Following Dad's death, I spent a little while off of school, perhaps a week or two, and when I returned, it was as if to everyone else, nothing had happened; no one seemed (from my memory) to talk to me about what had happened. It was as if it was 'business as usual'. This was hardly surprising coming from a Grammar School where we felt more like numbers on a league table than human beings with feelings. I felt I had no avenue to really process what had happened, and the way I was feeling as a result of my Dad dying. Because Dad died of cancer, we were offered free counselling by Force charity. I started going once a month if my memory serves me correctly. This was a terrifying experience as a 14-year-old to sit in a room with a strange lady and try to open up and explain how I was feeling. All I can remember discussing with her was the sheer level of anger I had in me. I also remember filling jars with different coloured sand, for what purpose I have no idea. I gave up on this counselling after a while, but all those feelings were still there and they wanted to find a way out. And one way I had tried to deal with those feelings was to self-harm. That rush of pain used to take my mind away from what I was really feeling for a short time. I learnt to cut shallow which meant I was never left with scars. I remember feeling like everything was just too much and had had thoughts of ending my life in the 1-2 years following Dad's death, but fortunately never acted on these. Then came the age of 16-17 where I began drinking alcohol, and I would drink a lot, to the point on one occasion my poor Mum and brother had to take me to hospital for fear I would need my stomach pumped. My family have never let me live this moment of being 'paralytic' down, and it gets raised at most family meals. I don't think they grasped what was really going on for me at the time, and I'm not sure they still do now when they talk about that night around the dinner table.

At some point, it all stopped hurting as much and the pain seemed to fade. I feel over time my memories of me and my Dad have also faded, whether this is truly the case, or I've *chosen* to forget them, I'm not sure. Time passed and life moved on, but as it did milestones appeared that made that pain rear its ugly head; being the only sibling to get in to University, graduating, completing my Masters, getting married, buying a house. All of these events reminded me of the fact that Dad wasn't around anymore. I found my wedding the hardest, knowing he wouldn't walk me down the aisle and share a dance with me. He was there in spirit though, and his photo was hung around my bouquet so that he would be with me on my walk down the aisle. It also felt like he was there in person as my brother is the spit of him, something that makes a grieving process difficult at first! I had made a point to my family and my Husband that I had not wanted a big fuss made over Dad not being at the wedding, as I would have been an emotional wreck for the rest of the day! I had the engagement ring he gave to my Mum on, his photo on my bouquet, as well his photo on display at our reception to make sure he was there with me.

Apart from reminders of him at my wedding, having reminders of him around the house is something I have never actively done, and I'm not entirely sure why. I did keep one of his zip-up hoodies and will wear this at times I miss him, just to feel like he's giving me comfort again. I also have a box I keep hidden away of lots of things that remind me of him, as well as his name card that was on his door at the nursing home. When I feel I need it, I'll bring the box out and look through it all. I have saved a birthday card with his writing that I want to get inscribed on to a piece of jewellery so that he can be with me all of the time. Then when something 'big' happens in my life, he'll be there with me. I'm also one of those people who believe a white feather is from a loved one passed on, and I don't see them very often, but when I do it makes me sad and comforted all at the same time. And this year I have already purchased a Bauble filled with white feathers to hang on our Christmas tree, so that he can join us for our first Christmas in our first home. Aside from physical reminders, the loss of my Dad steered me in to pursuing my current career path in Psychology. He's right there along my journey, pushing me to achieve my goals, as well as allowing me to understand the grief of others.

I'll be honest, over the last 15 years, I don't feel I've found anything that 'helps' with the grief, because I don't feel there is anything that can. But I find comfort in talking to those who lost a parent at a similar age to me, and even more so those who can relate to having lost someone extremely close to an important date. Every year now my birthday is not something I feel excited for, it's something that feels painful because of what the following day resembles. I've noticed this year that my grief has presented itself in a very strange way I had not expected. I had been working with an older male colleague with whom I had created a fantastic supportive friendship with. He valued my opinions, would check in on me as would I check-in on him. It wasn't until I had a new job lined up where I would no longer be working with this colleague that I felt myself grieving for my Dad again, but this time in a way I never had before. This male colleague represented an older male figure, some sort of father figure if you like, something I have not had in my life since Dad passed. And I think this is why I became so upset about leaving my job, because I would be leaving such an significant person in my life that had given me something I had not had in so long. I told a fellow colleague about this (who had also lost their Dad), and I felt so embarrassed saying it to her, it all seemed so ridiculous. But she understood and validated my feelings, something I'm not sure someone who hasn't experienced such grief would have been able to do.

Being able to talk to others who truly understand is comforting, but at times I still have to remind myself that there is no 'end point' to grief, there is not a point at which all those feelings suddenly go away, they're still there, just less intense and less frequent. What is also hugely comforting for me, is once in a while, sitting with my sister and watching Mrs Doubtfire and eating Burger King, both of which remind us so dearly of Dad.

41

Katie's Story

My Dad died in 2008, so I've spent quite a while hand in hand with my grief. I'm at the point where sometimes I don't know it's there and then every so often, maybe even out of the blue, it hits me, drowns me.

My Dad died in a sudden tragic accident in England whilst me and my husband were living abroad in Switzerland. I had a really great job, we lived in the mountains and my Mum and Dad visited regularly as they loved it too, so I didn't feel too far from them. Apart from of course when you are rushing back in an emergency, but I think any distance is too far then! I realised later that at roughly the time my Dad was involved in the accident, I was at a high ropes park, jumping off a bridge into a valley on the end of a bungee rope. I was on an absolute high which I couldn't wait to tell them all about, not knowing that my foundations had just been ripped out from under me.

People told me later that it must have been absolutely awful not having a warning of losing someone so special, not being able to say goodbye but I honestly don't think that would have been 'easier', what on earth do you say? How do you tell someone the extent that you love them? I think I was fortunate in that I had a great relationship with my Dad, even at 28 I was a proud 'Daddy's Girl' and would still sit at his feet to listen to his stories, so I feel safe in the knowledge he knew how much I loved and adored him.

My Dad was really quite a character. I had a fabulous childhood, full of fun and holidays and spending time with my parents. My brother was a very talented sportsman so we would spend a lot of weekends all together, travelling the country and abroad at times, going to his sporting events, which happened to be my Dad's absolutely favourite sport too. I wasn't much good at it, even though I entered a few races. But I loved being at these races and events and seeing my Dad in his element as my brother's coach, manager, mechanic, sponsor, and number one supporter. BUT my Dad ensured I didn't feel unsupported as when I played house netball matches at school, he was the only parent to come and watch. When I was in a play or musical, he would buy tickets to watch on several nights!!! I was so lucky, but I feel more fortunate now as I have such wonderful memories to look back on. Crazy, ridiculous thoughts take charge of your mind when grief is in control but at times it felt my Dad lived his life and was there for both of his kids, as if he knew it would be short.

So, back in 2008, I received what must have been the hardest call my Mum had to make. My Dad had been involved in an accident and had died. We frantically tried to get a flight home that day but couldn't make it so I had an agonising night before flying out the next day, to go and face my life that was never going to be the same again. One of my Dad's closest friends picked us up at the airport and I was so grateful but had to spend the journey in silence for fear of what might come out.

The funeral was horrendous, beautiful, gut wrenching and touching all at the same time. My Dad was a huge music fan, Eric Clapton, Pink Floyd, Jimi Hendrix kind of style. Several years before, me and my husband had sat up until 2am with him as we had told him that our laptop could 'burn' CD's, so he selected all his favourites to go on 2 CD's. At the end, he happily announced that this music would be his funeral music, so he took that job from us when the time came! He also told us that we would need 2 'slots' for his funeral so we could play his music so we booked the 2 slots!!! The sun shone brightly, huge amounts of people came, it was a good day to remember him and how full of life and fun he was. My thoughts were often with my Grandma who couldn't be there. I had lost my Dad who was my guiding light always, my safety blanket. As long as he was around, I was safe and making the right decisions. But my Grandma had lost her son, her child, I couldn't imagine that.

I spent about 3 weeks back at home, spending so much time with my family and friends. Sitting in this horrendous place in my heart and head but not wanting to leave it. I found moving back to Switzerland and 'normal' life was so incredibly hard. My Mum had to prompt me to return back there after the funeral, but it was so hard and confronting to know that the world moves on even though there is a gaping hole within me.

I think, what I would like to pass on, that came out of my experience is that grief is our own. It's so personal and you want to own it and live with it as it means we won't let go or forget that person. My grief was huge and I can't imagine anyone else's grief, but that's just the point, we CAN'T imagine anyone else's grief. A few months after my Dad's death, I was at a work event where I was talking to an elderly lady. She told me that she had recently lost her husband so I said how sorry I was for her loss and how difficult she must be finding things now. I opened myself up a bit (not something I did to people I didn't know usually as I found my grief so personal and something to be protected) and told her that I had recently lost my Dad too so I was very sorry for her loss. Unfortunately, she didn't take this in the way it was intended and maybe thought of it as someone saying they knew exactly the way she was feeling, but she turned to me and immediately said that "at least its not your husband" and walked away from me. Her friend apologised for her and followed her to see if she was OK. I was left utterly stunned but really angry as well. I wasn't trying to make our experiences the same, but she had taken it as an attack on her personal grief. But it stayed with me and still does. We have no idea how someone else is experiencing their grief, but we have absolutely no right to say whose is stronger, or worse, or easier. I think she was speaking from the depths of her experience, but it hit me when

Katie's Story

I was also pretty vulnerable and rocky, which she didn't need to do. So, listen to other's experiences. Only you know how you feel but similarly, we have no idea how someone else is feeling or coping and if it's someone we don't know well, then we don't know their personal narrative and life story. I know she was hurting, but I promised myself that I would not treat someone like that who was hurting as well, even if I inwardly thought my grief was more justified. I also did not need to hear from a lot of people that "things happen for a reason", they often don't and there was no 'reason' for me losing someone so dear to me.

I think my second point I would like to pass on was that I struggled for a long time and still do at times, with grief for what might have been. As I explained earlier, I had a fantastic childhood and I had always assumed that my Dad would be a huge part of my future family's life too. He was so much fun to be around, but he also just gave me the feeling that he would help me sort out all my problems. I didn't have children at the time, but was married and thought that obviously they would come later. My brother and his wife had just had their first child, so my Mum and Dad were first time Grandparents. My niece was 6 weeks old when my Dad died so we had a chance to get photos of him with his Granddaughter, but she and future Grandchildren had not felt his love and presence for themselves, they only have our stories to inform them of that. He would have made a fantastic Grandparent and would have been so involved in all our lives. I mourned for that missed opportunity. It tore me up that I considered for a while that I would not have children as he couldn't be there for them. The world turned and I found that it was our time for a family. I now have 2 children that have grown up hearing so much about a man they never knew. Children are direct, inquisitive creatures and sometimes they ask me things about him or make comments about him which I love to hear as he is still part of them, but I realise they will never really know the magnitude of this man, that is in their blood but not in their memories.

I wanted to give all his Grandchildren the chance to find out a bit about him in their own time, so I made a Life Story of him for each of them. I would thoroughly recommend doing this as not only did I love making it but I know they can pick it up today, tomorrow, next year, when they are parents, and find out a bit about him. I put in pages about his childhood, him meeting and marrying their Grandma (who they've only ever known as living alone so its been quite an eye opener I think for them), his favourite music, his hobbies, recipes of meals he liked and I finished each page with sayings that we used to hear from him very often, that are synonymous with my Dad. It sits on their bookshelves for when they are ready to look at it.

That's a little about my journey and my experience. It feels lonely at times, although I know so many of us are on our own paths. Tread carefully.

Email from: Marianne
To: Katie
Re: Your Story

Dear Katie,

It's perfect – you've done a wonderful job and it's moved me to tears. I love the idea of the books for the grandchildren – I might well steal that myself.

Your Dad was so fun & it explains so much where you get your own sense of adventure & spontaneity from! You write wonderfully and I can hear your accent too as I read it which I adore. He would have been and was, so proud of you. Thank you so much for writing this, it's poignant & will be so useful to so many I'm sure.

Much love,

Marianne x

> Some of the things discussed in the following story may be triggering to some. Not everyone is devastated when someone days and neither have all people who died been good people.
>
> All humans are born being deserving of love, care and protection. Unfortunately, though, that's not always people's experiences.
>
> As adults, insights about our upbringing and developmental experiences can cause us to reflect differently on our childhoods.

42

Fran's Story

I was twenty-two when my dad died a few weeks before Father's Day. I remember thinking that to the outside world, I looked like a young woman who had just lost her father. A tragic loss, especially at such a young age. Whereas, I'd never actually had a father, not in the real sense. We'd lived in the same house together for nearly twenty years, until I finally escaped to university, but I'd never had a conversation with him. To this day, the only stuff I know about him is what he shared at the dinner table and the little I've asked of other people since. I was terrified of him. Terrified to even talk to him. It used to take me the whole of dinnertime to pluck up the courage to ask him if I could watch a video.

I never liked him.

Not even when I was a young child.

He was in a permanent bad mood and the slightest irritation would set him off.

When I was 41 I had a type of trauma treatment called Eye Movement Desensitisation and reprocessing (EMDR). One of the images that came up was of me as a toddler, and my mum telling me that I had to wear a long-sleeved top to cover-up the bruises on my arms. My dad had lost his temper with me and physically abused me. Later, images were of him sexually abusing me. He was also emotionally abusive. He'd hidden behind a facade of respectability because he'd been in the police force for thirty years.

I found out he'd died during my year out from university. My mum had left a message for me to call her. I had a strange feeling about this message. When I phoned, she told me she was sorry but my dad had died. I was shocked. Not because I was upset, but because the thing I had been wishing about for the past twenty two years had finally happened. My dad was finally dead. I wrote in my journal about how surreal it was for my dad to be dead. I couldn't believe I was finally rid of him. I was then scared that he would come and haunt me because I was glad he was dead rather than despairing.

The next day I went home to see my mum. It was awkward knowing I was supposed to be upset when I wasn't. On the outside I tried to look glum because I knew my mum expected it of me, but inside the euphoria was bubbling-up. I was absolutely euphoric at finally being free of him. I left the house when I could contain it no longer, and skipped down the footpath near my mum's house singing "Ding-dong the wicked dad is dead" to the tune from the Wizard of Oz. I think a neighbour saw me.

Later on, people would come up to me and tell me how sorry they were to hear that my dad had died. I had to stand there and listen to their condolences while inside I was thinking, I'm not sad, I'm glad he's dead. I wasn't even just glad, I was ecstatic.

I had the same dream once a month every month for eighteen-months after he'd died. In my dream, the morgue had made a mistake and my dad wasn't really dead. He was coming home. The feeling of despair that I still wasn't free of him was overwhelming.
This was over twenty-four years ago.

My mum died eighteen years later when I was aged forty. I did cry when she died. I didn't know about her involvement in the abuse back then.

I now know my mum was implicated in the abuse as well and was likely the ringleader. I also know she was a narcissist. She would do things and then deflect the blame onto someone else, typically my dad. I'm still relived my dad is dead, but it's a shame I will never fully know to what extent the abuse was down to my dad, and how much of it was my mum who would then deflect the blame onto my dad.

I now celebrate her passing every year. I also regularly revel in the wonderful experience of not having any parents; dying was the best thing they ever did for me.

To: Fran
Email from: Dr Marianne Trent
Re: Your Story

Dear Fran,
Thank you for sending me your story.
I'm sorry to learn of what an abusive and traumatic childhood you had. Like all humans, from birth you deserved love, protection and support; I'm so sorry that's not what you got.
I'm glad you were able to access treatment to be able to help you process your experiences.
Thanks again,

Marianne

43

Sonia's story

of Grief and Loss

I have experienced many different losses in my life. Some of them I've coped with better than others and I've used different coping mechanisms which have aided my recovery. Some losses I've been able to move on from, others which have happened this year, are still so raw.

It's useful to mention some background information, to add clarity to the loss of my former sense of self:

I grew up in an abusive household where I was raised by an overly critical and controlling mother who mentally tortured and physically abused me regularly. I was also bullied throughout school, which only served to reinforce my mother's taunts and criticisms.

This meant that for a long time my sense of self was greatly influenced by my negative experiences. My mother made me believe that I was "thick", "had no friends, only acquaintances", that I was "a nasty piece of work", "selfish" and "lazy". She would constantly pick fights with me, then make excuses for my "bad behaviour". Despite evidence to the contrary, I gradually began to believe her. She mocked the way I walked in public and made me feel defective, but later denied it. She would start arguments with me over the smallest of things and would then twist the story, to make it look like I was at fault. She convinced my family and I that I was the problem.

of Grief and Loss

I suspected when I was 15 that my mother was mentally abusing me, but this wasn't confirmed until much later when I told a college tutor and my doctor. They did absolutely nothing to help me, so I started believing that I must be to blame or at least not worthy of help. After I left home, I managed to convince myself she had changed though, as she could be 'kind', 'nice' and 'helpful' sometimes. Then, last year when she 'gaslighted' me, I realised that she hadn't changed at all. I spoke to a therapist who told me that my mum was a narcissist who'd inflicted narcissistic abuse upon me. It was then, at the age of 38, that I realised that the kind, caring, helpful, empathetic and charming side of my mother was not real. I lost my former self-concept as well as my mother. I fear that I may also have lost my dad and older brother too as I suspect they were enablers and/or 'flying monkeys'. I am still rebuilding my life and I'm hoping that with time and therapy I will be able to develop a better sense of myself.

My mother made me homeless twice, once at 18 during my 'A' level exams and then 2 years later when I returned to Sixth Form to study for an Advanced **GNVQ** in Health and Social Care. I was free from her abuse, but I was homeless. I was also illegally evicted by a rogue landlord, who wanted his rent payments before they were due.

Losing my home was a horrendous experience, because I lost my sense of security and temporarily my belongings, which gave me a sense of identity. I think the worst of it was the unfairness and injustice when I knew I wasn't to blame. When my mother made me homeless twice for no reason she tried to twist the story to convince other family members and myself that "I chose to leave" which was a blatant lie. Luckily, I was able to stay with friends for a couple of days, and afterwards I stayed in a night shelter and the **YMCA**. I went on to live with 'S', but I never truly felt like it was my home, because he paid the rent. Today, I'm still scared of losing my home but I believe that once I am working again and able to contribute financially, I will feel more secure and able to recover.

I 'lost' my mother and possibly other family members, in a metaphorical sense. However, I also lost 4 people who *actually* died including 'S'. I knew 'S' for 13 years, we dated for a while and remained close friends after we split up. 'S' represented the family I never had. He was like an older brother who looked out for me, gave me a roof over my head and a bed to sleep in and cooked me dinner. He also visited me at University and in hospital, when I was admitted for my mental health. He died unexpectedly, 6 years ago, from a heart attack at just 40. I was living with him and my present girlfriend at the time, and I found him dead in his room. I will never forget what he looked like or how he felt, or the fly that came out of his nose. Rigor mortis had set in and there was nothing I, or the paramedics could do to save him.

When he died we had to move as my girlfriend and I couldn't afford the property between us and we also couldn't bear to live where he'd died. Luckily, there was an empty flat downstairs, otherwise I would have been homeless again.

There were a few things that I believed helped me to move on from my loss. Firstly, I received CBT for anger, which helped my partner and I to grieve without constantly arguing. Later on, I also found it really helpful attending a loss and bereavement group. They went through the stages of grief which helped me to make sense of what had happened and to process the event in a healthy way. I also felt less alone discussing my grief with others and hearing their experiences. I was also grieving the loss of my mental health nursing degree in the same year and discussed this too. I was subjected to mental health discrimination by my training provider, who would not let me make up 40 placement hours to complete my final year. This led to me being denied my degree and RMN status. I won't go into the detail of that here though.

After 'S' died and we'd moved downstairs, we started to hear noises coming from our kettle when it wasn't turned on. We still hear the clicking sound the kettle makes after its finished boiling, despite moving home again and buying 2 new kettles! Other people have heard the noise too, so we're not imagining it. 'S' loved his tea and I am convinced that he is responsible for the noise. Sometimes, I talk to him when I hear it and also talk to his picture, which helps me to feel closer to him.

His death prompted me to quit smoking, not because his death was caused by smoking, but because he had always wanted me to quit. I did, and never looked back, six years on!

'S' was cremated and his ashes were put in a plant pot by his family, so I couldn't visit him or do anything for him after he died. Giving up smoking was my gift to him...memorial ashes for cigarette ones if you like (!)

I also shattered my left foot and ankle after jumping from a balcony bare foot during a suicide attempt, 16 years ago. I am grateful to have survived, but I was left without the full rotation of my ankle and with osteoarthritis. I cannot run, even for the bus, and I can't play football or hockey. However, I have discovered a liking for swimming, which is good for my joints. I also enjoy watching women's and men's football and enjoy playing football and ice hockey video games. These activities are compromises that have helped me to adapt to my disability and deal with my loss.

44

Lucy's Story

I never truly understood grief until I was thrust into it full force. I always imagined grief to be the immense pain we feel for losing a loved one from the physical plane of existence, but my grief was different.

I had lost relatives in my childhood and adolescence, but I had not been close with them and had not felt that sense of grief I thought I would have. I berated myself privately for not having the experience that my preconceived idea of what grief should look like told me I should have. But as an adult I did not expect to grieve a relationship. After all, in most cases the ex-partner does not pass away; the relationship simply ends. Yet I grieved a relationship I had put my whole body and soul into. A relationship where we had planned to spend our lives together and I became entrenched in the picture of how it would be.

When my ex-partner decided he to my surprise, no longer wanted to partake in our relationship due to me carrying his child and not undergoing the abortion he wanted during my 16th week of pregnancy, I was crushed and ultimately devastated. He immediately disappeared from my life as if he were an enigma because I had not fulfilled his request. The saddest part was it was done via text message so my whole world was ripped from beneath me by reading letters on a screen.

I felt the breakup was like he had died as I was unable to speak with him and gain that sense of closure which I felt I ultimately needed. He had blocked me from all social media, texts and would not answer my calls. Now of course he wasn't dead and is still very much alive as I do see him in the street from time to time, yet still there is no chance of connection or communication. He shut the door to that so even though I see his physical body I still felt a sense of mourning of the loss of connection and communication we once had. I felt it was similar to when someone passes away and we are unable to speak with them again. Also, this break up catapulted me into uncharted territory. I had lost all my hopes and dreams for the future, I had lost my companion, confidant and all of our shared experiences both past and for the future.

During this time I was unaware that humans can grieve the end of a relationship I thought I had simply gone mad. But what I felt was definitely grief and I moved in varying speeds through the stages of grief entering one stage and returning back into another in what appeared to me to be an endless cycle of torment.

In an attempt to end my torment, I reached out to friends and loved ones but was branded obsessed and 'I should just get over it'. I was told to stop talking about it and to move on. I felt like no one respected or understood that even though he didn't die, I could still mourn what I had lost (imaginary and reality) and I could experience grief. Now I don't know if pregnancy hormones played a part in exacerbating my sense of grief but I know I felt lost, alone and with a pain unrecognised or validated.

However, life had not yet finished with me. My pregnancy as far as I was concerned was going well except for hyperemesis and a few stints in hospital to help manage this. At my 20 week scan I was told I was going to have a baby girl and she looked great. Then the blow came; I was told I was in fact pregnant with twins however 'twin b' could not be found, the placenta and sac were present, but no baby was inside. It was diagnosed as disappearing twin syndrome. I had never heard of this before and quite honestly, I never had to find out.

I felt confused and questioned why I hadn't been told about a twin pregnancy from my first scan. I was told however my growing baby was healthy and I should continue to carry her to full term with minimal issues. As I got home and digested the news, I felt guilt and torn. I questioned myself on how I could grieve for a baby I didn't know I was having? I blamed myself and began a cycle of self-loathing constantly telling myself it was all my fault and if I had done something differently it wouldn't have happened. Not only that, but I was even then questioning how is it even right that I feel sad when I still get to have a child when so many other women don't get to experience that?

I then started to feel a sense of resentment and anger toward my ex-partner that he had left me to deal with this on my own. I had the grief of a relationship to contend with and now this level of grief. My body and mind could not cope with the levels of grief. I became withdrawn and hopeless.

Yet, no matter how hard I tried to deny myself grief I still felt it, it was raw painful and confusing. Once again, I become stuck in an endless loop of what ifs and picturing how it could have been. Yet even though this time I had a societally legitimate reason for grieving, I kept it quiet to myself. I didn't feel I could share my pain this time through fear of judgement or remarks of 'well at least you still get to go home with one baby'. I already knew I was one of the 'lucky ones.'

I kept my grief from my breakup and loss of my unborn child to myself, I began to feel like it had become all encompassing. It began seeping into other aspects of my life. It caused family tensions, displacement of blame and a deep-set anger which I felt unable to shake. Ultimately, through repressing my grief I believe it manifested into postnatal depression.

I had my daughter and felt joy and happiness for the first time since my ex had left. But a string of guilt oozed in for not holding 2 babies instead of 1. I felt like a failure that my own body had not managed to do what it was intended to, but then felt foolish because it was, and it was carrying and keeping one baby safe. I tried to brush off my feelings of grief and continue focusing on my new baby and journey into motherhood, yet it would seep in when my mind was still.

My thoughts had become consumed with a furious negativity that my baby would die. I would lay awake at night staring at the small vulnerable child next to me and I would be fearful that if I slept, I would wake up next to her lifeless body. I had gone a week with minimum sleep of a couple of hours here or there, but I always woke filled with that dread and sense of urgency to check the Moses basket next to me. I finally confided in my health visitor my fears and she responded with "if she is going to die, she'll die there's nothing you can do about it." I immediately broke down. I felt even more of an urge to protect her and I felt failed that I had opened up and had not received any form of reassurance or even understanding of my thoughts. To make matters worse, I became extremely ill physically one week after giving birth as the delivery team at the hospital had not checked for Twins B's placenta and unbeknown to my it had been left for a week to rot within my womb. I only became aware of it as I gave birth to it in my shower. Rushed into hospital and experiencing sepsis, I was on the brink of death myself. However, luckily, I survived. Then the negative thoughts manifested from my daughter dying to I would die, and she would be left alone with my body and no one to care for her.

It has been 6 years now, and even though I am what I would describe "good," I am still experiencing the aftermath of the level of grief I experienced. I did not process or deal with my grief and it can pop up at any time and with out warning like a sucker punch. Only recently have I felt able to open up about my experience and being to process what had happened. As a result, I feel I am making steps forward. Although I still hear that inner voice tell me that "stop being pathetic" and I still battle with overcoming societal norms with regards to what constitutes acceptable grieving.

I don't often talk about it losing a baby as I feel too much time has passed and no one wants to hear about losing a baby especially 6 years ago. I feel I have still had not been able to process losing a baby and it is if my mind had blocked such event from its awareness. When I speak of it now it was if it happened to someone else rather than me. Some may say that it is a defence mechanism however I feel upset that I am still unable to process what had happened. But one thing is for certain I felt like a piece of me is missing, like I will never be whole again and I yearn to hold my baby in my arms. But I try not to think too deeply as I feel I have no right to grieve when I was blessed with one child when so many others don't get to take a baby home.

One thing I have learnt from my experience is there is no right or wrong way to grieve but there is a right way and wrong way for you. Only you can be the judge of that. Not everyone grieves the same way and that's ok. I have also learnt to listen to those who need it when they are in need of support; I didn't have that and I wish I did. I feel my story would have been very different if I did.

45

Surina's Story:

I'd like to get off this rollercoaster please (p.s. strokes suck)

Grief is mostly spoken about with regards to a human or an animal passing away. But what about the loss of who somebody used to be? How your life used to be? This is what I'd like to talk about.

In 2015, my Dad had a stroke. He survived but our whole lives changed forever. There's a complicated mix of feelings you feel when someone you deeply care for survives a life-threatening health issue but now, they are no longer who they used to be. How do you explain to someone that you're grieving a person who is still alive?

My Dad was never perfect by any means; he drank a lot, smoked a lot, had an unhealthy diet, was a frequent liar, and had a hot temper. But whenever I needed to go somewhere, he would give me a lift, as if my personal taxi. He always endeavoured to get everything that was on mine and my brother's Christmas lists every year as children, especially the newest Pokémon game for me, because he loved to see his kids happy. He also cared for animals even if he didn't want anybody to know that and always denied it. It's so easy to idolise the person that passes away as if they were perfect, we do the same thing when going through a break-up, like some form of self-inflicted torture of make-believe. For me personally, I've found it easier at times to deal with the rollercoaster of emotions by remembering that my Dad was never perfect to begin with and perhaps the stroke emphasised the negative parts of him that were always there. Regardless though, I loved him and I still love him.

The first few weeks after his stroke, he became the gentlest man. He oozed serenity. I remember my Mum and I talking about how perhaps this wasn't such a disaster, maybe this was a blessing in disguise. Every cloud has a silver lining, right? The dynamic at home shifted following the stroke but in a positive way – it felt a lot calmer, the air felt easier to breathe. Unfortunately, this all came to an end. We don't know what the trigger was, if there was one at all, but his new calm version of my Dad was replaced with a rude, angry, and verbally aggressive one.

Life is very different now; I live in a constant state of fight or flight, never knowing what the morning is going to bring. My Mum, who is an actual angel might I add, bears the brunt of my Dad's verbal outbursts. The demands, the insults, the shouting, the impatience, the way he humiliates her in front of others "for a joke". Watching this all go on but feeling so helpless is unbearable and torturous. I'm lucky in the fact that he's nice to me, but I'm not entirely sure why. My brother also bears some of verbal abuse too, but he's always been one to hide his feelings and pretend he is some emotion-less robot, but I know that's not true. When my Dad had his stroke, it was the first time I ever saw my brother cry, and it was only a glimpse that I caught when his tough bravado crumbled on his way to his room to escape anybody seeing him. One thing I am grateful for is that this brought my brother and I closer together as we can bond

I'd like to get off this rollercoaster please (p.s. strokes suck)

over the shock of it all and the huge impact it has had on our lives. Our lives have been changed and we can't keep pretending that it's all okay, because it isn't. I want to scream at the top of my lungs about how much everything sucks and how exhausted I am. I want someone to come up to me and tell me it gets better; tell me it won't feel like this for much longer and he'll go back to when he was calm and serene. I've always liked the quote "everything happens for a reason" because it's comforting and hopeful, but what if actually the world doesn't care about you? What if the world is just incredibly unfair and we just have to make the best of the hand we've been dealt?

Walking on eggshells every day, wondering what the next trigger will be, is draining. Every demand that comes from his mouth has to be answered so as to avoid any verbal outbursts and triggering his anger which can last many weeks until one day suddenly he's acting as if everything is fine and offers to make everyone breakfast. I adore the days when he's happy, he teases us playfully, and makes his stupid Dad jokes while laughing his mischievous, but also child-like laugh (intermittently broken up by his smoker's cough). His love language is very much through food these days, so we always know it's going to be a good day when he's offering to make my Mum lunch and a cup of tea.

We're learning to revel in the good moments and push through the bad ones by holding onto knowing that they will pass. We don't know how long it will take, whether it's hours, days, or weeks, but it will pass. It's become difficult to celebrate things and to feel genuinely happy because we are always anticipating when things will go south again.

When people hear "stroke", they think walking issues and speech problems. What you don't hear about are the changes in the brain. Fortunately, I come from a background in psychology, so I was aware of the impact this could have on his cognition. His pre-frontal cortex has been affected and thus he now acts in a much more impulsive way. He has impaired executive functioning which impacts on his ability to plan ahead and make decisions. His impulsivity has meant we've suffered financially because he'll just suddenly buy things that he deems necessary but just aren't; including multiple bikes for himself which he cannot ride, multiple cars that don't work, a treadmill that doesn't work, and a huge loan for no reason at all. God forbid you try and reason with him or stop him buying something, you might as well have invited the devil to come and stay for a couple weeks!

My heart breaks at the thought that he might not be there at my wedding day (I think that's why he's pushing for me to get married because he fears the same thing), or to see his grandchildren one day. Some days I don't think I can handle it, some days I hope I don't wake up so I can get off this rollercoaster for good. The one thing that keeps me going is my Mum; the kindest, most loving, most selfless woman in the world. I don't want to ever do anything to hurt her more than life already has. She's lost unborn children through 2 miscarriages, she lost both her parents at a young age, and now the man she married is no longer who he used to be. So I'm not going anywhere, I'm going to stay by her side as we walk through this hell together, arm in arm. I dream of a day that I can whisk her away somewhere for a peaceful life.

Being an Indian family, there is a lot of shame around mental health and asking for help. I'd love for my Mum to attend therapy and get the support she needs, but I know that that is a battle I will be fighting for a while to come, maybe one day she'll give in, but she knows I will always be there for her. It's hard when nobody in your extended family has an idea of what you're going through (and Indian families are huge), because your Mum doesn't want to worry anyone or come across as weak or needing any help.

I've gone on to actually work as an assistant psychologist on a stroke ward following this experience, I wanted to help others going through a similar experience. I want to offer support to not just the stroke survivor, but also their families. I'm angry that my Dad was not offered psychological support when he was in hospital, I wonder if things would have been different if he had. I still wish for things to go back to how they were before the stroke, but not all wishes come true and that's just how life works unfortunately.

I've become painfully aware that our parents won't always be there, which is a terrifying thought when you've been fortunate enough to have them in your life for 25 years like I have. I can't even begin to imagine what life would be without them and just thinking of it just now as I write this, made me feel sick. The impermanence of life terrifies me. It's strange because I don't fear my own death at all, but the death of loved ones is unbearable for me to think about. I don't know if I want to live in a world where my Mum isn't there.

Going out is now a different experience too. I can never fully relax; the idea of my phone dying when I'm away from anything that can charge it sends me into a panic. What if I miss the call? What if today is the day that he has another stroke and takes his final breath? What if something has happened to my Mum or brother now? Watching others laugh and smile and be carefree fills me with envy, and I hate myself for feeling that way. I long to feel that feeling. Having a support network has been so important. Only recently have I actually felt more able to just reach out to friends and cousins to have a shoulder to cry on or to distract me from my current reality, and now I don't know how I got this far without doing so. I'm also now that person that always has a portable charger in her bag…

Please don't bottle up how you're feeling; write it down, tell somebody, scream it into a pillow, do whatever you need to so

I'd like to get off this rollercoaster please (p.s. strokes suck)

you can release how you feel in a safe way. There is something so incredibly raw and human when you grieve. Going through what feels like an unstoppable flood of tears, your balled-up fists cramping, your burning throat, the nausea. Things will never be the same again, but they do get easier as time passes. Be kind to yourself and allow yourself to grieve repeatedly for as long as you need, grief has no timeline. As I write this in September 2020, it's already 5 years later and I'm still angry and I'm still grieving. There is no right or wrong way to grieve, find what helps you and seek support from professionals and loved ones because human connection is so important for our mental health.

There's a quote that I quite like, the origin of which is unknown:

> "Pain is inevitable, suffering is not".

We can ease our suffering through acceptance of the reality of life and learning to tolerate feeling uncomfortable because we cannot escape pain. Just like as if you're stuck in quicksand where struggling makes it worse but remaining still (and lying on your back) allows you to float to the top and survive.

> To anybody reading this, I hope you know you won't feel the pain you're feeling forever and that there will be good times again.

I'd like to get off this rollercoaster please (p.s. strokes suck)

May you use your experiences to make you all the more resilient to weather anything that comes into your path.

> Email from: Dr Marianne Trent
> To: Surina
> Re: Your Story
>
> Oh Surina!
>
> It's wonderful, you've done such a good job with it. Well done.
>
> I'm sorry to hear what an impact this all has on you and your family. It certainly seems like you are doing a superb job but that it definitely has its toll, do know that it's okay to ask for support as and when you might need it.
>
> Thanks again,
> Marianne

46

Vanessa's Story

My grandmother was one of the most hard-headed, put together people I have ever met. She always took charge of situations and would fight to the death to protect her family. I have fond memories of her smuggling my sisters and I cookies saying "don't tell your mom" when my mother had told her we'd had enough cookies already!

When I was 12, she was diagnosed with Alzheimer's, at the time I was not sure what this was or how it would affect her but as time has continued I have slowly learnt what this means. To this day my grandmother is still fighting her battle (I told you she was hard-headed) but unfortunately, she would be considered in the last stage of this now. It has been harder and harder to come to terms with losing my grandmother despite her not passing. It feels like she has already left us. Every time we would visit, she would remember us less and less and to see how this affected my family too was heartbreaking. One thing that has given me solace from this is for whatever reason, when we would visit she would always want to hold my hand. My grandmother has always hated being touched by people and if anybody else has tried to hold her hand she would refuse. This has helped me somewhat deal with the circumstance to believe that possibly a tiny part of her may still spark inside and seek comfort from her family.

The only other things to help me deal with this has been talking about her, looking through family photo albums and mindfulness. My parents will tell us funny anecdotes about times they spent with her, funny things she used to say and do. These stories always make us laugh and somewhat alleviate the pain we're feeling as we know her memory still continues through us even if it doesn't for her anymore. Being able to look through photos of when she was my age, wedding photos and photos of how I remember her are very therapeutic for me as I through this I am still able to feel an attachment to her. My family and my partner are a big coping mechanism for me as my family always ensure we are there for each other. So, we all lean on each other when we go through hard times. I believe it will yet again be difficult when she passes away, but I believe we will continue to share our stories to cope.

Mindfulness is useful for me to be able to understand how I'm feeling, address it and deal with those emotions. It's something I have implemented when I feel distressed or upset and helps me to deal with underlying issues I may have. I think the big thing people forget in these circumstances is that it IS okay to cry, to feel and express that to others no matter who you are. There is no right way to grieve and if something gives you a glimmer of happiness or helps you to release the pent up pain and anger and frustration, DO THAT! In circumstances like my family's it is difficult to convince yourself it is okay to be happy. Sometimes when remembering the current situation with grandmother it is easy to feel like you should be miserable all the time, to continuously grieve but really no one's loved one would like them to feel this way. My grandmother would ask us "what are you being silly for?" It doesn't make you a bad person to be happy despite the circumstances. It is good to laugh and smile when recalling memories of your loved one, that is how they would want you to deal with this. To celebrate them, not mourn.

I think my grandmother will always be one of the most hard-headed people I would ever have had the pleasure to know and will continue to live by her teachings; don't let anyone get you down, no one is ever better than you are and "chocolate quenches thirst"(okay maybe not that one!)

I take comfort in the fact that SHE was my grandmother and nothing will ever change that.

> Email from: Dr Marianne Trent
> To: Vanessa
> Re: Your Story
>
> Dear Vanessa,
>
> Your story is very powerful and very nicely depicts how it is possible to grieve for someone who is not dead.
>
> I'm so pleased you've been able to find a place for mindfulness in your life and also that you allow yourself to feel the emotions which you will inevitably feel what with you being human!
>
> Thanks again for your story, I'm totally going to adopt the mantra of chocolate quenching thirst!
>
> Thanks again,
> Marianne

47

Hold my Hand in Death:
Katherine's Story

Reflecting 14 years ago, I held my mother's hand as she took her last short, shallow breaths. In my 22 years of life, I had never watched someone die, and I had no idea what to expect. I remember tears streaming down my face watching her lips turn a light purple, her hands already feeling cold and stiff. Oddly this moment felt easy, it was so peaceful, and I was thankful my mother was no longer in pain. Her cancer battle was over, no more pain, no more chemo, radiation, drugs, hospitals, doctors, tubes, bedsores, infections, blood, vomit, and tears; it was simply over. I thought maybe the hard part was over for me; watching my mother suffer was done, and I remember thinking how odd that I had cried almost every day when she was battling cancer and caring for her, but I couldn't cry at her funeral. I don't know if this was because I was happy, she wasn't in pain anymore, or I didn't have any more tears in me.

I had no idea of the grief and pain that was ahead. I want to share with you some of the moments in life that have been difficult for me.

1. I had no idea how hard it would be for people to talk about my mother. People knew she had passed, but some didn't come to the funeral; some would see me and not mention her at all. Others would talk to me about her, her life, and her death, but usually, this meant

I would cry at some point, and eventually, they didn't want to talk about her anymore. My father was different in this way; anytime I wanted to talk about her, he wanted to. Even 14 years later, we can talk about her as if it was just yesterday that she passed.

2. I believe time has helped me cope in many ways, especially now that I can talk about anything without crying.

3. I had no idea it would change me emotionally. I was never a crier growing up; I could watch sad movies like Titanic without a drop. But something changed in me; I could relate to others' pain as if it was my own. I can watch a sad movie and cry like it is real and happening to me or someone I love. In 14 years, this has never gone away.

4. Birthdays, holidays, anniversaries are hard. I started to hate the month of September; she died in September, two weeks before her birthday, also in September. Now every year, September never disappoints; something horrible happens to me in September.

5. I had no idea what my wedding would be like without my mother. I feel like I held it together pretty well, even when the photographer said, "now a photo of the bride with her mom." My friends quickly corrected the poor photographer before I could even respond. Honestly, I didn't want to talk about my mom that day; I just wanted it to be a day without sadness.

6. I had no idea what it would be like to have a child without my mom nearby. My child had a rough start to his life. I did everything I could to keep him well and get

him on the right path. I remember thinking so many times; I wish my mom were here to help me.

7. I had no idea what it would be like to raise a child without his grandma. There are still so many things I want to ask her, but I simply can't.

I am so grateful for the time I had with my mom, and I try to focus on good memories with her. On her last Mother's Day, she was feeling well, and we went out for ice cream and planted some petunias. Now every year on Mother's Day, I plant petunias in my yard. Planting flowers has become a very positive ritual for me each year.

Katherine Pendergast, also known as Kat Socks is an award-winning and 1# best-selling author. Her books include Pickles the Dog, Adopted in North Dakota, Pickles the Dog, A Christmas Tradition, Pickles the Dog, Goes to School, In Loving Memory A Child's Journey to Understanding a Funeral and Starting the Grieving Process, In Loving Memory A Child's Journey to Understanding a Cremation Funeral and Starting the Grieving Process and Babies of the Badlands.

Kat is also the creator of a line of soft sole baby shoes called Kat's Socks. With Kat's boutique, a small portion of the sales is donated to local animal shelters near her. Kat lives with her family and two Great Danes in Bismarck, North Dakota. Her Great Dane Carmela, is a certified pet therapy dog. Kat and Carmela volunteer at a local facility with youth children.

48
Her Name Was Leah

Once upon a time, I was one of those people that didn't want to talk to people about their grief. Not all grief, just one kind of grief in particular. Baby loss grief. The thought of it made me uncomfortable and a little bit sick, because if you talk about it, you kind of put yourself in that position and imagine what it would be like to have that experience. No thank you. I didn't mean it in a selfish way, just thinking about it and talking about it might have made me cry and that wouldn't help anyone. The bereaved parent has enough on their plate without having to deal with someone else's pity. It felt better all round to skirt around the issue unless completely unavoidable.

Then, once upon a time, I became one of those people who was more than comfortable talking about it. Since this is a book about grief, you will know exactly where this story is going. I lost my only daughter during the second trimester of pregnancy in January 2019.

I wanted to share my story about my journey of the short life we had together whilst I was carrying her and what that path has been like since, for many reasons. The top reason is because I want to share that a wound as deep, dark and painful as this one can be healed. My experience is that yes it can. If you believe it can be and if you want it to be. As part of my journey, I've read my fair share of baby loss literature in books and forums and what made me most sad was that many people didn't want to feel better at all and felt guilty if they started to feel better or started to let thoughts of other things fill their minds. I saw over and over mothers telling other more recently bereaved mothers, that the pain of loss never gets any easier, ever.

I don't believe it makes you a bad person, heartless or inhumane, if you want to want to finish grieving at some stage. I didn't think I deserved to be desperately unhappy indefinitely. I realised for me it would be a choice; I could choose to remain unhappy and not move forwards and in doing so lose some of the joy of raising the two sons I already had, or I could work hard to feel better.

Somehow, I've always known I would be a Mum that raised boys. I knew I was pregnant with my daughter for 13 long, painful, gut-wrenching emotionally and physically draining weeks. The only hurt I can compare the pregnancy with was that that I felt in the last few days of my Auntie's life, when we learned that she was terminally ill. I knew it was coming, right in the pit of my stomach. Not exactly when, but all the time that painful pressure building up and up; the more time that passes, the sooner that time would come and our world would be changed for the worse.

I had a troubled, traumatic pregnancy with multiple early episodes of threatened miscarriage. The routine dating scan confirmed my worst fears that something was wrong with my baby, which resulted in us needing further testing. In the absence of chromosomal and genetic abnormalities, the areas of swelling and other markers pointed towards a heart defect. The plan was fortnightly scans to monitor the heart's progress as the baby grew until 24 weeks when they would be able to give a more specific diagnosis, prognosis and treatment options for once the baby was born.

The additional testing also revealed that we were expecting a girl. Although this didn't come as a surprise based on my intuition, it still filled me with unease, I had said to my husband before that if the baby was a boy then everything would be alright, but if it was a girl it wouldn't. The night we found out, we settled on her name with a high five. A happy moment, yet with an unspoken thought that this way, I would never have to name a dead baby. In family tradition, when a baby is named, we add their name and a cartoon picture to the family list on our Netflix account. Not that our babies watch telly (no judgement if yours do) it was just something we did that finalised our decision.

Deep down, at 16 weeks and 6 days pregnant, I knew Leah was gone on the evening of Thursday 24th January 2019. I didn't dare share my thoughts with my husband as saying it out loud would have made it real. I wanted to believe I was overthinking, that my gut instinct had let me down.

For the last few evenings in a row, once we had sat down for the night after having put the boys to bed, we had both been able to feel the baby kicking. It was in the same spot each time, in the gap where my stomach muscles had separated already due to the intense vomiting that had been happening this pregnancy. Since we had named her and then feeling her presence, I had started to allow myself to think that I might actually get to have her, to let my guard down, to love her. This Thursday night, I didn't notice any kicks. Part of me reasoned that it was still really early to get a regular movement pattern and at a day short of 17 weeks, the baby was too small to always be in a position where movements would be felt.

If that was the only reason, I probably wouldn't have felt so on edge. It also happened to be the first day that I hadn't been sick in about 9 weeks. I had hoped that the sickness would have passed at the end of the first trimester and when it just carried on with a vengeance, I had come to the realisation that it might be there for the duration of the pregnancy. I don't know how it had escaped my attention until this late in the day considering the amount of time I spent with my head down the toilet!

I put these thoughts to the back of my mind and looked forwards to our regular foetal medicine scan appointment that was due the next day. That morning, I got ready and looked at my bump in the mirror. I went to take a picture, but something inside stopped me, the same way as it did every time before that I had considered taking a photo. If there was one thing I could go back and do differently, it would have been to take that photo.

So we went to what was the 7th scan that pregnancy. You would think after that many scans in such a short space of time that I would have immediately realised something was wrong. The first thing they always do without fail is scan the heart and say 'there's the heartbeat'. Well that didn't happen. What I focussed on was the crystal-clear view of a little pair of feet. I can still hear myself now as I said in a little giggly high-pitched voice "ah look at the little feet!" The next thing, the consultant was saying she was sorry. I can still picture her face as she was speaking and remember my confusion that she didn't immediately go on to elaborate. I thought she was going to say she was sorry that the baby definitely needed surgery. No, she was saying there was no heartbeat.

All along I had been convinced my baby would die, I had worried myself for weeks about it and vividly imagined what it would be like, how I would find out, to the extent I had panic attacks and vomited, yet here I was, not spotting all the warning signs that this was turning into exactly that scenario. Because on the other hand, there is hope. I also had the perception that heart defects, whilst serious in babies and children, are a fixable thing. This is the area of medicine where miracles happen, odds are defied, right? Having been real about what could happen all this while, here I was in denial. I could hear my own heartbeat pumping in my ears and I remember crying out 'no no no,' and shaking my head violently from side to side like a toddler that hasn't got their own way, determined to override the decision, and then in the next second realising my worst fears were reality. I then became acutely aware that I needed to shut up. Everyone in the waiting room would be aware of exactly what was happening if I didn't quieten down. Everyone in that waiting room was there either because there was something wrong with their baby or because there was a strong possibility of there being a problem, this wasn't what they needed. They needed hope unless definitively told otherwise that there was none.

I don't know how I wasn't angry that I had been through absolute hell with this pregnancy and it hadn't all been 'worth it' because I didn't get my baby, but I wasn't. Running through the 'what if's' in my mind, there was no blame, no negligence, no finger to point to justify any anger. I just felt guilty that I should have loved her sooner when I had the chance, rather than trying to distance myself to protect myself from the pain of losing her.

What I learnt was that for someone suffering from anxiety, that the experience of worrying about what might happen is just as bad as that event happening in real life. The shock, pain and grief I experienced through imagining her being dead, imagining not ever getting to hold my warm, snuggly new born girl, not getting to see her grow up, were just as difficult to endure as when it finally happened. The sweats, racing heart, tears and emotional pain were all just as real despite being 'just' anxiety. I can truly empathise with those who live with anxiety on a permanent basis.

The next few hours were a blur of repeat scans and decisions about what should happen next. It was starting to get towards time when we needed to make arrangements to collect my oldest son from school, which I would have done myself had the day gone to plan. My husband had already called into work and explained he wasn't going to be back, so I said that there was no point him sitting here with me waiting for some medication, there was nothing he could do for our dead baby but he could make one little boy's day by surprising him and picking him up from school. In that moment, all I could think about was everything I had to be grateful about.

The baby loss literature I have since read always seemed to discourage thinking 'at least' suggesting it as belittling of the grief. Certainly many 'at least' comments from well-meaning people deeply offend the very people they are trying to comfort. But for me, they have really helped me to accept what has happened and live a life with considerably more gratitude than if this had never happened:

- At least I knew losing my daughter was a possibility. It wasn't out of the blue. We had known there were problems. I was able to prepare myself to some degree.
- At least I wasn't faced with reaching 24 weeks pregnant to find out the full severity of the heart problems and having to have a termination for medical reasons. I cannot imagine the pain of having to make an ethical decision based on love to lose one you love and want so badly. I am truly grateful not to have been put in that position.
- At least I have children. **Never say this to anyone who has lost a baby at any stage,** it is up there as the number one thing not to say, but for me and my situation, this is

how I feel. Already having children means my heart, whilst hurting, is never empty. I was not left with an empty womb wondering if I will ever have my own family. I got to go home and hug my children and carry on doing normal family things. There were times in the first few weeks where I felt so depressed I couldn't get myself out of bed, but on the whole, my children gave me the purpose I needed to carry on.

I was scheduled to go back to the hospital in two days' time to 'have' the baby. In the meantime, I had to go home and try and have some normal family weekend time. Our sons were 5 and 2 at the time and had no idea I was expecting, but my eldest would have had an idea something was up. It is hard to describe what it feels like knowing you are carrying a dead baby around, the phrase 'dead weight' is as close as I can get, an acute awareness of something heavy inside my tummy trying to make me sink to the ground. I felt like I had the weight of the world on my shoulders.

The next day we went shopping. I remember the boys excitedly running up and down the isles of a sports warehouse and behaving like wild animals. The next shop, my husband went to try on some trousers and I was so tired I flopped onto one of two stools by the shoes. I can definitely say that its true that children can sense when something is up and in turn act up as they both started fighting over who was getting the other seat. I offered my lap but there was no interest just pushing and shoving and shouting. People were staring, I could almost hear their judgements on me for just letting it play out. I wanted to shout and scream about just how hard it is to stay standing knowing your baby is in there, dead. I could feel myself getting warmer but thankfully the trousers fitted and it was time to go.

That night at bed time I explained to my eldest that Mummy hadn't been very well for a while (no surprises there when one doesn't get to vomit without an audience!) and was going to hospital tomorrow and that I would come back feeling better. I told myself that that was not a going to be a lie. Going to bed that night, I felt some sick, twisted form of excitement as I knew the next day I would get to see my baby.

When I arrived at the ward to be admitted I was asked what I was here for and I was completely lost for words, I didn't know what to call the process. Not to have a stillbirth, as my named, loved baby that I had felt moving just days earlier was too small to be considered a person by law. My face must have explained for me, as I was ushered into a side room.

Once she had arrived, the nurse dressed her in a little dress and put her in a tiny moses basket the size of a regular ice cream tub. She would have fitted in my open hand, but she was too fragile. I held her tiny hand and it was stone cold. I just looked at her and those little feet I had felt kicking and cried. She was just a little girl who had fought so hard for her chance to grow and live. My body had tried to reject her within days of me knowing of her existence, but she was feisty. But it wasn't enough, it wasn't fair. Within the hour, her dress was starting to stain as she started to disintegrate. If there was any realisation and acceptance that hadn't already happened by then, then that certainly nailed it. It was so distressing to watch that I asked for her to be taken away.

Once she was gone, all I was left with a ward-based birth certificate and a memory box. Inside the box was a miniature book of the story 'guess how much I love you'. It made me break down at the sight of it. This was a story I would read to my children at home. I felt sad at the wasted opportunities I had to love my girl because I was being to cautious of loving her for fear of losing her. I didn't take the box because I felt I wouldn't forget what I had been through.

The next evening, I got under the covers with my oldest son for his story. He let me choose the book and I chose 'guess how much I love you'. As I started, it hurt to read the words, they started as a croaky whisper and some secret tears rolled down my cheeks. I felt like I was punishing myself in some way whilst accepting it was also a huge privilege that I had the full-size book to share with my full of life boy.

Telling everyone the news was really difficult, but I was overwhelmed by the support I received. Friends visited, took me out, cooked for me, plied me with chocolate. People even picked up the phone and chatted. One of my university friends cried down the phone to me. If roles were reversed, I wouldn't have felt able to call in fear of me crying and upsetting them further, but actually having someone share a tear was sharing in my pain and it helped. My Mother in Law having to leave the house in tears when I returned home from the hospital just felt like an act of solidarity, sharing in my grief, it helped.

I totally understood that some people didn't say anything at all; maybe for the same reasons that I can remember choosing that option before. Maybe they didn't want to rock the boat. Maybe, hopefully, they had no personal experience to draw upon, so they felt they had nothing to add to conversation.

My husband just picked up doing everything that I dropped doing and 'got on' for me, as well as listening to me saying the same things over and over again. I learnt that people can experience the same loss in different ways, in different time frames and that's perfectly acceptable. It is not a competition to see who can feel the worst and demonstrate that most effectively.

I made the decision that I wasn't going to let myself feel hurt or offended by anything that anyone said. I reasoned that I wasn't going to be speaking to anyone who would say anything mean, but that there would no doubt be things that people would say that I could agree to disagree with. To date, only two things spring to mind that I had to completely disagree with. The first being that what happened would be down to me having taken anti-sickness medication in pregnancy. The evidence available at this time suggests that this was not the case; the medication has been taken successfully by millions of pregnant women worldwide who have gone on to deliver healthy babies. Also, the signs that this pregnancy was not going to have a happy ending were consistently present for many weeks before I began the medication. Secondly, the statement that my baby would 'always be with me'. Well, yes, if you consider having ashes in an urn shoved at the back of my wardrobe until I come up with a better solution for them an ideal way to always have your child close by. Personally, I would rather watch my child grow and spread their wings and go and live on the other side of the world than keep them tucked up in my wardrobe for safe keeping!

What I found was that it was the things people didn't say or do that hurt more than anything that was actually said. When you have a baby, the first thing people ask is what you called them and can they see the pictures. Well nobody in our family asked what we had called our baby, even though we had said weeks prior that we had decided on a name. They didn't ask if we had any photos. She felt very quickly forgotten. So, for the record, her name was Leah. To feel better about that, I focussed on the things that family did to support me instead, after all, they couldn't be expected to mind read what it was that I wanted. My children were cared for when I wasn't in a good place, my home was looked after. They were maintaining my world for me and I am truly grateful for that. If you are reading this and are in this situation, please ask those you love very specifically for the help and support you want, otherwise how are they going to know? If you are supporting someone with no idea how, they will appreciate if you ask how you can help.

As I said at the beginning, I believed that at some point, I would feel healed. I didn't know when, but I knew that I could be happy again, that I would be at peace with losing Leah. I will try and explain what feeling healed means to me. It doesn't mean no longer caring about what happened, but I don't allow her loss to consume my thoughts on a regular basis. The therapeutic writing experience involved in contributing to this book was certainly deeply uncomfortable because it involved taking myself right back there to that place and time in my life. Thankfully that painful place isn't somewhere I feel the need to frequent very often and when I do, it is less vivid each time.

Using the common analysis of the storm, with the weather being the grief, I feared the storm rumbling in the distance. I feared the havoc it could cause. As predicted, that storm hit with full force. It was so strong, the hail battered me to the ground, each stone bruising me deeply, making me curl up tight into a ball; I didn't want to face it. Gradually, the storm became lighter and moved off into the distance and life carried on without constant thought of that storm. Most days are now warm, sunny, happy days. I acknowledge that stormy weather may always return, but that it will never be as strong as before. It won't stop me putting on wellies and raincoat and going about my day, living my best life.

One day, about a month later, a few days before I was due to return to work, I realised I was genuinely doing well the majority of the time. The tears had dried; I could sometimes find happiness where there was opportunity. We were out as a family when I faced my first test. We had gone to soft play and our boys had found another family with two brothers of a similar age to them and were happily playing. We started chatting to their parents, when their mum looked at her boys and asked if I had ever wondered what it would be like to have a girl. She spoke openly about them considering having another child and the potential challenges that would bring to the family life balance they currently had and how it might feel to raise a girl, but on balance it was not going to happen and she would just have to wonder. The look on my husband's face, I could see the fear that he was worried about what I would say or do next. I can't honestly remember what I did say, but I wasn't hurt. I didn't feel the need to say, yeah, actually, I had a really good chance to think about that as I was expecting a baby girl, but she died a month ago. I didn't cry, I didn't fall apart. It was the start of me accepting my life as it was.

I won't say time alone was the healer, I had to work on myself, to learn, to talk with others with similar experiences. I had the support of my bereavement Midwife and the support group. Because of my loss, I have met some wonderful people, that without losing Leah, I would never have met. I used to attend the group once a month and I would nine times out of ten sit there and cry. My husband didn't understand why I went when it upset me when I had got to the stage that I would only cry about Leah when I was there. But I don't think I would be in the place I am in now without facing the discomfort head on. Those thoughts would have hit me in waves at some point in the future, so better for it to happen in a safe supportive environment than to catch me unaware when I'm least expecting it. Because those moments still happened. Turning on Netflix one day to find out cartoon Leah wasn't watching any more was one of those moments that stung unexpectedly. I think I've worked through all the different thoughts I could ever have now. I'm prepared for whatever people ask or say, I'm comfortable with my memories (or accepting of them).

10 and a half months after losing Leah, I gave birth to my third son. Pregnancy after loss is a difficult time, but the hope of new life and love outweighs the fear of loss. Our son is reinforcement for our family, we are stronger with him. He

brings laughter and happiness (as well as attitude and sleepless nights) but he is not a replacement for the baby we lost.

> I love that you've called your story "Her name was Leah" in place of your own name and that you talk with such honesty about your experiences.
>
> I personally have taken something from your approach to decide how to respond and this is something I know I will continue to think about. Even as I was bathing one of my own children this evening and laughing at something silly we were doing I was conscious of your words. So thank you.
>
> I am so sorry for the loss of your daughter. The miniature book and full-sized book and child comparison is such an emotive scene. My heart really went out to you as you described that time when your own must have been breaking.
>
> Thanks again for your story, Take care of you and your army of boys.
>
> Thanks again,
> Marianne

49

Lynsey's Story:

Grateful for the time we had, with nothing left unsaid

I was backwards and forwards as to whether I wanted to put down on paper about my grief of losing my mum in 2017. The reason being I'm very good at pushing things out of my mind, it goes in a little box where my grief stays until something ignites it, usually a memory, a conversation or a programme on the TV that brings my grief flooding back. This is when the tears don't stop, my husband stares at me in shock because he thinks I'm okay, which is the illusion I give of 99.9% of the time.

I find it hard to explain how grief makes me feel, I just can't put my finger on it, it's a depth of sadness like nothing ever, a sickness in the pit of my stomach, an emptiness, sometimes it even feels like a physical pain. The hardest thing is not being able to pick up the phone and speak to my mum every day like I used to do. There was so many times after she initially passed away that I went to make this call before that horrendous realisation hit me that I'd never speak to her again, ever, and that would break my heart all over again.

I think my grief actually started when my mum got her diagnosis of cancer, it absolutely knocked me sideways, I didn't know how to deal with it, what to think, not my mum, my mum was my everything, someone I could talk to about everything, someone who never judged. However, I couldn't speak to her about the sadness I felt about her diagnosis, I didn't want to put my feelings onto her when she had so much to deal with herself, So I spiralled, struggled with everyday situations, I felt like sad news was attracted to me, everyone I spoke to seemed to have a poorly parent, or knew somebody who had died recently. Eventually I went to see the Doctor who gave me medication, which really helped me to just function.

I also took the plunge and began to see a counsellor on a weekly basis as my mum struggled to get a definitive diagnosis; it felt good to speak to someone outside of the family. I cried the entire time, a whole hour every week, it exhausted me, but Jackie gave me clarity, helped me make decisions. I was living 260 miles away from my parents and felt so out of the loop, my dad either wasn't asking questions to the doctors or was trying to protect me by holding information back from me, either way, I felt helpless. Jackie encouraged me to call the doctors myself to get the answers I needed, which I did and I realised the situation was much worse than I'd anticipated. In the following months, I spent a lot of time with my mum, my husband was great and just told me to do what I needed to do, he kept the house and family strong whilst I was crumbling.

I was with her for the last 10 days of her life, I stayed at the hospice with her and held her hand as she took her last breath, I'm so grateful for this, I'd have definitely regretted it had I not been with her. For as long as I can remember, my family have never shown their feelings, we never said, 'I love you' and whilst I always felt loved, it was never spoken about. Jackie, my Counsellor encouraged me to write my mum a letter, with all the things that I wanted to say but had never had the courage to do. I never realised how much this would help me, I actually read it to my mum on what would be her last day with us. I read it to her, and she said to me for the first time ever that she loved me, this is something I will never ever forget. Reading this letter to her, knowing that I said everything that I wanted to say to her really helped me to feel at peace when Mum passed, I have since had a framed picture made with her favourite flower and the words 'grateful for the time we had, with nothing left unsaid.' I have this in my kitchen which I often look at it and reminisce, with a feeling of huge gratitude.

The biggest thing that I have taken from this situation is that what you see on the outside, rarely reflects what's going on inside. Many people are carrying a burden and a pain that no one knows anything about. People think I'm strong, they say that I've done so well working and continuing everyday life. It's because of the little box that I put my feelings in. I'm not sure my feelings will ever come out of that box properly, they try to pop out (they even tried to whilst I was writing this, but I took a little break and pushed them back in). I do worry that the grief I feel will always be locked away, I know that this isn't healthy, but I hate being out of control and people seeing me upset, I hate to be a burden and for people to feel sorry for me and feel that they need to make me feel better. It's impossible for anyone to do this. But I do want my own children to know that it's okay to not be okay, that you don't have to be strong all the time, I'll be honest, I'm not sure how to do this, But I am hoping that over time, I will figure out a way.

50

Alice's Story:

Guilt – A Stronger Emotion than Love

I did not grieve for my Dad when he died or for my mother when she died five years after Dad.

I say five years, but I actually lost them both on the same day.

I had driven to an interview for a new job one hundred and sixty miles away from my home. The job, if I was successful, would be a promotion, an opportunity to escape an un-relenting, bullying boss and an opportunity for me to move closer to my ageing parents, who, in the very near future, may need me for support. Needless to say, everything I hoped for was 'pinned' on my being offered this job. As I drove out of the car park following my interview I hesitated; it was only 12.30pm, should I turn right and drive to surprise my parents or make the return journey home? If I visited my parents it would be hard not to tell them about the interview and I had a 'bad' feeling that I had not presented well to the three managers I had just left. Both Mum and Dad would be very disappointed if I were to tell them later that I had failed and would not be moving back to be nearer them after all. I turned the car and drove home.

As I pulled into the drive my husband appeared at the door. He told me that my Dad had been admitted to hospital that afternoon; he was okay but they wanted to keep him in for observation overnight. Apparently he had gone to his medical centre to pick up a repeat prescription. Whilst he was there, he had become very 'light headed' and so an ambulance had been called.

It was not the first time Dad had such a 'turn' so I was not overly worried, but I was angry with myself that I had this morning decided against a surprise visit to see Dad and Mum. I could have at least been there to re-assure Mum.

I was awoken at three thirty the following morning; my husband answered the phone, Dad was dead. I remember saying over and over again as I pulled on my clothes 'My Dad is dead? My Dad is dead?' I don't remember getting into the car and driving the two hundred miles to the hospital.

As I pulled into the car park, my phone rang. It was one of the managers who had interviewed me the day before offering me the job. It was only when I said 'My dad is dead; he died this morning', did I feel overwhelmingly 'lost' and a great deal of sadness that my dad would never know that I was coming home.

I was taken to see my Dad by a nurse who showed me into a general ward where patients were being served breakfast. My Dad was in a bed in the middle of the ward with an inadequate curtain pulled around. He had been dressed in a weird kind of gown with a high ruffed collar and long sleeves. My Dad would have HATED it. All around me the sounds and smells of breakfast were there. Patients and staff talking loudly and here lay my Dad - quite dead. I felt an anger rise inside me that was to remain with me for the following five years.

I left the hospital with my Dad's clothes and shoes in a plastic bag given to me by a nurse. All my Dad's clothes had been bundled, seemingly, without care into the bag. I noticed with surprise that Dad's shoes had mud on them. Dad polished his shoes every day till they shone. He would have been horrified that his shoes were in this state. I hurried to my car; I had to get to Mum. She would be waiting anxiously for me.

My Mum 'was' waiting for me but not in the emotional, anxious

Guilt – A Stronger Emotion than Love

state I had expected. She was instead looking very angry. When I attempted to put my arms around her she pushed me away with surprising force. I said: "I'm so sorry Mum". She turned from me and went into the lounge. My son, who had taken Mum to the hospital during the night when the call came from the hospital, told me she had refused to see Dad; she had returned home with my son and had gone straight to bed. She had got up at her usual time and carried on as though nothing had happened.

This behaviour from Mum continued for the next five days as I attempted to arrange Dad's funeral. She became very angry when I asked for access to my Dad's personal files. Years ago he had shown me where everything relating to his demise was kept but I felt it impolite not to ask Mum first.

Mum would have nothing to do with the arranging of the funeral. She just kept asking why I was doing this. From time to time she would say angrily: 'So where HAS he gone?' or 'When is he coming back?' She started to 'bad mouth' my Dad at every opportunity. The rest of the time she carried on as normal.

By the end of the week, Mum was telling neighbours and all those who called to pay their respects that Dad had left her without any money. Even when her solicitor arrived for the reading of Dad's will she behaved as though he was there on a social visit; chatting and laughing but slipping into the conversation how badly off she was financially.

I had arranged for my Dad's funeral to take place in Scotland where all our family live. My daughter and her husband flew up from London and immediately commented on how cheerful Mum's mood seemed. We had booked into a hotel the night before the funeral and Mum was in her element with the coming and going of visiting family members. She behaved as though we were getting ready for a huge family celebration.

The day of Dad's funeral found Mum still in high spirits. As my Dad's casket was carried into church and laid across the alter, my Mum said in a loud whisper: -'who is in the box?'

Guilt – A Stronger Emotion than Love

At my Dad's wake, Mum seemed to enjoy it all, chatting happily to her family like the hostess of a huge happy family gathering.

When I took Mum to her home, she became hostile again about Dad. I tried to tell myself that I was upset, but it was anger I was really feeling. Anger that my Dad had died and was not being missed by my Mum. He was not being mourned by his wife of sixty-one years. I also knew that these feelings were completely unreasonable, but I could not stop the waves of anger washing over me as I listened to Mum's tirades about Dad.

I returned home one week after the funeral. Mum was not tearful, just matter- of- fact as we said our goodbyes. As I drove away, I automatically looked in my rear-view mirror for Dad. He always came to the gate and waved me away until I was out of sight. I would never see him again in my rear-view mirror or anywhere.

Mum managed to look after herself for the next few weeks. I drove back every weekend and telephoned three times a day. I dreaded making those calls because Mum would rant about Dad. I had taken medical advice on how to handle Mum's refusal to accept Dad had died. It was suggested that I just go along with her and gently ask if she had thought of anywhere he might be? This approach did not work. One evening, about 9.30pm, I got a telephone call from a police constable. He said he was sorry to tell me that my Dad had gone missing and that he was sitting with my Mum who was very concerned about my Dad. When I told the PC that my Dad was dead, he was completely shocked. For over two hours, my Mother had managed to convince three PC's that her husband had gone out before tea without a coat and had not come home; other officers had already been alerted and were out looking for Dad.

As the weeks rolled on Mum became increasingly agitated. I took some time from work and took her to see the doctor. He ran Mum through the usual test: 'what day is it?' Who is the Prime Minister?' etc. She was able to recall the name and address he had asked her to remember at the beginning of the test and she answered all questions successfully. Only when he questioned her about Dad, did she become angry explaining that Dad had walked out on her.

The doctor told me that Mum 'probably' had 'vascular dementia' and that I should consider care.

After the very unhelpful consultation, it was a year before I gave Mum up to residential care. Within three weeks of seeing that doctor, Mum was admitted to hospital with bowel problems. She went into hospital with much of her faculties intact; when she was discharged five weeks later, she was hardly even able to carry out her own personal care. Her time in hospital had been humiliating for her. I arrived to find faeces in her hair and fingernails. There were Modern Matrons in those days; I took up the fight with her. Mum was rushed to a private room where she was washed and changed. Mum was severely dehydrated and put onto a drip. The profuse apologies for inadequate care were just the first of many I was to receive from The NHS during the last four years of Mum's life.

I could not maintain working full time and making the four-hundred-mile journey every weekend to visit Mum. The carers I had employed were calling me day and night with their concerns about Mum. Often she would not allow them access and had sabotaged the key safe I'd had installed. I did not want to take Mum out of her environment, but I had no choice and so she came to live with us. We converted our dining room downstairs into a bed-sit for Mum. She kept asking to go home; she was deeply unhappy. When I was at work Mum would not allow the carers access. She started to get up during the night trying to leave the house. She cried constantly and continued to 'bad mouth' my Dad. It had become almost impossible to communicate with her. I employed a carer to take Mum to some social activities in our area, hoping that she may be distracted from her mental torment for a few hours at least. But Mum hated these outings and eventually the carer advised that she felt it was 'doing more harm than good'.

I began visiting residential care homes, twelve in all, before I finally decided on the one which I believed to be most appropriate for Mum.

The day I took Mum to the home was the very worst day of my life. I am still unable to describe how I felt. It is said that the feelings of guilt are stronger than feelings of love. For me, I know that to be accurate. Years later I can never think of my Mum without the horror of that day clouding out any good memories.

After only three weeks at the home, I took Mum away. She was not being cared for and had deteriorated further. She was being left in the resident's lounge overnight as it was less 'trouble' than putting her to bed. Something Mum had started to resist. They had also changed her room from the one I had originally chosen for her. The new room was the size of a cupboard. No wonder she did not want to go to bed.

Mum settled into her new home reasonably well. It was not perfect but at least the staff were very caring; they liked Mum even though she was not easy to care for.

I employed a consultant who is a specialist in Mental Health. He spent over two hours with Mum talking to her. His diagnosis was Mum had suffered something akin to PTSD. He felt that if this had been diagnosed at the beginning it may have been arrested and Mum may well have recovered.

During Mum's remaining years, I fought just about every aspect of her care; GP's who failed in their duty to visit the home when requested, The CQC who in my opinion were not fit for purpose, District Nurses who were unkind and often aggressive in their approach. It was at the hands of one of those nurses that my Mum finally went into a coma from which she never recovered. She was finally euthanised with the use of a syringe driver in the care of The NHS. I received yet another apology from the CEO of the local Health Trust when following Mum's death I was invited to his office. He corrected me when I stated my mother had been abused by the district nurse. He said 'No, your mother was ASSAULTED by the nurse for which I am deeply sorry'.

At my Mum's funeral I only felt relief. Finally she was free from her 'tortured' life. She died believing my Dad had abandoned her. She had not grieved for him, but instead had come to hate the man she had loved for over sixty-one years.

My Mum had been a medical secretary in a large NHS teaching hospital. All her life believed strongly in The NHS and then they were not there for her when she needed them most.

I began by saying that I lost my Mum & Dad on the same day; from the time she was told my Dad had died, The Mother I knew no longer existed. She became a tortured soul lost inside her own head where she could not be reached.

I have let both my Mum and Dad down very badly. I had once promised my Dad that I would never put my Mum into care should something happen to him. I let my Mum down because I could not help her in the way she so needed.

> To this day, when I look at their photograph, which sits on a small table my Dad made for me, I am racked with guilt a 'stronger emotion than love'.

Email from: Dr Marianne Trent
To: Alice
Re: Your Story

Dear Alice,

I am so sorry for what you went through with the loss of both of your parents. It must have been such a bewildering and painful time for you and for your family.

I honestly think it sounds like you did everything you could do in such an impossibly painful situation. To quote the words of my EMDR trainer, I do find myself wondering "How much of the guilt you feel do you need to hold on to and how much can you let go?"

Thanks again,
Marianne

51

Hena's Story

Grief can catch you off guard, as the obvious time for grief is after someone has died. Sometimes described as 'passed away' or 'passed on', as we believe, when their soul has left this world.

My mother was still present and alive, but the grieving process for me had already begun. My mother had an illness which meant I lost pieces of her, when her energy and humour went, it was like she was a different person and I yearned for the person she was. She couldn't be the grandmother to my baby she wanted to be and like the one I had dreamed or imagined. She was ill for around 7 years, but really poorly for the last year of her life. Although it has been 7 years since she died; it still feels really raw.

After she died I felt some relief as she wasn't suffering anymore and I felt like she had returned to the person she was. I dreamed about her well and healthy which helped me to process her loss. There are always regrets, so many things I could have done better, so much of my relationship I could have improved, sadness and anger that she experienced so pain and indignity through her illness. This is woven into the grief like a tapestry of emotions that I can't tease apart. The physical pain of grief sometimes can't be described, deep in your gut, or your chest, a wave from your head to your toes when you remember something.

You miss them in ways are unexpected. I spent a long time looking at the time on the days we would usually speak, wondering why she hadn't called yet. I think I did this for a year.

I missed the feel of her hair, the sound of her laugh, her funny comments, especially in Urdu as there were very few people who spoke like her. If I hear someone speaking from her hometown, I get so excited and will attempt a conversation for just for a small reminder of what I have lost.

52

Maxine's Story

We've relocated to a new county and are embarking on much needed fresh start for our family. I'm married to the love of my life, Lawrence and together we have three beautiful children, Bella, Frankie and Theo. However, missing from that list is my stepdaughter, Georgina. I raised Georgina full time from when she was three and a half years old until our family broke down and fractured when she was ten and a half years old. Georgina was my first child really. She was the first child I walked to school on their first day and sat boasting about at teacher-parent consultations.

I can't talk to many people honestly and openly about giving up a child. It was the toughest decision of my life having to step back and say 'No more'. The guilt and grief you feel is unique and gut wrenching, compounded by the fact that very few people will understand what led you to make the decision you had made.

Georgina had a very troubled early years and was passed around to a lot of different caregivers. Due to her Mother's financial issues, Georgina came to live with me temporarily fulltime in the middle of my degree when she was only three and a half years old. I was hesitant at first towards taking her in as it would involve getting a fulltime job alongside my degree to pay for her nursery fees enabling my husband and I to continue our studies. I felt it would be too hard, but at the end of the day, Georgina is my husband's little girl. There was no saying 'No' to this. When Georgina moved in, I was swept up in the visions of Lawrence and I being 'a real family' with a child together now. I engulfed myself in preparing for Georgina's bedroom, her wardrobe, liaising with nursery providers and applying for any financial help to support my husband and I through this transition. Happily enough Georgina slotted into our world perfectly, we rented a nice home with a large garden and Georgina stayed with her Mother at weekends.

To begin with, my world was complete and I embraced the Mum role to this little girl who I became the primary carer for. However, one evening we received a phone call in the middle of the night asking us to come and collect Georgina from her Mother's house. There had been an alcohol-fuelled fight between her and her partner and Amanda had to be restrained and taken away. The police informed us of the poor living conditions in the house and that social services would be in touch. Lawrence and I already had growing concerns over Amanda's behaviour and the state of her home, but any queries we had were met with verbal abuse. Recognising that Georgina's Mum was unstable, Lawrence and I started the process of applying for a residency order. We felt Georgina would be safer with us and we could offer her a better quality of life than her Mum. Our degrees, work and going to court against Georgina's Mother was a tough road, but we were eventually awarded the residency order. Any contact between Georgina and her Mother had to be supervised and having had no concerns Social Services left us to manage everything ourselves. Supervised visits between Georgina and her Mother were awkward for everyone involved and Georgina began to resent our supervision. Our biggest mistake was not supervising conversations between Georgina and her Mother because as she aged her behaviour towards Lawrence and I started to change. Georgina quickly became destructive, defiant and challenging. In desperation we approached Georgina's school for advice and Asperger's syndrome was suggested. After some extensive reading and an expensive private diagnosis Georgina was diagnosed with Autism. After her diagnosis I felt a wave of relief having for a long time feared Georgina's behaviour towards Lawrence and I and our younger children; Bella and Frankie was due to her not liking us or our parenting. However, Georgina being autistic felt to me like if I read enough I could manage her condition and we could become a happy family again.

After time, Georgina's behaviour turned more violent and threatening; we found bleach on our toothbrushes, she attempted to push my daughter Bella down the stairs, and Georgina had taken to smearing faeces and urinating around our home. It got to the point where we needed an alarm on Georgina's door to hear if she was wandering around at night damaging our belongings. Attachment disorder was later diagnosed informally through CAMHS and once again we were given information to navigate through. A lot of different institutions tried to talk to Georgina to work out just exactly what was going on. It always came back to this idea in Georgina's mind that if she was naughty enough we would send her away to live with her biological Mother. Amanda hadn't changed much over the years and had lost another daughter to social services for neglect and alcohol related issues. Contact between Georgina and Amanda had dissipated after Amanda lost her second child and Georgina eventually revealed she had heard and witnessed domestic abuse by her Mum towards her partner when she had stayed there. Unfortunately, Georgina had never shared with us the full extent of what she was seeing at her Mum's and her Mother masked the conflicts and drinking very well.

Due to a mix of issues, Aspergers, Autism and attachment disorder we felt we needed a psychoanalysis to help us properly understand what was going on with Georgina. We never got the psychoanalysis as the stress, destruction and conflict eroded our family unit. Lawrence and I couldn't meet Georgina's needs and against Social Services advice we kicked Georgina out of the family home. She was ten and a half years old.

It was the darkest time of our lives. My husband and I could not talk to each other properly because the grief washed over us. Once I'd shut Georgina's bedroom door when she went to stay with relatives, the door wasn't opened again for 6 months. Georgina had urinated on the carpet and smeared all over the walls, I couldn't bear the smell or the pain of being in that room so our house became a two bedroomed home and I just pretended it didn't exist. When I told family and friends about our decision to kick Georgina out there was mixed responses. Close family and friends felt that we had done the right thing as the situation was becoming unmanageable, others cut us completely out of their lives as they were disappointed that didn't stick it out. Giving up Georgina was compounded by the fact that her Mother had also abandoned her and put her through such a traumatic time in her early years. Georgina had experienced seven years of family celebrations and traditions with us that now stung me to think about, but she wasn't safe and happy in our care. I couldn't help but resent the fact she had turned on us in misplaced loyalty to a parent who had often been neglectful and absent. Georgina ended up living with my Mother-in-law. She appears to be thriving in the quiet house and having my in-laws undivided attention. My Mother-in-law is incredibly relaxed with Georgina's routine and Georgina is relishing the freedom and power that comes with that. Although my heart aches that my mother-in-law has had to burden such a task in her 70's I'm also happy to see Georgina's needs being met by someone who hasn't experienced the conflicts we have. I'm sure Georgina plays up for my mother-in-law also, but for the time being I'd like to pretend that everything will be OK.

I attended trauma counselling where I let out absolutely everything I couldn't tell anyone else. I told the counsellor how much I hated Georgina's Mum, how I resented Social Services and CAMHS for not helping my family more, how I resented the family members who accused me of not loving Georgina enough or lacking in some way. But I also shared with the counsellor my internal fears I couldn't admit out loud. How much I missed Georgina, how hurt I felt that seven years of being her step-mum didn't amount to much and she left my family showing no remorse or sadness. I spoke openly about the strain all this had on my marriage and somewhere in all the talking I found some peace. I came to accept the anger, hurt and frustration I felt about what we had been through. I couldn't even look at photographs of Georgina's face or talk to her directly when we went around to visit. To me at the time it felt like someone had died. I lost my little gingernut, my wild girl, my first child, my shadow and she had seemed to become someone else entirely. Someone cold, aggressive, and calculating, who smiled sweetly at strangers but terrorised me behind closed doors. I lost seven years of fond family memories that now pained me to recall, I lost family members who disapproved of the steps we had taken to salvage ourselves. More worryingly, I lost myself in doubt, anger and confusion. Could I have done better? Could I have prevented this? Did we do the right thing? Will my marriage survive this? Will my family get through this?

The answer to all of that is yes. Eventually I stepped into Georgina's bedroom and scrubbed every inch of that room. I redecorated and ripped up the ruined carpet and the room became a bedroom to my new baby, Theo. Two years later I finally managed to make idle chit-chat with Georgina in Grandma's garden about a mutual interest in illustration and graphics. Grandma watched us eagerly from the corner of the garden knowing full well how long this step had taken me. It was the first time I could look Georgina in the eyes and talk comfortably. I also started accepting my feelings more the way they were. Part of me screamed internally 'she's a child, suck it up and talk to her, cuddle her' but my lips wouldn't move, my body would freeze. Acceptance was a long road that I'm still treading even now.

My story is a bit different to others as I gave up my first child. My feelings are conflicted because despite the longing I have for Georgina to come home I feel so much safer and happier now that she's gone.

The grief is changing and becoming easier to shoulder but I feel it every Christmas, Birthday and family tradition when I look over at the spot where Georgina should be.

>
> Email from: Dr Marianne Trent
> To: Maxine
> Re: Your Story
>
> Dear Maxine,
>
> I'm so sorry to read about your grief for Georgina and that you lost your shadow. It must have been such an exquisitely painful time for you. I definitely think there is something about the absence at family gatherings which is so incredibly poignant.
>
> Thanks again,
> Marianne

53

Bernice's Story:

Grief to Anger to Love

My older brother Jerry died three years ago at the age of forty-three. It was absolutely the saddest experience of my life. Jerry had a rare type of cancer that was brought on by the use of steroids for bodybuilding. Jerry only appeared ill during the final year of his life and survived for about five years after his diagnosis. In the last year of Jerry's life his illness and the challenges of taking care of him were complicated by the dysfunctions of my extended family. The main source of dysfunctional behaviours in my extended family is my mother. 'Mummy Dearest' as I sometimes call her is the epitome of a mother hen. This 'Mother Hen' syndrome as I call it, focuses on control and instantly lashes out at anyone or anything that can interfere or reduce her control of a person or situation.

My brother Jerry moved in with our mum about six months before his passing. His presence in her home presented mum with a most convenient object of control. Mum exercised her dominion by regulating who could visit and monitored all aspects of conversation and physical interaction between Jerry and his visitors. At the time Jerry lived with mum I happened to be in her bad books. As a result, my younger sister became mum's lieutenant or partner in executing the crime of control. They operated a tag team security service vetting, monitoring and subsequently bullying or harassing all visitors. As Jerry grew weaker and the news spread about his condition his ex-wife and three sons reached out to him. His son's ages ranged from fifteen to twenty-five and neither they or their mum had seen

Grief to Anger to Love

Jerry for at least a year. The boys instantly reconciled with their dad and seemed to grow closer to him during each visit. Observing this occurrence, both my mother and sister went on the warpath by harassing, antagonizing, and proclaiming the boys unworthy of such intimacy with their dad. My mum judged the boys as inadequate sons because they had in her opinion sided with their mother ten years prior during their parent's divorce. Both my mum and sister so antagonised Jerry's sons, the daily visits were reduced to once or twice a week.

As my mum and sister grew in their determination to isolate and control him, Jerry and his sons grew more dependant on myself and my then eighteen-year-old daughter for support. We soon became the main conduit of emotional support between Jerry and his sons. I also became Jerry's main advocate and defender against our 'Mother Hen' and her 'Lieutenant.' I found respite from my grief with my new found duty to be strong and fight to make each day of Jerry's life the best it could be. In the midst of all this hostility, Jerry and his ex-wife also managed to heal their friendship. This was only accomplished because his ex-wife a "mother hen" herself managed to bulldoze her way to his bedside. In the final weeks of his life it was primarily left to myself and my daughter to provide Jerry his only respite from his captivity. On several , Jerry requested certain meals and massages. In order to fulfil such simple requests, I had to withstand battles from the kitchen to his bedside. In order for Jerry to enjoy a simple meal, I had to stand guard while he ate. Failure to do so had resulted in my mother literally removing the plate in the middle of the meal.

On a daily basis my emotions seemed to swing from extreme sadness and despair to rage and anger. Managing my anger was the most challenging task, since an emotional outburst or expression of anger could result in my banishment which would then leave Jerry almost totally isolated. It became apparent that Mum's focus was not on Jerry living or his comfort; instead she became obsessed with his impending death and the attention it would bring to herself. My mother grew increasingly angry that while Jerry lived, he was the central focus of attention. In his death she surmised, it would be the heart broken grieving mother at the centre of attention and she was not about to share the spotlight with anyone, not even Jerry himself. As he grew weaker, Jerry requested that I massage his legs and feet more frequently. These requests seemed to particularly irritate both my mother and sister. On many occasions my mother would illicit my sister's support. As the massage started my sister would enter the house loudly exclaiming "pay him no mind he's just spoilt". The only time they seemed to control their displeasure was when my daughter did the massaging or stood with me while I did it. Finally, Jerry took his last breath and another scene of the drama began.

At last "Mummy Dearest" was to be the centre of attention, the grieving Mother. Jerry's passing brought on an intensified attack on his sons and ex-wife. My mother and sister sought to exclude Jerry's sons from all aspects of the funeral. Jerry's life and untimely passing paled in comparison to my Mother's need to be centre stage. I barely managed to advocate for the boys getting two of them to be pallbearers. The hostility towards Jerry's sons increased after the funeral and it was mandated by my mother that they be socially and relationally disinherited. This mandate was adopted by all of my extended family and is still in force. The pain and anger of this unbelievable absurdity brought me closer to my nephews. Our having a common adversary was part of the glue that strengthened our bond. As the months and years go by however, we found a stronger more enduring glue in love. This love was purified in the fires of 'hate control' and my mother's utter self-indulgence. The love I share with my nephews is more than an equal compensation for what we have suffered and lost.

Email from: Dr Marianne Trent
To: Bernice
Re: Your Story

Dear Bernice,
Thank you for your story. You write beautifully.
I'm so sorry for what you and he and his sons endured. It sounds like it was such a difficult situation. Your nephews are so lucky to have you in their lives. Thanks once again for your story.

Marianne

54

Yasmin's Story:

When a Child 'Dies'

There are a few key moments that really stand out to me in the last four years:

1. Holding my wonderful Mum's hand, telling her I will never let go, and promising I would one day dedicate my doctoral thesis to her.
2. Two years later, arriving at my Dad's house to see an ambulance, and screaming 'I'm a fucking orphan' into my little brother's arms.
3. Making that same promise to my Dad.
4. Missing out on an interview for doctoral training that year by seven places.

In that moment, on the 11th March 2019 when I screamed, I screamed so hard. Noticing the realisation hitting me that our family of four was now just the two of us, I let out: 'What the fucking fuck do I do now?' That was the moment that I felt I too had died inside, everything I ever knew, felt as if it had gone. I was 23 and my brother was 20, and I still felt like a child. Although technically classed as an adult, I didn't know how to change a tyre by myself, manage my finances, and was I still learning the ropes of working full time. Never would I have thought that at the age of 23, I would feel so alone. I remember so strongly in the weeks and months after each of my parents passing, getting my phone out to text and ask them a question;

just to realise the guidance I needed and 'adult' to turn to wasn't there anymore.

I also never would have imagined that on the day my Dad died, one of my family members would say to me: 'yeah but you will be able to cope with this Yas, you work in mental health!'

Now, not only am I supposed to step up to the plate and go through the trauma of grief again, I was now also expected to hold my family together too! Apparently 'I have it all figured out'. So now, I felt like a child who was hurting, with the expectation to 'cope', and then return to work as a mental health practitioner just six weeks later. I remember feeling so lost, confused, and helpless that day.

The condolences started pouring in 'I'm sorry for your loss'. I was surrounded by flowers in my home, being told to 'grieve', and being asked if I was going to turn my father's ashes into a ring or a necklace. I remember being angry with myself that I didn't feel better when someone said: 'I am here if you need me'. Although my house looked beautiful, and I was out of vases to display all the lovely bunches of flowers I had received, I was in a lot of pain. Why did I feel guilty for not feeling better?

I turned to the internet and started to intellectualise my confusion. There must be a reason as to why flowers didn't automatically bring me comfort and relieve my pain? I felt really lucky to work in mental health services, and be exposed to incredible research, practice, and clinicians. Someone who has always inspired me is Brené Brown, whose research mainly revolves around shame and vulnerability. One morning, when I was feeling really empty, I came across her YouTube video on Empathy, and something in me just clicked.

What I took away from this video was when I was 'grieving', I think people were unsure what to do or say to me. As normal human beings do, we try to 'silver line' a bad situation to make someone feel slightly better. Unfortunately, 'At least you could be there to say goodbye' just didn't cut it for me. The reason I didn't share my pain with others, is because I was scared that I was going to have my pain turned into a 'silver lining', or to be told that: 'I just need to keep going'. From the messages I had received, to the flowers delivered at my door, I remember feeling really resistant to open a dialogue of telling myself:

- At least I had parents to grow up with.
- At least they didn't die at the same time.
- At least I have other family and friends who care about me.
- At least I have a home, a husband, and a dog to live with.
- At least I have a full-time job.
- At least I am in a position to have a stable lifestyle without them here.

As Brené Brown says in her video, 'Rarely can a response make something better, what makes something better is connection'. What I did find really helpful when recovering from this trauma, was finding someone I could feel safe to connect and be vulnerable with. Surprisingly to me, that wasn't my husband. It wasn't colleagues at work, or family members. It was someone who had also lost a parent. Someone who could connect with the pain they had experienced themselves, in order to help me lean into the pain I was feeling too. I felt a huge sense of relief when we became friends. There were no 'silver linings', no 'at least...'s, and there was a great deal of connection. I strongly remember being sat in a restaurant over dinner and hearing her share: 'I don't even know what to say, this is just so shit' and I nearly cried. I couldn't believe I had found someone who actually understood, could sit with that emotion and didn't try to change it or make it better!

So what am I trying to say? Something I found helpful in the midst of grief was connecting with who and whatever made me feel safe. This is my experience, and it is ok to feel whatever shows up for you. If finding 'silver linings' is helpful, that's ok too. It just didn't work for me, and everyone's experiences will be different. Even now, I think of grief as a balancing act. I try to be kind to myself, and nurture that little child inside me who is in pain. Some days, I can create space for that grief, and some days, I definitely can't. For me, I have taken great comfort in words over the past year and connecting with those who have been through similar experiences. On the days where I feel I would like to feel closer to my parents, I go to the last line that was read in my speech at my Mum's funeral. I would like to share it with you, in the hope that you can connect with it too.

> *'How lucky am I to have something that makes saying goodbye so hard'*
> — A.A. Milne

Email from: Dr Marianne Trent
To: Yasmin
Re: Your Story

Dear Yasmin,

Your story is beautifully written and I'm so pleased you were able to find your own 'Grief Collective' in your friend who had also experienced loss. I too found it to be an incredibly validating process which helped so much. I'm pretty sure I'm going to use your story to close the book because it so nicely demonstrates the importance of the collective and why I wanted to put this book together at all. For those who get grief, 'get it' and that makes the experience for the bereaved so much more bearable.

Thanks once again for your story.

Wishing you all the best with your future Doctoral applications.

Marianne

An email to the Contributors

Email from: Dr Marianne Trent
To: All 54 Contributors
Re: The Grief Collective

Dear *Grief Collective,*

Thank you so much to all of you for being so willing to put your complex thoughts and feelings into your individual grief stories for the book.

I was blown away by the honesty within them and by just how helpful I know reading them will be to people who are struggling on their own grief journey, or those who are trying to learn how best to support them.

I have so enjoyed the process of this book from its initial ideas, to the story reading and up to and including the editing! I've learned so much about humans, grief and of course publishing too!

Thank you again,

Marianne

Reflections on Writing

Many of the contributors told me that writing their stories for the book had been therapeutic. It reminded me of the evidence for a therapeutic approach called narrative therapy. There's evidence that this type of approach can help process and assimilate trauma and distress into people's life stories just by the very experience of writing it down from A - Z. Of course, we know that when writing, things rarely come together in a linear fashion and sometimes it can seem a bit more like: A, B, D, F, B, Q, Z, A, R, S,T, U, back to A and so on! Actually, the evidence for that type of backwards and forwards approach to storytelling is also firmly embedded within the trauma literature too. To further demonstrate how helpful a process writing can be I thought I would include some of the contributor's comments.

> I'm so glad you liked it! It was a very interesting process to go through trying to organise my thoughts and experiences. I think one of the things I realised through writing it, is that it's incredibly hard to find the words to describe grief and loss. Maybe that's one of the reasons why we find it so hard to talk about...words just seem terribly lacking to describe such a deep and profound experience.

> I have been very private with my grieving because that's my kind of default setting. So I haven't always reached out as much as I should have. Even my partner wasn't always aware of what was going on for me and we live together! He read my piece and he was quite shocked by getting an insight into my experiences. So, thank you!

I have really enjoyed writing the piece for the book and look forward to reading it when it comes out. It has really helped my sense of understanding my own feelings and I hope that by doing so I can help other individuals who are experiencing the same feelings or individuals who are trying to support those through a bereavement. After losing my mum at 5 years old and being too young to remember this I had no idea what to expect from my dad's passing and the grief that follows. I keep a scrapbook of photographs however I feel that writing is a great way to capture how things have been for me, I haven't done this until now, so I just wanted to say thank you. It's so much easier to write something that is real and experienced.

It was difficult at times, especially writing about the recent discoveries. The loss of my former self-concept, has also left me a bit confused but I'm hoping that with time and therapy I will recover. It was also helpful to write about historic events as it allowed me to express loss and the associated feelings, without having to explain to someone who may not have the time to hear or the inclination to listen. So, in that sense, it was quite a cathartic exercise

Writing this was hugely therapeutic for me to do actually, so thank you for providing that opportunity. I hope your editing goes well and I look forward to reading the finished product!

Reflections on Writing

Now you've read this book, if you feel inspired to write your own grief story I'd love to know how you get on. Please also feel free to come and give us a wave over at the Facebook group: The Grief Collective Book

> I also wanted to take this moment to thank you for giving this opportunity. It felt so liberating to reflect in-depth on my personal story of grief after so many years and just having the chance to contemplate, see things from a different perspective.

> I've made it very honest and have definitely gone through many emotions through writing it. I did have to stop at one point as it became hard to type through the tears but it felt very therapeutic to get it all out on paper in hope that it helps someone going through something similar to know they are not alone.

Emotional, Practical & Mental Health Support for Contributors

Sometimes we all need a little extra help. That's absolutely ok; as mammals we're not meant to battle through things alone! Where, in their narratives if it seemed were still struggling but hadn't mentioned support I empathically made a clinical recommendation as to which type of support I thought might help meet their needs at this time. For some, this was a particular book, for others a particular service and for others a particular type of therapy. This was a different recommendation for each story as appropriate.

If you are struggling please check out the information on the following page and the helpline information on page 4.

Helpful Resources and Ideas:
summary of things suggested as useful in this book

Books:
- A Manual for Heartache, by Cathy Rentzenbrink
- The Reality Slap, by Russ Harris
- Finding Meaning: The Sixth Stage of Grief, by David Kessler
- Always and Forever, by Alan Durant
- Muddles, puddles and sunshine activity book for children, by Diana Crossley

Activities
- Writing poetry
- Listening to music
- 'The Laundry Cupboard'
- Calm app
- Grief podcast
- Art / pictures
- Reading
- Grief blogs
- Yoga Running / Gym
- Eating Well / Self Care
- Ball in a box pain button analogy
- A memory jar (see Samantha's Story)
- Peaceful Warrior Film
- Family photo shoot

Support
- Bereavement Midwife
- Facebook Groups; including Widowed & Young
- Child Loss: www.karaclinicalpsychologistinsussex.co.uk

Helpful Resources and Ideas:

Useful Helplines
- NSPCC - 0808 800 5000
- National Domestic Abuse Helpline - 0808 2000 247
- Victim support - 0808 168 9111
- Mind - 0300 123 3393
- Cruse Bereavement - 0800 808 1677
- Action on Elder Abuse - 0808 8088 141
- Childline - 0800 1111
- Respect - Men's Advice line - 0808 801 0327
- Centre for Domestic Violence - 0207 186 8270
- Samaritans - 116 123
- Shout TEXT helpine - 85258
- Winston's Wish - 0808 8020 021
- Papyrus Hopeline UK - 0800 068 4141
- The Mix (under 25's) 0808 808 4994
- Saneline - 0300 304 7000
- Youngminds - 0808 802 5544
- Campaign Against Living Miserably - 0800 58 58 58
- Rethink - 0300 5000 927

Therapies
- EMDR
- CBT
- Bereavement Group
- Counselling
- Therapy
- Mindfulness
- Journey Therapy

Suppliers

Mumma's Doodles, (Facebook & Instagram)

Our Glass at Cockington, Mail Order Memorial Paperweights for humans and pets.

Acknowledgements

Thank you first and foremost to all of the contributors who have so freely shared their stories with me. I know, from first-hand experience, but also because you've told me, just how emotional writing about grief can be. When you submitted your stories, I think pretty much every one of you said to me 'you don't have to use it, it might not be what you're looking for,' or something along those lines. The very idea that you would bare your soul and your most exquisitely painful thoughts and feelings with me in the name of this project and then I wouldn't use them makes me shudder! I have used them and treated them with respect and I thank you for your courage and trust in sharing these with a wider audience. Welcome to the collective but know that I'm so dreadfully sorry that you had to go through these experiences in order to earn your place in 'the club no one wants to join!' Thank you for the creative, practical and emotional ideas about how to cope and what to do. They shall live on within me and will continue to be recommended to clients I work with and also considered by me too at such a time as I prepare to earn more 'stamps' on my grief club card.

Thank you also to my husband and my children for just allowing me to get on with my wacky project of writing a book in a month. It means that they've seen even more of the back of my laptop than usual. Thanks also to my husband for helping me photograph and design the covers. I probably also ought to thank my oldest child for dropping his aquabeads all over the table which then led to the inspiration for the cover design!

I'd of course like to thank my Dad Norman. God, I loved that man. I miss his smile. I miss the sparkle in his eyes and I really miss his laugh. Thanks for the wrists Dad.

Thank you also to the original members of my 'Dead Dad Club.' It was in part, your support and love at the darkest times of my life which allowed me to survive. I'm sorry that you had to earn your own stamps but I'm so fortunate that you and your grief ticket were in my life when I needed you most. Some of you didn't feel able to contribute to the book or weren't able to do so within a month. Please know that you are here in spirit and that I think so fondly of the

Acknowledgements

warmth, validation and containment you showed me. I know how it works in grief club, it's reciprocal; sometimes we can allow ourselves to be the knowledgeable but compassionate supporter and at other times it is us who needs the supporting.

Thank you to my fabulous Virtual Assistant, Hannah. Her organisation, flexibility and memory have been so important and helpful in getting this project complete. I couldn't have done it without you and 'Index Bingo' wouldn't have been right with anyone else on board!

Thank you to Dr Tim Mahy for his instigating the challenge to write a book in a month which I duly accepted! Thanks also to Professor Amy Brown for her openness and honesty about the book writing process. She's recently launched her 6th or 7th 'book baby.' Thanks Amy, you're an inspiration, incredibly wise and also supremely funny; the perfect combo!

A bit of a random mention but I wanted to thank Lee Stuart who owns and runs Project RapidFit. Talk about phoenix from the flames! Prior to lockdown he earned his money running fitness bootcamp classes and doing personal training. Lockdown of course stopped all of that. Lee then started doing free daily HIIT classes and quickly acquired over 3,500 page fans – many of whom were exercising with him from their homes each day at 6am – for FREE! Towards the end of lockdown, he decided he was going to launch the business as a Community Interest Company (CIC), meaning that he'll be continuing to help people across the UK and the world to get fit everyday - for free! I think it's really commendable and he's a great motivational speaker. If I ever hear myself say "I can't", then I can imagine Lee saying: "yes you can!" I'll warn you; he swears a bit but if you're putting off until tomorrow what you can do today, be that fitness, diet career goals or something else entirely then it's well worth checking out his Facebook page!

Lastly, thanks to you dear reader. I can't know why you are reaching for this book. It could be because you want to know how to support a loved one who is experiencing grief. It could be because you are experiencing grief yourself. It could be that you're a professional wanting to learn more about how to support other's who are experiencing grief. Whatever the reason; I'm delighted and humbled that you found the Collective and I do hope that you find it useful.

The End

Website: www.goodthinkingpsychology.co.uk
Instagram: @GoodThinkingPsychological
Facebook: Good Thinking Psychological Services
Facebook: The Grief Collective Book
YouTube: Good Thinking Psychological Services
LinkedIn: Marianne Trent

Compassionate Flow 1

May you be happy and well.
May you spend as much time as you like tinkering with and riding vintage motorbikes.
May you be free to watch Only Fools and Horses, Last of the Summer Wine & Dad's Army on repeat.
May you enjoy Cheese & Crackers on your kitchen chair with your feet up on the side!
May you enjoy trips to the pub with Bob, safe in the knowledge that the 'Greasers' tin is there to foot the bill.
May you be free from pain and distress.
May you rest in peace.

Compassionate Flow 2

Within Compassion Focused Therapy we encourage compassionate flows to others, from others and to self. You may find reading this or something similar aloud to yourself helpful.

May my troubles float away from me like leaves on a stream.
May I find a way to live in the present which still allows me to reflect mindfully and meaningfully on my past.
May I be free from pain and distress.
May I find a way to assimilate grief into my life.
May I find a space to breathe and be myself.
May I be freed up to imagine and hope for a vibrant and enjoyable future for myself.
May I be happy and well.

Index

If you're looking for a quick reference guide this is a good place to refer to. the page number listed refers to the start page for a related story.

A

Abroad
78, 81, 137, 244
Abuse
4, 250, 254, 263, 292, 302, 322
Alcohol/drinking
22, 68, 72, 97, 111, 143, 177, 239, 302
Alone/Lonely
11, 22, 28, 36, 50, 59, 68, 91, 100, 111, 132, 137, 143, 152, 168, 177, 190, 218, 244, 254, 258, 276, 312, 317, 231
Anger/Angry
36, 42, 68, 72, 78, 91, 97, 100, 103, 108, 137, 146, 168, 173, 177, 187, 204, 215, 218, 239, 244, 254, 258, 263, 263, 270, 276, 292, 300, 301, 308, 312
Anxiety / Anxious / Worried
22, 28, 36, 50, 72, 81, 84, 87, 103, 111, 129, 132, 143, 152, 168, 177, 190, 204, 215, 218, 263, 276, 289, 292, 302
Anniversary
47, 132, 168, 177, 190

B

Battle / Fight
42, 50, 54, 91, 100, 103, 137, 177, 254, 258, 263, 270, 276, 273, 302, 308, 321,
Bereavement group / support group
2, 11, 15, 42, 47, 72, 87, 190, 254, 276, 277, 317, 322
Birthday
28, 50, 54, 100, 111, 137, 177, 190, 204, 239, 273, 302
Blame
91, 103, 111, 173, 177, 190, 250, 254, 258, 276
Bond
22, 36, 54, 263, 308
Brain
15, 22, 28, 59, 72, 81, 137, 190, 277, 239, 263
Broken
47, 50, 68, 81, 91, 97, 100, 111, 132, 137, 143, 152, 160, 165, 173, 177, 187, 190, 204, 218, 258, 263, 302, 308

329

Index

Brother
22, 28, 47, 50, 54, 59, 72, 78, 84, 111, 129, 137, 143, 152, 160, 165, 168, 173, 204, 213, 214, 225, 226, 239, 244, 254, 263, 276, 308, 312

Buried / Bury
50, 60

Burden
78, 81, 218, 289, 308

Bursting/ Outburst
50, 59, 97, 132, 137, 204, 218, 263, 308

Baby
4, 28, 81, 84, 108, 111, 160, 190, 218, 258, 273, 276, 300, 302

C

Calm
4, 54, 100, 129, 137, 143, 177, 190, 215, 263, 322

Cancer
42, 84, 91, 97, 100, 103, 111, 129, 137, 143, 168, 177, 204, 239, 273, 289, 308

Cat
152, 277

CFT
22, 54, 103, 111, 190, 323, 327, 336

Child/ Children
4, 72, 28, 47, 50, 59, 78, 81, 97, 100, 111, 137, 146, 160, 168, 177, 190, 215, 244, 224, 244, 250, 258, 263, 273, 276, 302, 312, 322, 323

Christmas
22, 84, 100, 103, 111, 137, 143, 152, 160, 177, 204, 239, 263, 273, 302

Church
20, 59, 111, 165, 177, 292

Coffin
47, 50, 59, 152, 190

Compassion/ CFT
22, 54, 103, 111, 190, 323, 327, 336

Cope
22, 54, 59, 78, 81, 103, 111, 132, 177, 190, 204, 225, 258, 270, 273, 312, 324

Coping
42, 59, 68, 78, 132, 160, 165, 177, 190, 215, 217, 244, 254, 270

Counsellor / Counselling/ Therapy
28, 72, 78, 81, 84, 91, 103, 111, 168, 177, 227, 204, 254, 263, 273, 318, 321, 322, 389

Cousin
47, 165, 204, 215, 263

COVID-19
17, 59, 72, 103, 204, 227

Cremation / Cremated
152, 227, 239, 254, 273
Critic / Criticism
103, 254
Cry / Crying
15, 19, 22, 36, 42, 50, 59, 68, 72, 78, 81, 84, 87, 91, 97, 100, 111, 129, 132, 137, 143, 152, 160, 165, 168, 173, 177, 190, 204, 213, 214, 218, 227, 250, 263, 270, 273, 273, 276, 318

D

Dad / Daddy / Father
2, 11, 15, 19, 22, 36, 42, 47, 50, 54, 59, 68, 72, 78, 81, 84, 87, 91, 97, 100, 103, 111, 129, 132, 137, 143, 146, 152, 160, 165, 168, 173, 177, 187, 190, 204, 213, 218, 224, 225, 227, 239, 244, 250, 254, 263, 273, 289, 293, 308, 312, 317, 324, 327
Daughter
26, 54, 72, 108, 111, 143, 146, 152, 190, 204, 225, 226, 244, 258, 276, 292, 302, 208
Depressed / Depression
2, 59, 108, 168, 218, 258, 276
Diagnosis / Diagnosed
42, 50, 72, 81, 84, 100, 103, 111, 137, 143, 146, 168, 173, 204, 227, 258,270, 276,289,292, 302, 308
Difficult / Difficulty
15, 36, 54, 59, 78,103, 111, 129, 132, 160, 177, 190, 204, 215, 218, 227, 239, 244, 263, 270, 273, 276, 308, 317
Divorce
100, 308
Dog
28, 50, 111, 204, 227, 273, 312
Drugs / Meds
97, 111, 146, 177, 190, 276, 273, 289

E

Eating / Appetite
68, 72, 103, 111, 168, 173, 177, 187, 204, 213, 239, 322
EMDR
103, 111, 168, 250, 322
Emergency
59, 68, 111, 129, 173, 244
Enjoy / Enjoyment
28, 36, 72, 87, 91, 111, 137, 146, 160, 177, 204, 227, 254, 292, 308, 317,327
Excited / Excitement
11, 22, 36, 111, 152, 160, 168, 187, 190, 218, 227, 239, 276, 300

Index

Exhaust / Exhausting
28, 42, 72, 103, 111, 146, 168, 215, 263, 289

Expected / Unexpected
28, 50, 54, 59, 68, 78, 91, 97, 108, 111, 132, 137, 165, 204, 215, 218, 239, 250, 254, 276, 292, 300, 312

F

Facebook
2, 11, 18, 317, 322, 323

Family
22, 28, 36, 47, 50, 54, 59, 68, 72, 78, 81, 87, 91, 100, 103, 108, 111, 129, 132, 137, 146. 168, 173, 177, 187, 190, 204, 215, 218, 227, 239, 244, 265, 258, 268, 270, 273, 276, 289, 292, 302, 308, 312, 322

Father / Dad / Daddy
2, 11, 15, 19, 22, 36, 42, 47, 50, 54, 59, 68, 72, 78, 81, 84, 87, 91, 97, 100, 103, 111, 129, 132, 137, 143, 146, 152, 160, 165, 168, 173, 177, 187, 190, 204, 213, 218, 224, 225, 227, 239, 244, 250, 254, 263, 273, 289, 293, 308, 312, 317, 324, 327

Feeling / Feelings
2, 4, 11, 19, 22, 28, 36, 50, 54, 59, 68, 72, 78, 81, 84, 87, 91, 100, 103, 111, 129, 132, 137, 146, 152, 160, 168, 173, 190, 204, 215, 218, 224, 239, 344, 250, 258, 263, 270, 273, 276, 289, 302, 312, 317, 324

Fight / Fighting
42, 50, 54, 91, 100, 137, 168, 177, 254, 263, 270, 276, 292, 302, 308

Flowers
72, 97, 103, 177, 187, 190, 273, 312

Friend / Friendship
11, 19, 22, 28, 36, 47, 50, 54, 59, 68, 72, 78, 81, 84, 87, 91, 97, 100, 103, 108, 111, 129, 132, 137, 143, 146, 152, 160, 168, 177, 187, 190, 204, 213, 214, 218, 227, 239, 244, 254, 258, 263, 273, 276, 302, 308, 312

Funeral
36, 42, 47, 52, 54, 59, 68, 72, 78, 84, 87, 100, 103, 111, 137, 143, 146, 152, 160, 165, 173, 177, 187, 190, 204, 213, 214, 218, 227, 239, 244, 273, 292, 308, 312

Funny
36, 42, 72, 91, 111, 137, 152, 224, 227, 239, 270, 300, 324

G

Grandad / Grandfather

Index

22, 50, 59,78, 81, 119, 137, 146, 152, 160, 165, 177, 187, 204, 213, 225, 227,
Grandma /Grandmother / Nan
22, 28, 36, 47, 59, 78, 81, 84, 111, 108, 160, 187, 244, 270, 273, 300, 302,
Grandparents
22, 28, 36, 47, 59, 78, 97, 111, 132, 165, 177, 204, 205, 227, 244
Gratitude / Grateful
22, 28, 42, 50, 54, 59, 78, 111, 132, 146, 152, 160, 190, 218, 244, 254, 263, 273, 276, 289
Grief – see whole book!
Group
2, 11, 15, 42, 47, 72, 87, 190, 254, 276, 277, 317, 322
Guilt
22, 36, 42, 59, 68. 72, 78, 87, 91, 100, 137, 146, 152, 160, 165, 173, 177, 190, 204, 215, 225, 258, 276, 292, 302, 312

H

Hand/Hands
11, 22, 36, 81, 103, 111, 143, 160, 168, 190, 204, 218, 227, 244, 263, 270, 273, 276, 289, 292, 312
Happy/Happiness
42, 78, 81, 87, 108, 129, 132, 137,146, 160, 165, 168, 177, 190, 204, 215, 258, 263, 270, 273, 276, 290, 302, 327
Healing
22, 68, 72, 111, 160, 218
Health
2, 4, 11, 17, 36, 50, 54, 68, 72, 78, 81, 87,91, 103, 111, 146, 152, 160, 187, 190, 204, 215, 218, 227, 254, 258, 267 276, 292, 300, 312, 321
Heartbreak
17, 28, 54, 177, 190, 270
Hope
4, 11, 15, 17, 18, 19, 28, 36, 42, 50, 54, 59, 68, 72, 87, 103, 111, 129, 137, 146, 152, 160, 173, 187, 190, 204, 227, 258, 263, 276, 279, 312, 317, 322, 324
Hospice
36, 100, 111, 177, 204, 289
Hospital
22, 36, 42, 47, 50, 54, 59, 87, 100, 103, 111, 129, 143, 146, 152, 160, 168, 173, 177, 190, 204, 227, 239, 254, 258, 263, 273, 276, 292
Husband
28, 36, 72, 78, 84, 87, 100, 111, 146, 177, 190, 204,

333

Index

213, 239, 244, 276, 289, 292, 302, 212, 224

I
Illness
42, 50, 111, 300, 308
Internet
103, 137, 312

J
Job / Working
18, 22, 42, 50, 59, 78, 91, 103, 111, 129, 132, 146, 152, 187, 190, 204, 215, 227, 239, 244, 254, 289, 292, 302, 312

K
Kind / Kindness
19, 22, 28, 42, 50, 54, 68, 81, 87, 91, 100, 103, 111, 152, 160, 165, 168, 177, 187, 204, 218, 224, 225, 244, 254, 263, 276, 292, 312, 317

L
Laugh / Laughter
24, 28, 50, 54, 72, 81, 87, 91, 97, 100, 108, 111, 137, 143, 160, 165, 177, 190, 204, 213, 215, 218, 227, 239, 263, 270, 276\, 292, 300. 324
Learn / Learning
11, 28, 36, 42, 59, 81, 84, 87, 91, 100, 111, 132, 168, 173, 177, 190, 204, 227, 239, 250, 258, 263, 270, 276, 312, 317, 324
Loss
4, 11, 17, 19, 22, 28, 36, 42, 47, 50, 54, 59, 68, 72, 78, 81, 84, 87, 97, 100, 103, 108, 111, 129, 146, 152, 160, 165, 173, 177, 190, 204, 213, 215, 227, 239, 244, 250, 254, 258, 263, 276, 300, 312, 317, 322
Lungs / Lung
59, 84, 91, 103, 111, 146, 177, 163, 289

M
Mental Health
4, 72, 103, 111, 146, 254, 263, 292, 312, 321
Miscarriage (& Stillbirth)
160, 190, 263, 276
Mum / Mother
11, 18, 22, 28, 42, 47, 50, 59, 72, 78, 81, 84, 87, 97, 108, 111, 132, 137, 143, 146, 160, 165, 168, 173, 177, 190, 204, 213, 215, 218, 224 225, 227, 239, 244, 250, 254, 258, 263, 276, 289, 292, 300, 302, 308, 312, 317, 323
Music

Index

28, 36, 54, 72, 91, 111,
129, 137, 146, 177, 187,
190, 218, 227, 239, 244,
322

N
Nephew
177, 213, 308
Normality / Normalising
17, 36, 42, 47, 59, 72, 81,
87, 100, 103, 108, 111,
132, 137, 152, 160, 177,
190, 204, 215, 218, 227,
244, 276, 292, 312

P
Palliative
11, 22, 42, 111, 129, 173,
204
Pandemic
17, 59, 103, 204
Panic
81, 168, 253, 276
Parents
11, 36, 42, 47, 59, 78, 81,
97, 100, 111, 132, 137,
143, 146, 165, 177, 187,
190, 204, 215, 218, 227,
250, 263, 270, 276, 289,
292, 312
Photos / Photograph
19, 20, 22, 28, 36, 42, 47,
54, 59, 111, 132, 146, 152,
173, 190, 204, 239, 244,
270, 273, 276, 292, 302,
318, 322, 324
Pregnancy

108, 111, 146, 160, 190,
258, 276

Q
Quiet / Quietly / Silent
28, 54, 68, 100, 111, 137,
146, 168, 190,192, 215,
244, 276, 302,

R
Reflect / Reflection
28, 36, 42, 54, 68, 87, 137,
143, 146, 218, 244, 289,
318
Regret
72, 87, 108, 111, 129, 137,
146, 177, 187, 289, 300
Relationship
50, 54, 59, 68, 91, 108,
137, 177, 187, 204, 215,
218, 227, 244, 258, 300
Remember / Remembered
22, 28, 36, 42, 47, 54, 59,
68, 72, 78, 81, 91, 97, 100,
103, 111, 129, 132, 137,
152, 160, 165, 168, 177,
187, 190, 204, 213, 215,
218, 224, 225, 239, 244,
250, 263, 270, 273, 276,
289, 292, 300, 312, 318
Running
42, 81, 97, 111, 204, 215,
218, 227, 276, 322, 324

S
Sad / Sadness

335

22, 36, 42, 50, 54, 68, 72, 78, 81, 84, 87, 91, 111, 132, 146, 152, 160, 165, 168, 177, 187, 190
Stillborn / Miscarriage
160, 190, 263, 276
Stress / Distress
22, 50, 72, 78, 137, 146, 152, 160, 190, 204, 218, 227, 270, 276, 302, 317, 327
Stroke
59, 160, 263
Struggle / Struggling
11, 15, 28, 36, 42, 59, 78, 81, 91, 103, 108, 111, 146, 160, 168, 173, 177, 190, 204, 215, 227, 239, 244, 263, 289, 317, 321
Suicide
4, 28, 72, 91, 108, 754
Support / Supported
4, 11, 17, 18, 28, 36, 54, 59, 78, 87, 103, 111, 129, 132, 137, 146, 152, 160, 177, 187, 190, 213, 215, 218, 239, 244, 250, 258, 263, 276, 292, 302, 308, 317, 321, 324

T

Terminal Illness / Terminally Ill
59, 111, 42, 137, 143, 177, 204, 276, 289

Therapy
11, 15, 28, 42, 72, 78, 81, 84, 91, 103, 111, 168, 177, 204, 254, 263, 270, 273, 276, 318, 321, 322,
Tired
152, 204, 276, 111

V

Vulnerable / Vulnerability
28, 50, 68, 160, 204, 244, 258, 312

W

Widow
28, 36, 87, 322
Wife
59, 111, 137, 177, 190, 227, 244, 276, 292, 308
Working
22, 36, 42, 50, 59, 78, 91, 103, 111, 132, 146, 152, 187, 190, 204, 227, 239, 254, 289, 292, 312
Worry / Anxiety
22, 28, 36, 50, 72, 81, 84, 87, 103, 111, 129, 132, 143, 152, 168, 177, 190, 204, 215, 218, 263, 276, 289, 292, 302

Y

Yoga
28, 111, 322

Printed in Great Britain
by Amazon